Seasons of the
HORSE
A practical guide to year-round equine care

Jackie Budd

T.F.H. Publications, Inc.

Seasons of the HORSE

Project Team
Editor: Mary E. Grangeia
Copy Editor: Joann Woy
Indexer: Dianne L. Schneider
Design: Mary Ann Kahn
Cover Design: Mary Ann Kahn

T.F.H. Publications
President/CEO: Glen S. Axelrod
Executive Vice President: Mark E. Johnson
Publisher: Christopher T. Reggio
Production Manager: Kathy Bontz

T.F.H. Publications, Inc.
One TFH Plaza
Third and Union Avenues
Neptune City, NJ 07753

Printed and bound in China
07 08 09 10 11   1 3 5 7 9 8 6 4 2

Library of Congress Cataloging-in-Publication Data
Budd, Jackie.
  Seasons of the horse : a practical guide to year-round equine care / Jackie Budd.
    p. cm.
  Includes index.
  ISBN 978-0-7938-0611-9 (alk. paper)
  1. Horses. I. Title.
  SF285.3.B83 2007
  636.1083—dc22
                                  2007013816

This book has been published with the intent to provide accurate and authoritative information in regard to the subject matter within. While every reasonable precaution has been taken in preparation of this book, the author and publisher expressly disclaim responsibility for any errors, omissions, or adverse effects arising from the use or application of the information contained herein. The techniques and suggestions are used at the reader's discretion and are not to be considered a substitute for veterinary care. If you suspect a medical problem consult your veterinarian.

tfh
The Leader In Responsible Animal Care For Over 50 Years!®
www.tfh.com

CENTRAL
Garden & Pet

Table of Contents

Preface

Anyone who has been responsible for the care of a horse throughout a whole year knows that few experiences will ever bring us closer to the natural world around us. Nature impinges on us constantly: while trudging through a muddy field in the lashing rain, flashlight in hand, calling for a horse in the gathering gloom of a winter's evening; while worrying over the effects of fast-appearing spring grass on our horse's waistline; or perhaps while battling the annual appearance of tormenting flies as summer temperatures rise. Although we might not appreciate it, while hauling hay on a freezing January morning, this contact with nature is one of the great privileges of being a horse owner.

It is equally true that it takes a full 12 months to be able to say that you truly know the animal out there in your field—the way he puts on weight in summer but needs careful feeding to keep that condition in winter, how he interacts with others in his social group, what regime keeps him both happy and healthy. As our horses' bodies and behaviors respond and adapt to the altering demands of their environment, every month of the year brings its own horse-care challenges.

The horse was bred to live out in the open, with no limits on his freedom.

Nature's Horse

These continual, year-round changes remind us that, despite centuries of domestication, our equine friend remains nature's horse, body and soul. When it comes to coping with the seasons, there isn't much we can teach him. Throughout millennia, evolution has fine-tuned the horse's survival skills. Unrestricted by fences or walls, wild horses have succeeded in searching out the tastiest grasses and freshest water supplies, finding shelter and shade to protect them from fierce winds and scorching sun.

We can still see evidence of the same tried-and-tested coping strategies in our own mounts. Despite the bags of food piled ready in our feed rooms, our horses continue to busily store up fat reserves over summer so they are ready when winter drains the goodness from the grass. And they insist on growing a coat fit for a polar bear, oblivious to the small fortune you spent last week on the latest in thermal blankets and the fact that the clippers are oiled and prepared for action!

Of course, horses never forgot how to look after themselves when they came to live with us. However, by confining them to fields and stables and denying them their ability to control their own surroundings, we changed the rules of the game. Survival techniques that have worked so well, for so long, suddenly don't always fit the circumstances in which our horses now find themselves.

For Better or Worse

The world over, from moorland ponies to mustangs, those horses who do still live a feral life (without overcrowding), remain predominantly fit and healthy, even in the harshest living conditions. Most of the diseases that threaten the welfare and even the lives of their pampered domesticated cousins, including colic, laminitis, and allergies, are virtually unknown in wild horse communities. Only when humans came on the scene and started trying to "help out" did most of the horse's problems begin!

For our convenience, we want our horses living beside us, in a small, fenced field or barn, not running free on the plains or the mountains with free access to natural resources of feed and shelter. We like them clean and tidy, with their natural, all-weather, protective coat grease brushed away. The warm, slow-burning fuel supplied by low-quality grass alone is no longer enough—not by human standards; equine digestive systems now have to handle buckets of grains bursting with protein and "go-faster, jump-higher" carbohydrates.

Having commandeered almost every survival decision and claimed virtually total responsibility for our horses' welfare, we have set ourselves up as the experts on what is best for them, but we have not always gotten it right. At last, a more thoughtful approach to the horse's true management needs is spreading throughout the equine world. Horse lovers are finally realizing that it is up to us to do as good a job for our horses as they could do for themselves.

Horse Care for *Horses*

This isn't as illogical as it sounds. The key to knowledgeable, appropriate, year-round management is horsemanship, in its broadest possible sense. It is about knowing your horse inside and out, both as a member of his species and as an individual with a personality and special needs all his own. It is also about making the sort of choices on his behalf that you know he would make for himself if he could and, wherever possible, giving him the chance to choose.

Approaching horse care from the horse's perspective does take some particular skills: practicality, common sense, flexibility, and courage. Everything we do should be assessed based on the answer to one vital question: Is this really in the horse's best interests—even if it isn't necessarily the quickest, easiest, or cheapest way (although it often is!), or the way I was taught, or the way it has always been done?

Fortunately for the horse, there is a growing realization that horsemanship is about more than a tidy muck heap or a neat clip. Horses must be allowed to live as closely as possible to their natural lifestyle and, in those areas of care where we have moved the goal posts, it is up to us to help them adapt to our alternatives with a minimum of stress, both physical and mental.

Arranging your horse's care to suit him first and foremost doesn't mean life gets more difficult for you—in fact, quite the opposite. It is possible to keep your horse in a way that suits you both, whether your ambition is simply to trail ride or to achieve the highest performance levels. By keeping an open mind and thinking practically, combining new ideas with the best of traditional know-how, you will be rewarded with a fitter, more contented horse to enjoy all year round. Your horse, meanwhile, will have the best of all worlds.

If you are in tune with your horse, you will understand his needs.

The Right Start

Owning a horse is a dream come true for the equine enthusiast, but it brings with it a huge amount of responsibility. You are making a commitment to care for him in "sickness and in health" and, perhaps more significantly, "in summer and in winter." Looking after a horse is a year-round occupation, but the workload steps up steeply during the winter months. As luck would have it, this coincides with the time when opportunities to ride are minimal.

Chapter One

Lifestyle Options

*I*f you plan ahead, you will be able to make the best possible use of time and still ensure that your horse gets the care he needs. In many cases, horse health problems are directly related to errors in management— so, by learning and understanding good management skills, problems can be avoided.

Make sure you are a good friend to your horse in all senses of the word. Build up a good and trusting relationship with him. And, even more importantly, find out what his needs are and provide for them to the best of your ability.

Your Horse's Priorities

As far as your horse is concerned, his primary needs are:

Freedom: The lifestyle of wild horses encompasses complete freedom to move wherever they choose, avoiding threats as necessary. Access to loose exercise is essential, not a luxury.

Friends: Horses are social creatures for whom isolation, whether in a stable or in a field, is extremely stressful.

Food: Equine digestive systems are built to deal with a continuous trickle of high-fiber food. Equine brains are designed to be continuously occupied with finding and processing that food.

Your Priorities

Bearing in mind the crucial requirements just listed, you must find the type of accommodation that is most likely to suit your horse as well as your own lifestyle.

Keeping Your Horse at Home

Where is your horse going to live? This is probably the most important decision you will make, so take time to weigh the options that are available.

If the facilities are there, keeping your horse at home is an option. It is much easier having your horse outside the back door than 10 miles up the road!

Independence and convenience are the main advantages. You do things your way, with complete control over how your horse is kept. Any compliment on how well he looks is that much more rewarding when you know it's all because of your efforts! Close contact, day in and day out, builds and strengthens your relationship as you and your horse get to know all there is to know about each other.

In addition to saving on travel time, it is easy and reassuring to pop in at any time to check on your

equine friend or simply say "Hello." Being there for the vet or farrier is so much more convenient when you can wait in the kitchen with a cup of coffee.

However, when keeping a horse at home you must also consider the following:

Turnout: Many owners have space for a stable at home, but without access to sufficient turnout, you are shortchanging your horse's needs and creating a lot of extra work.

Company: A "home-alone" horse is an unhappy horse. Your facilities and timetable must be able to cater to at least one companion, even if it is just a small pony.

Muck Disposal: Muck heaps have a way of quickly becoming muck mountains. Is there room for yours? How will you deal with it? And most importantly, will it be tolerated by the neighbors?

Storage: Hay, bedding, and feed need their own dry storage areas. If storage space is restricted, you won't be able to save by buying in bulk.

Commitment and Expertise: Sole responsibility is a commitment that you and your family must be ready for. Are you sure you know what is going to be involved? Are your abilities on the nitty-gritty of horse-keeping up to scratch? When (not if) you need advice, will you recognize that you need it? Where will it come from? Who will take over in an

The horse is a herd animal who needs the companionship of other horses.

If you keep your horse at home, you can make all the decisions regarding his care.

emergency when you are on vacation or if you are ill? Is that person up to the job?

Setting Up: Plans to build your own stable or field shelter, or to convert existing outbuildings, need careful preparation well in advance. Factors such as siting, access, and materials must also be taken into account. Permission and building/construction permits may be needed from the local authorities. Be sure to budget properly and build to last, with consideration given to all your current and potential future needs.

Boarding

Keeping a horse at home may be the ultimate goal of many owners but, in reality, most of us have to settle for choosing between various kinds of boarding options. Boarding barn services generally fall into one of four broad categories: do-it-yourself (DIY), part, working, or full.

Do-It-Yourself Boarding

Do-it-yourself (DIY) boarding is based on the rental of grazing land and/or stabling only, direct from the land or barn owner, either for your sole use or within a barn with other horse owners.

The Pros: DIY's main advantage is its relative affordability, making it especially attractive to those on a tight budget. Many of the plus points that go along with having complete control over your horse's care also apply.

Renting with other owners in a barn situation provides company for your horse and you, plus potential sources of advice and help (including the possibility of sharing duties).

A barn owner or farmer may also be able to provide and store hay, bedding, and even feed for you at a reasonable cost.

The Cons: The downside, of course, is the very fact that you literally must do it all yourself.

As for the home-horse owner, every last water bucket refill and pile of manure is up to you to deal with. The difference is that you also have to build traveling time into your daily schedule.

Regardless of how tired, off-color, or fed up you feel, or how busy you are, a significant slice of every single day is going to be taken up with looking after your horse. This commitment, too, must be understood and accepted by parents (particularly if they provide the rides), friends (if you expect a social life), and partners (especially if that means they must take on the child care while you do the horse care!). You also must consider the following:

Emergency Coverage: Who is available at short notice to stand in when you can't make it or are held up? Proprietors soon tire of owners who take them for granted, abusing goodwill by calling once too often to ask "Could you possibly...?"

In a shared barn where everyone gets along well, joining forces can work if everyone is reliable and a mutually convenient schedule can be arranged and adhered to.

If you are out on your own, you may have to look further afield if no one capable and reliable springs readily to mind.

Sharing: Shared facilities usually come with their own built-in frustrations. Company all too often also means barn politics—gossip, interference, and unsolicited comments. Items of equipment mysteriously "disappear" or are borrowed and never replaced. And it may not be just the owners who don't get along. You may have little say in who your horse shares his field with, and a bad mix can cause all kinds of problems.

Accommodation: Renting a field only is the most economical way of keeping a horse, but what happens in the case of illness or injury? Plan in advance to find a roof over your horse's head at short notice, if need be.

Who's in Control?: Some boarding barn owners are never seen week-in and week-out, leaving horse owners to do as they like in DIY-rented facilities. You must sort out at the outset who is responsible for overseeing repairs to fencing and other maintenance issues. In a shared barn situation, it helps to have some "house rules" set up and to establish a good working relationship with the proprietor. This means disputes between renters can be aired, and everyone feels able to discuss adjustments or improvements to the established system.

Partial Board

Partial board is an excellent system for those who want to be involved in their horse's care but can't guarantee always being at the barn every morning and evening. It is also a sensible option if you don't have the confidence to go solo just yet.

In partial board setups, the person in charge of the barn (usually the owner) takes responsibility for

If you opt for DIY boarding, you are committing yourself to a heavy workload.

some of the daily chores (often mucking out, morning feeds, and turning out), charging for each service rendered.

The beauty of partial board is its flexibility, especially for working owners. In addition to having peace of mind because you know someone is always there to care for your horse, you also have a knowledgeable person around for advice, as well as having other owners for company. A farm offering partial board may well have better facilities than a DIY-oriented one.

If you decide to opt for partial board, be aware of the following:

Doing It Their Way: You will not be able to dictate how your horse is managed. You will have to fit in with the way the barn owner does things, which may include the type of feed used, the amount given, how your horse is handled, what time he comes in from the field, and which other horses he is put out with. Can you put up with this (within reason)? If you must insist on certain things, such as shavings used as bedding or soaked hay, discuss these and be prepared to pay for any extra labor involved. Look for a barn owner who is prepared to listen.

Who Does What?: The owner is likely to be a busy person, so deal with her courteously and patiently—and expect the same in return. The key to staying on good terms is to be sure about who is doing what and being clear about exactly how services are being charged (agree on what is "standard" and what is "extra" in advance, and ask for an itemized bill). Keep the owner informed of any changes of plan, giving as much notice as possible. Calling at the last minute to ask her to bring in your horse and feed him won't go down well!

Sharing: Sharing facilities in a large barn brings its own ups and downs and requires compromise.

Working Board

With a working board setup, for a reduced boarding fee, your horse is looked after by a riding school in return for being used in lessons. This can be a useful stepping stone for new owners who are unsure of their abilities, those who may be tight on time, or anyone unsure about how committed they are to the whole horse-owning business.

Many newcomers choose this way to maintain a link with the place where they learned to ride. The arrangement can provide a gradual introduction to ownership in familiar surroundings with help on call.

At a reputable establishment, a horse on working board might be ridden by very capable clients or staff who can improve his schooling. (If you would prefer competent adults only on board, a training barn or college that offers equestrian courses is a better option than a riding school.) Your horse will be kept fit and well, ready for whatever plans you have for him, and there are no worries about making it down to the barn every day.

As a system, its success depends on everyone being completely clear about how the contract works. Above all, you must have total confidence in the establishment and the people who run it not to abuse either the agreement or your horse's welfare. Any compromises you sign up for must not be at your horse's expense—but always remember that he will be considered a "working" animal in a commercial barn.

Partial board is often a good compromise.

Before comitting to a working board contract, bear in mind the following:

Terms and Conditions: Discuss these in detail beforehand. How will your horse be kept? How much turnout will he get? How often and by what standard of rider will he be used? Be sure the arrangements will suit you. Will your horse be available to ride when you want (remember, weekends are the busiest days of the week for most riding schools)? Will he be covered by the barn insurance?

Handing Over: You will have little say in how your horse is kept and potentially little to do with his care either. Are you sure you will be happy with that?

Trust: Trust is all-important. Working board horses frequently end up getting more work, or have a poorer standard of rider on board, than the horse owner has agreed to. Keep a close eye on things to make sure the terms of your contract are followed.

"Get me outta here!": Not all horses are made for riding-school life. It's a nonstop, bustling environment, where the people handling and riding your horse constantly change. Individual horses upset by this are not suited to working board.

Full-Care Board

The priciest option is full-care board; the barn takes care of every aspect of your horse's care for you. Your obligation stretches to turning up for a ride when you feel like it. Full board means that, however busy life gets, you can still enjoy owning a horse, riding him when you have the chance, and knowing his needs are being fully met. For those short on experience, it's an opportunity to learn the ins and outs of horse care with none of the responsibility.

Full-care barns also frequently boast additional facilities, such as an all-weather riding ring, an indoor arena, and jumps, making the system ideal for those who want to compete seriously but are pressed for time, perhaps due to a demanding career. Factors to consider are:

How "Full" Is Full Care?: Confirm precisely what is included in the deal. Some fees include everything right down to exercise, tack cleaning, and braiding up for competition; other facilities will have a long list of extras.

Cost: Top-class care does not come cheap, so be prepared to dig deep into your pocket. Fees that seem an out-and-out bargain mean corners are being

Find out how much your horse is going to be used before agreeing to working board.

cut—probably at the expense of the horses in that barn's care. Before committing yourself, work out a whole winter's bill now (complete with extras!).

Horse Ownership at Arm's Length: Will you be content to hand your horse's care over wholesale? Do you have complete confidence that the barn will consider his needs as much a priority as their commercial considerations? Will he be cared for as an individual and sensitively ridden, or does he simply have to fit in?

Barn Search Checklist

Having decided on the system that's going to best suit you both, the next step is to track down a barn that fits the bill. It's the lucky person who can find the perfect home for his horse right around the corner.

Realistically, it is a case of determining if any compromises you need to make are acceptable to you. A checklist of essentials and preferences can help when making comparisons between possible locations.

Bear in mind that a good barn doesn't have to mean neat rows of red-brick or mahogany stables surrounding a gravel square. Horse facilities with happy occupants can take many shapes and forms, as long as the vital ingredients are there.

From the horse's point of view, a barn should offer the following:

Sufficient Grazing Land: The grazing land should be well managed, with adequate shelter, clean water, and solid, safe fencing. Be wary of large, full barns with limited grazing. Too many horses on too small an area soon leads to overcrowding, which in turn, contributes to horse-sick pasture that rapidly becomes a quagmire during a wet season. Ideally, enough pasture should be available to allow all areas to be regularly rested. Check whether mares and geldings are turned out together or separately, and inquire about the barn's policy on colts and stallions.

Proper Housing: A large, solid, well-ventilated stable with a wide door is a must. Expect a minimum size of 12 x 12 feet (3.7 x 3.7 m) to 14 x 14 feet (4.3 x 4.3 m) for 16.2hh+, but the bigger the better. All horse

Short on Knowledge?

The broader your equestrian experience, the more responsibility you can comfortably take on yourself. Novice owners are best in a situation where reliable, trusted help is close at hand. Be honest about your capabilities.

To be in exclusive charge of your horse's welfare, you should have practical experience in all horse-care responsibilities, be confident at coping with all everyday issues, and recognize when you need more expert help. If your hands-on experience is patchy, limited, or rusty, then acknowledge this and don't risk going it alone just yet.

What you can do:

- Spend time helping out at a local riding school or boarding barn.

- Offer your services to a hard-pressed owner in return for the practical horse-care experience.

- Find out if your local riding school or local college offers part-time stable management or other horse-care related courses.

- Join the United States Pony Club if you are under 21, or the British Horse Society, and find out about education programs.

housing should be in good repair—in addition to the safety factor, awkward doors and gates are frustratingly time-wasting.

Daily Turnout: Not all barns offer year-round turnout because some are reluctant to see their fields churned up during the winter. But, because overconfinement can lead to endless health and mental welfare problems, several hours a day outside are a must. Preferably, this should be loose at grass but, failing this, every horse must have at least the

chance to stretch his legs in a safe, enclosed area. Immediately discount any barn not able to offer this. Remember, the more limited the amount of natural exercise your horse gets, the more daily ridden exercise you must provide. Again, if you are considering a big barn with restricted turnout facilities, check how things are organized. You may find that your horse is getting very little time out if only one field is available for a barn full of horses.

Companionship: Horses need the company of their own kind. The more settled the group of horses, the better. The high client turnover of some barns is stressful for the horses there because they will constantly be readjusting their relationships within the "herd." Ideally, thought should be given to the compatibility of horses within grazing groups, and new introductions should be made carefully.

Forage and Feed: Quality forage and feed should be given according to your horse's individual nutritional requirements. What if your horse needs a special diet, or is a particularly poor or good keeper? Must you use feed supplied by the barn, and, if so, is it of good quality and reasonable in price?

Daily Attention: Daily maintenance must come from caring, competent people who are observant enough to notice and take action on any worries they might have.

From your own perspective, the barn must:

Meet Your Horse's Needs: Does it get good marks for all the factors listed above? If not, can you make up for any inadequacies? Do you have confidence in whoever is in charge?

Be in the Right Place: The nearest barn may not fit the bill, so be prepared to travel if necessary. On the other hand, be realistic about the difficulties of transport. If you intend to do most or all the work yourself, traveling 20 miles across town to a barn you

Lifestyle Options

marginally prefer, or where your friends are, simply won't make sense during a big December freeze-up. Look for facilities near your place of work if nothing is available close to home, or for a barn situated en route between work and home. Having a stable near your workplace means that a lunchtime visit (even a ride) may be possible, and although weekend trips may be longer, you'll have more free time then. Proximity to home, on the other hand, allows for a late-evening visit too. Many horses are left unattended by their DIY owners from late evening to late morning—and a lot can go wrong in that time.

Have the Proper Facilities: In riding terms, the facility should offer access to quiet trails and a range of off-road riding, preferably not all on routes likely to turn to knee-deep mud. During fall and spring, it may be possible to ride in the field, but don't blame a barn owner for banning this as the weather worsens—it's your horse's food that's being trampled on! Never underestimate how hard it is to find time to ride in winter, especially when you are trying to

keep a horse fit for competition. Paying more for a place with an all-weather riding ring, or even an indoor arena, is worth considering.

Barn Facilities: Look at general barn facilities, too. This may seem picky, but when the wind is blowing, and it's been raining cats and dogs for the third week in a row, you will be thankful for choosing a place with a few modern conveniences.

Consider the following:
- How close is the feed room/haystore to the stables?
- How many water taps are there, and where are they?
- Where will you have to haul the muck?
- Is there a tack room, and how secure is it?
- Are fences, gates, and stables in good repair?
- Is an undercover area available where field-kept horses can shelter to dry off, tack up, be shod, and leave blankets to dry?

Your horse will need a large, solid, well-ventilated stable.

Daily turnout should be considered essential.

- Can you store your own food, mucking-out tools, and other equipment safely?
- How secure is the barn? Preferably, someone should be on-site 24 hours a day.
- Is there an electricity supply? What about a phone, and a bathroom?
- Is there ample, secure parking, plus trailer room?

The barn should be reasonably tidy and, above all, safe. There should be somewhere to put away mucking-out tools, and there should be easily accessible fire-fighting equipment. All areas to be used by horses should be clear of dangerous garbage. Remember, if your horse has an accident, any claim of negligence against a proprietor is compromised if you knew those lengths of rusty barbed wire were left coiled up right next to the trough, but you still kept your horse in the field without doing anything about it.

The barn should offer the services you need. If you have decided you need part board, then the barn must be able to do all the care jobs necessary when you need them to. If you would like feed and bedding supplied by the barn, it should be of a quality you are happy with—and given in the quantities you request (and pay for).

If dust is an issue, ask if a bed of shavings or paper is available instead (and check that it's not adjoining a straw one). In all cases, turnout time should be as much as you want for your horse. Ask if the barn turns out, brings in, and feeds all the horses together, or when you request.

Reasonable house rules are important. With part and full board, you want a barn owner or manager who takes a real interest in your horse and is prepared to be flexible, within reason, about meeting his individual needs. Well-run barns also bring up the subject of insurance (many will expect you to have at least third-party coverage, perhaps also veterinarian fee coverage). They will expect you to sign a boarding contract. Read this carefully before committing yourself. Confirm the use of facilities and charges (what's standard and what's extra), and the barn's policy on important care issues like turnout, worming, and standard veterinary care. This may seem a bit demanding, but many a bitter disagreement can be avoided if everyone knows the score from the start.

It is helpful to share space with other owners you can get along with. Of course, this is difficult to tell until you have spent some time at a barn, but even a brief visit should be enough to get an impression of whether the other clients seem to share your approach to horse care. Would you be happy to spend time with these people, or to have them help with your horse? Is there a match age-wise—a barn full of children and ponies may not be your scene.

Settling In

Horses thrive on the security of familiarity, so changing homes is a traumatic time, especially for sensitive types. Forethought and planning will hopefully help you avoid having to repeat the exercise too often.

When buying a new horse, find out as much as possible about the routine he is used to and stick to it for the time being, making any changes gradually (particularly those to do with diet).

The change of scene and the routine of moving to a new barn will unsettle any horse. Continuing your established routine and spending extra time with him will ease him into his unfamiliar environment. Careful introductions to new companions are crucial.

Most horses find changing homes very stressful.

Chapter Two

Principles of Feeding

Feeding a horse is a year-round occupation, although there are times when it becomes more important, such as during the cold winter months. Whatever the season, providing the correct diet is one of the most difficult aspects of horse ownership. It is all too easy to get bogged down with the technicalities of nutrition and lose sight of the individual horse's requirements. For this reason, it is worth a look at the basics of equine diets and establishing a few fundamental points.

Food is fuel. Just as with people, horses need fuel to:
• grow and maintain their bodies
• keep up their body temperature
• breed and pass on their genes
• provide energy to escape from threats to their safety
In other words, food is about individual and species survival.

How a horse eats is as vitally important to his well-being as *why* he eats. The horse has a digestive system designed to process a slow but steady trickle of small quantities of low-quality fibrous food. Eating for most of the day (16 to 17 hours) is not only a physical but a mental need. Keeping that constant stream of food coming in is the be-all and end-all of a horse's existence. No wonder that the way to his heart

is through his stomach—not because he is greedy, but because everything about both his digestive system and his attitude toward food is driven by that overwhelming need simply to keep on chewing.

To sum up, your horse's feed must supply him with three things:

- essential maintenance nutrients and energy so his body runs efficiently day to day
- additional energy for the extra activities we expect of him
- and equally important but too often ignored, his feed must fulfill his physical and mental drive to chew and keep his digestive system on the go

By checking your horse's diet against these essential criteria, you won't go wrong.

What Should We Feed?

To satisfy overall nutritional needs, the ingredients of your horse's diet must combine to provide a minimum level of five nutrients:

- protein for muscle and cell growth, maintenance, and repair
- fat for warmth and slow-burning energy
- carbohydrates for faster-burning energy
- fiber to keep the digestive system functioning efficiently
- vitamins and minerals to support the whole system by maintaining the correct balance of chemicals in the body

Any work we expect the horse to do increases his body's energy requirement. To avoid depleting essential energy reserves needed for day-to-day living and to fulfill the need for additional energy, we must provide extra calories, either in the form of fast-burning carbohydrates or slower-burning oils and fats.

To fulfill your horse's physical and mental drive to chew and keep his digestive system on the go, you must supply sufficient quantities of just one

thing: fiber. A horse will chew 2 lbs (1 kg) of hay up to 6,000 times before swallowing, compared to 1,000 times for the same amount of concentrated feed. Thus, satisfying that urge to chew using concentrated feeds alone would be impossible. The continued movement and whole equilibrium of the digestive system depends on fiber.

Grass: The Complete Feed?

Does any one food contain all these essentials in the right proportions? The answer is yes—and no. In theory, grass can provide everything your horse requires for health and survival, and it is the ideal and only truly complete feed for horses. The equine body took millions of years to evolve into a super-efficient fiber-processing machine able to extract all its energy and nutrient requirements from the steady passage of grasses through the gut, together with a regular drink of water.

Theoretically, grass should supply a horse with all his nutritional needs.

Principles of Feeding

The problems horse owners face are threefold. First, grass is no longer what it was. Constant access to unimproved, permanent pasture with a diversity of plant species is a luxury few horses enjoy. Most have to make do with limited exposure to modern grassland that is often overgrazed and covered with plenty of weeds, but has very little in the way of beneficial grasses and other herbage.

Second, we want our horses to do much more than just exist and survive. We want them to look healthy and lean, with glossy coats that impress the show judge. But we also want them to school for an hour, gallop and jump cross-country, or go for a 20-, 50-, or even a 100-mile trail ride. As a result, grass alone is not generally sufficient to satisfy either their full range of nutritional requirements or their full energy needs.

Finally, we want energy level and condition kept constant all year round. Grass, however, is not consistent in its nutritional makeup or value. As summer progresses into fall and winter, grass becomes increasingly fibrous and indigestible, insufficient in feed value to replace the extra calories used up to keep warm. Only with the onset of spring does the carbohydrate and nutrient content begin to increase—and then intensify—before leveling off and then dropping once more.

Wild horses adapted to this nutritional roller coaster by storing up fat reserves in the summer to be drawn on during winter. With their extra energy expenditure, our horses need their tank topped off, especially during the lean winter months.

That being said, good-quality grass (or its dried forms) single-handedly goes a long way toward fulfilling our three criteria. As such, grass, together with other forms of digestible fiber, should always be considered the staple ingredient of every horse's diet.

Providing Fiber

Deprived of sufficient fiber, a horse will suffer physically (being prone to colic, ulcers, and other digestive problems) and psychologically (turning to other things to chew, such as woodwork, blankets, or

Fiber Tips

- Shake out hay before putting it into the net or rack. All kinds of things can fall out that accidentally got into the bale. If you disappear in clouds of dust, soak the hay and change your supply.

- Typically, a slice of hay weighs about 4.4 lbs (2 kg), but it is worth weighing your hay to be sure how much you are giving. Bales vary in their density. Big, round bales are far less tightly packed than small, traditional ones.

- Reduce waste in the field by using sheep hayracks, cattle feeders, or making your own wire/plastic mesh containers and securing them in the right positions.

- Check droppings. The length of fiber in them indicates how well your horse is digesting his roughage.

- Six hours is the maximum time your horse should be without forage to eat before it adversely affects his gut function. Overnight, provide enough hay (or slow down his rate of eating what he is given) so that you can be sure it will last until long past midnight.

gulping air). Digestible fiber (forage or bulk feed) can be provided in the form of grass and hay or, in lesser amounts, within feedstuffs such as sugar beet pulp, bran, and complete pellets.

Grass

A 1,100-lb (500-kg) horse on good pasture will eat about 110 lbs (50 kg) of grass a day. This amount seems vast until we remember that fresh grass is up to 80 percent water, so a horse needs to eat that amount just to get the necessary level of nutrients from the remaining 20 percent. To get the most feed value from grass, it pays to take care of your grazing land.

The Right Start

How much nutrition a horse is getting from the grass depends on the time of year and the types and quality of grasses that make up the pasture. During spring and summer, well-managed pasture can support up to four horses per acre, with extra feeding only needed for animals doing hard work. But in winter, the same space will represent barely more than an exercise area for a single horse. When its quality is low or quantity insufficient, grass is likely to need supplementing with other fiber sources.

Hay

Providing hay is the main way of keeping fiber supply up when a horse isn't at pasture (or when pasture quality is poor). Hay is grass that has been harvested at its most nutritious in late spring or early summer, dried, and baled. Again, the feed value of hay varies enormously depending on the pasture from which it was taken.

Choosing Hay

Hay may be good, adequate, or plain old bad for your horse. It all depends on the nutrient value of the grass when the hay was cut and how well it has been harvested and stored. Knowing what you are looking for when choosing hay not only means you can get lots more nutrition for your money, but it can also, literally, be a lifesaver.

Don't be fooled into buying bad hay; buy the best you can. After all, it is going to be the foundation of your horse's diet for most of the winter and early spring, and possibly all year if he is stabled throughout the spring and summer, too. When searching out supplies, ask for several bales to be opened so you can look right inside, take out a handful, and give it a good sniff. It is well worth having hay (and grass) analyzed so that you know exactly what you are getting in terms of nutrients.

Quality

Select hay on the basis of quality and type.
Good hay should:

- have a clean, fresh appearance and a pleasant smell
- be a uniformly green, greenish beige, or clean, bleached color (gray or brown coloring suggests mold growth and weathering)
- be free of mold and contain very little dust
- be free of weeds (watch out for ragwort in the United Kingdom)
- contain grass leaves rather than too many stalks or seed heads (which indicate it was cut late and so has lower feed value)

Dust and mold spores are the real villains. Any nutritional deficiency can always be made up using concentrated feeds and supplements, but dust or mold can do irreparable damage to your horse's lungs.

Hay must be of good quality and correctly stored.

Grass hay.

Seed hay.

Type

Choose a type of hay that has the nutritional value best suited to your horse's needs.

Grass Hay: Grass hay is taken from established pasture. It usually contains a variety of grasses and other plants with soft, thinner stalks and leaves. It offers a medium-to-low protein level.

Seed Hay: Seed hay is produced from specially sown rye grass. Stalks and leaves are coarse. It offers a higher protein content.

Legume Hay: Legume hay is grown from alfalfa (lucerne) and clover. (In the United Kingdom, it is more commonly fed in small quantities as *chaff*, which is chopped-up hay sold in bags.)

Storing Hay

Hay continues to dry in the stack, so ideally it should not be used until it is at least 5 months old. It is best eaten within 12 to 18 months.

To keep its feed value, store hay in a clean, dry place, free of vermin. Keep hay off the ground on pallets or by lining the stack with straw bales, which also help to draw out remaining moisture. Hay must breathe—never store it wrapped or covered in plastic, or condensation will build up and promote mold.

Soaking Hay

Despite a horse's digestion being geared up to receive its nutrients in a diluted form (for example, in grass), the forage you provide over the winter period is invariably dried. Wetting or damping forage (and concentrated feeds) brings it closer to natural feeding and makes it more easily digested.

Dry forage is also potentially dusty and is therefore bad news for the respiratory and digestive systems. Whether changes in climate, modern production methods, or increasing sensitivity in our horses are to blame, there's no doubt that getting good hay is becoming more difficult. Even the very best hay contains a certain amount of dust, however well it is harvested and stored. To guard against the risk of lung damage, all hay is best fed soaked—to all horses, not just those with existing respiratory problems.

The purpose of soaking is to swell any dust particles and mold spores sufficiently so that they are swallowed with the hay and not breathed into the respiratory tract, where they irritate and inflame the delicate lining of the lungs. In the past, it was recommended that hay be soaked for 12 or even 24 hours, but this prolonged soaking is unnecessary and problematic. Most of the offending particles are swollen within half an hour of immersion. Longer exposure only allows nutrients and flavor to leach away into the water, which itself then becomes polluted with toxins.

Guidelines for Efficient, Effective Hay Soaking

- Use a container that is big enough for the amount of hay to be soaked and easy to fill and drain (one that contains a whole bale is best).
- Split the slices and submerge the hay completely, using a heavy object to keep it down.
- Soak for 10 to 45 minutes, depending on quantity.
- Drain completely before using.
- Use fresh water for each soaking.
- Feed while wet, because once the hay dries the particles become airborne again.
- Sodium, potassium, and phosphorus are all lost during soaking, so replace these with a teaspoon of salt in each feed and a vitamin/mineral supplement.

Purpose-designed hay-soaking units are available, but these are costly for small barns or individuals. An old trough or tub does the job just as well.

Some owners steam hay as a quick alternative to soaking. Steaming is less effective, but it is better than feeding hay totally dry. Steaming is useful if you are in a hurry, short of water, or the soaking bin keeps freezing over. You will need a kettle and a large plastic sheet or sack, or a waterproof container (for example, a trash can) with drain holes. Pour boiling water over a loosely filled hay net, put it into your steamer container, and immediately cover tightly. Add another kettleful once it has boiled. Leave for at least 20 minutes, and feed right away.

Feeding Hay

Feed hay in a way that minimizes waste and provides an eating position that is as natural as possible for your horse.

Off the Ground/Floor: Ground feeding allows for a natural eating position, helps mucus to drain, and keeps dust down and away from the nostrils. Make sure the floor or bed itself is clean. A safe container, such as an old laundry basket, helps to reduce waste.

Racks and Hay Nets: These must be carefully positioned to be at a comfortable chest height, but not so low as to be potentially unsafe in a stable. Both create more of a dust hazard than does ground feeding.

It is important to shake out hay before feeding.

Alternatives to Hay

When hay is in short supply, perhaps due to a wet summer, other forms of fiber must be fed to compensate. Fortunately, hay replacements are available that are not only useful in times of hay shortage, but are also a boon for the owners of dust-sensitive horses or older animals who find chewing difficult. Each has its own features, so choose carefully according to your horse's individual needs. Remember to introduce any changes gradually. Assess how the alternative fiber source will affect the overall balance of your horse's ration, and try to make sure it nutritionally complements his hard feed.

Use fresh water for each hay soaking.

Principles of Feeding

Oat Straw

Low in calories, high in bulk, oak straw is a suitable hay replacement for ponies and other "good keepers."

- Oat straw is dry compared to hay, so dampen it before feeding and up the horse's water intake (for example, add succulents or soaked sugar beet to concentrated feed).
- Harder to chew and digest than hay, oat haylage is only suitable for horses with sound teeth.
- Don't allow hungry horses to overeat oat straw, or impaction colic becomes a risk.
- Verify the variety before buying—other straws, such as wheat, are very indigestible.

High-Fiber Pellets

Another hay alternative, high-fiber pellets are made from grass meal and cereal fiber, which is ground and compressed into shape with added vitamins and minerals.

- Although high-fiber pellets are a useful addition to fiber intake, they are unsuitable as a complete replacement for long roughage such as hay because the pellets are eaten and digested too quickly.
- Pellets are helpful for overweight ponies, resting horses, or to supplement poor grass.

Sugar Beet Pulp

Sugar beet pulp is a by-product of sugar production. Molasses is added to the beet pulp and fibers before drying and shredding or pelleting.

- This food source has a high energy value but slow release because the energy comes from digestible fiber, not carbohydrate.
- Products without molasses reduce the carbohydrate level further.
- Sugar beet pulp must be soaked in plenty of water for up to 12 hours (shreds) or 24 hours (pellets) before feeding.

- Because it will ferment, use it immediately after soaking.
- Up to 4 lbs (1.8 kg) can be fed daily.

Haylage

A cross between hay and silage, haylage is produced by baling hay before it has fully dried (at 50 percent moisture rather than 20 percent) and vacuum-packing it to seal in nutrients. It is popular in the United Kingdom, but it is not often used in the United States.

- Compared to hay, haylage contains half the fiber per pound (kg), but it is more digestible so it has greater energy content. Feed 1 1/2 times (by weight) more haylage than hay.
- Haylage adds more fiber when mixed with soaked hay, chopped alfalfa, or oat straw.
- It is dust-free and consistent in feed value.
- Due to its wetness, haylage is a more natural feed than dry hay.
- It's easy to store, but check that the bales have not been punctured; open bales may contain mold.
- Because haylage is very palatable, use a small-hole hay net or one hay net inside the other to slow down the horse's eating rate.
- Different feed values of haylage are available. Select a low-energy, high-fiber type for hot horses or those in light work.
- Only consider buying big-bale haylage if you are certain it has been made specifically for horses by a reputable producer and you are feeding five or more animals. Make sure that each bale is eaten within 4 days. Silage produced in clamps for cattle is very acidic and may be a risk for botulism and digestive problems in horses.

Sugar beet must be soaked before feeding.

29

It is important to shake out hay before feeding.

• It is dust-free.
• Alfalfa is higher in energy and protein than grass hay, so it is not a direct replacement, but it is useful for competition horses as an extension to the hay supply.
• Grass hay/alfalfa mix is better for horses who are working less. It's also a good source of calcium, and it's useful for older horses.

Supplying Nutrients

Nutrients and energy that cannot be provided by your horse's forage must be supplied in the form of concentrated feed. Exactly what he still needs depends on his individual requirements (which is why no single diet suits all horses) and what feed value he is getting from the grass, hay, and other fiber sources already in his diet. This requires a nutritional analysis of his diet.

We will be planning an individual horse's diet later, but first let's look at what is available in terms of concentrated feeds and what is likely to best suit your horse.

Concentrated feeds all belong to one of two groups: They are either basic cereal grains or compounds (mixed feeds like sweet feed, a grain containing molasses).

Chaff

Chaff is hay, oat straw, alfalfa, or a mixture of all or any of these chopped into short lengths to be added to concentrated feed. It is often coated with molasses, which increases the energy value and makes it more palatable. Chaff is commonly used in the United Kingdom, but not in the United States.

• Chaff is most useful for boosting the fiber content of the diet and aiding digestion by extending concentrated feeds.
• It can be a partial, but not complete, replacement for hay on a weight-for-weight basis.

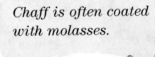

Chaff is often coated with molasses.

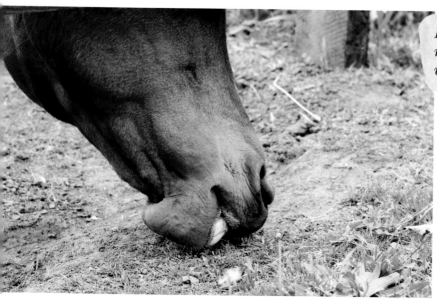

In some cases, forage may need to be supplemented with concentrated feed.

Compound Concentrated Feeds

It's important to learn about the different properties of the various straight cereals because they are the basic ingredients of all compound concentrated feeds. The proportions of different grains used in compound mixes and pellets determine how suitable that compound is for a particular horse.

Compounds are essentially a formulation of grains, other nutrient sources (e.g., beans, peas, grass, or milk pellets), vitamins, and minerals. They are produced either in a granola form or ground and pressed into pellets or cubes. Compounds have been a revolution in horse feeding because they are prepared by the manufacturer to provide a correctly balanced diet. Along with forage and water, they provide all that your horse needs.

Other advantages of compound concentrated feeds include:

- Different formulations are made for horses with different energy and protein needs, from maintenance to those in hard or competition work, brood mares and ponies, to old horses. There is one to suit every horse.
- It's hard to go wrong with compound feeds as long as you feed according to the manufacturer's instructions and don't unbalance the ration by adding other feedstuffs yourself.
- Because they are a complete diet in one bag, compounds save time, money, and storage space.
- There is usually no need for supplementation if fed in the recommended quantity for the horse's body weight.
- Consistent quality is guaranteed.
- Palatability helps to tempt fussy feeders.

Straight Cereal Grains

Straight cereal grains used for feed are oats, barley, corn, and the like. Horses, of course, did not evolve to eat bucketfuls of cereals, so these grains have generally undergone various processes to ease digestion, such as rolling, crushing, micronizing (cooking), or extrusion. Traditionally, all horses were fed a combination of cereals, but this involves numerous drawbacks:

- Cereals are all high in starch (and therefore fast-burning energy), but their protein is poor in quality and their mineral content is low or out of balance with the horse's requirements (in particular, the necessary calcium:phosphorus ratio is reversed).
- The horse's digestive system is designed to cope with fiber passing slowly through the gut. Starch can only be digested in the relatively small stomach and foregut, so they should be fed only in limited quantities (no more than 5.5 lbs/2.5 kg) per feed. Unabsorbed nutrients will simply be wasted.
- Creating a ration containing the correct balance of nutrients, vitamins, and minerals by mixing cereals is virtually impossible without scientific analysis.
- Many myths surround cereal feeds. Whole oats, for example, contain less energy than barley, especially once soaked.

The Right Start

In theory, the advent of compound concentrated feeds has simplified diet planning immensely. Market forces being what they are, however, there is now such a bewildering array of compounds available, covering every shade of purpose, that owners struggle to see the forest for the trees.

To stay competitive, most manufacturers produce a range to cover most needs. One approach is to settle on a brand you can trust and that is readily available to you, then phone that manufacturer's own advice line for help in planning a diet suitable for your horse. Many major feed companies have their own nutritionists whose expertise is available free of charge, so why not take advantage of the service?

A horse on poor-quality or limited grazing may benefit from supplements.

Balancers

A relatively recent innovation, balancer pellets or mixes also aim to take some of the hard work out of calculating a nutritionally correct ration. There are two types available:

Feed Balancers: Feed balancers are designed to be fed along with straight grains and forage to correct the protein and mineral deficiencies in the cereals. They are frequently used in performance horse/racing yards to balance an oat-based ration.

Forage Balancers: Forage balancers are designed for feeding along with good-quality forage. They fully or partly replace all-concentrate feed by creating the correct environment in the hindgut for maximum efficiency in absorbing nutrients, vitamins, and minerals from forage in the diet. An extremely versatile system, they are in harmony with the horse's natural digestion. They work well for all types, ages,

and uses of horse and pony. Those with high-energy needs can be given a complementary high-calorie supplement.

Succulents

Apples, carrots, and root vegetables or sugar beet all make a horse's diet more interesting and provide the succulence lacking when grass intake is limited. Think of fruits and vegetables as an add-on rather than as a diet mainstay—it is possible to overfeed them. Be sure to cut them up carefully, too, slicing them lengthwise to avoid choking hazards.

Supplements and Additives

A huge variety of extras is available to put into your horse's bucket. But the important question is: How much supplementation is really necessary, and how much simply exploits our concern to make sure our horses are not missing out on anything that could do them good? First, it's important to appreciate the distinction between supplements and additives.

Supplements

Supplements correct a known deficiency in a diet and might include specific vitamins (for example, biotin to improve horn quality), minerals (limestone flour, high in calcium), and electrolytes (body salts). A broad-spectrum vitamin/mineral supplement will contain a range of micronutrients and trace elements to boost the levels of these in an otherwise balanced diet.

Before rushing out to buy a supplement, confirm that your horse genuinely has a deficiency in his current

Compounds are designed for horses with differing energy requirements.

diet and, if so, identify what it is. Otherwise, it is impossible to know what supplement, if any, he needs. The only sure way to find out is to have the major part of his diet (his grass/hay) nutritionally analyzed and checked against what you are providing in the way of concentrated feed. A horse on good-quality grazing being given the full amount of concentrated feed recommended by the manufacturer for his size is unlikely to require a supplement.

Supplements are most likely to be needed by:
- horses being fed no concentrated feed or small quantities of concentrated feed below the manufacturer's recommendation (on a maintenance, invalid, or low-energy diet)
- performance horses eating high levels of grains with limited access to grazing
- horses on poor-quality feed, grazing, or hay
- horses under stress—competition horses, growing ponies and brood mares, old horses, and invalids

Additives

As their name implies, additives are substances added to a diet that is already balanced. The addition should be for a specific, identified purpose. Commonly used additives include probiotics ("friendly" fiber-digesting bacteria used to recolonize

Storing Supplements

All supplements and additives must be protected from light and damp and used while as fresh as possible.

Storing Concentrates

Concentrated feeds must be handled with care to do their job properly, which means giving thought to storage. Storage areas should be cool, well ventilated, clean, and secure.

No feedstuff has an indefinite shelf life. How long a bag will keep depends on what it is—whole oats, for example, will go bad in 3 weeks, whereas cooked cereals stay fresh much longer. Always check the expiration date on the bag, and remember, that once open and exposed to the air, the vitamin content starts to deteriorate. Rats and mice also love nothing more than bags of grain left stacked in feed rooms. Store unopened bags well off the ground, and put open bags in vermin-proof containers. Make sure all the old feed is used up and the container is cleaned before adding in a fresh bag.

Feed rooms need securing from horses, too! No escapee from the yard must be able to get at feed containers. Clearly labeling each bin and putting up a chart that shows each horse's diet helps to prevent feeding mistakes and means everyone knows what each individual needs.

the hindgut), yeasts (to promote the right gut environment for these bacteria to thrive), and enzymes (to stimulate effective digestion).

Herbs

Herbs are natural alternatives to synthetically created supplements and additives. The same rules apply to all herb-based products: Identify the need, treat them with respect as the medicines they are, buy only the best quality, and use and store them with care. Remember that many drug ingredients are derived from or related to herbs.

Planning a Diet

Having established the elements that make up your horse's diet, you now need to determine how much to feed.

Flexibility is very much the name of the game in diet planning. A good owner will be constantly looking with a critical eye at her horse's shape and energy levels and assessing whether his diet is meeting his needs. Those needs will be different for every horse, so in any barn where the occupants are all given the same ration, a lot of horses are being improperly fed.

The main factors that determine the makeup of an individual ration are:
- condition
- size and build
- type
- workload
- temperament
- age
- time of year
- the horse's management system and health status

How each of these fits into the overall picture will be explored further as we go.

Working out a ration seems daunting, but in fact it breaks down into four straightforward steps.

Step One: Assess Condition and Calculate Body Weight

As a general rule, the bigger the horse, the more food he requires to fuel him. Body weight is a much more accurate indicator than height because a well-built 15hh cob can easily weigh more than a rangy 16.2hh Thoroughbred (TB).

Knowing your horse's weight is vital not only to feed him correctly but also to judge how much wormer or medicine he may need. Don't make guesses. The average 15.2hh TB may weigh 1,100 lbs (500 kg), but researchers weighing 500 animals fitting that description found weights ranging between 904 and 1,212 lbs (410 and 550 kg).

If you do not have access to a weigh bridge, use a weight tape or simply use an ordinary tape to measure around the horse's barrel, just behind the withers, as close to the forelegs as possible (the heart to girth), and use the body weight table.

The next questions are: Is that body weight ideal? Are you happy with the amount of condition your horse is carrying? Does he need building up, slimming down, or maintaining as he is?

A fat horse obviously needs to eat less and/or exercise more, just as we do when we are trying to lose weight. Most leisure horses in the Western world are grossly overfed for the work they do, and a fat horse is certainly not a healthy one. On the other hand, a thin horse is not receiving enough fuel to work and retain sufficient reserves to keep him well covered with warming layers of fat. (Bear in mind that fit performance animals need to be "lean and mean," whereas it's

Replacing Body Salts

Essential body salts must be replaced with electrolytes added to the drinking water before and after extreme exertion, particularly in hot weather. Salt itself (sodium chloride) is essential for all horses. Although it is added to compounds, it is worth providing a salt lick or adding a teaspoonful to each feed for horses not being given the full, recommended amount of feed.

fashionable—although that doesn't make it right!—for show animals to carry a lot of "condition.")

Monitor your horse's weight about every two weeks or you may not notice weight loss until it has gone so far that it takes a lot to regain lost pounds. Practice assessing the condition of every horse you see throughout the year because this will help to give you an eye for what looks right. Don't confuse the issue by taking a horse's belly into account (an animal might have a huge belly but sticking-out ribs), involving conformation (individual shape or build), or mistaking loss of muscle tone for loss of condition.

Condition scoring gives you an objective assessment and useful guideline for what your goals are.

The diet you feed is dependent on your horse's workload.

Skinny, Fat, or Just Right?: Condition Scoring

Condition Score	Quarters	Back and Ribs	Neck and Shoulders
0 Extremely emaciated	Deep cavity under tail and either side of croup. Pelvis angular. No detectable fatty tissue between skin and bone.	Processes of vertebrae sharp to touch. Skin drawn tightly over ribs.	Ewe-neck (neck shaped like a sheep's neck); very narrow; individual bone structure visible. Bone structure of shoulder visible. No fatty tissue.
1 Thin	Pelvis and croup well defined, no fatty tissue, but skin supple. Poverty lines (deep lines running down hindquarters either side of tail) visible, and deep depression under tail.	Ribs and backbone clearly defined, but skin slack over bones.	Ewe-neck; narrow, flat muscle covering. Shoulder accentuated, some fat.
2 Moderately thin	Croup well defined, but some fatty tissue under skin. Pelvis easily felt, slight depression under tail. Not obviously thin.	Backbone just covered by fatty tissue, individual processes not visible, but easily felt on pressure. Ribs just visible.	Narrow but firm.
3 Moderately fleshy	Whole pelvic region rounded, not angular and no gutter (depression) along croup. Skin smooth and supple, pelvis easily felt.	Backbone and ribs well covered, but easily felt on pressure.	Shoulder not obviously thin.
4 Fat	Pelvis buried in fatty tissue and only felt on firm pressure. Gutter over croup.	Backbone and ribs well covered and only felt on firm pressure. Gutter along backbone.	Neck blends smoothly into body. No crest except for stallions. Layer of fat over shoulder.
5 Obese	Pelvis buried in firm, fatty tissue and cannot be felt. Clear, deep gutter over croup to base of dock. Skin stretched.	Back looks flat with deep gutter along backbone. Ribs buried and cannot be felt.	Very wide and firm, marked crest, even in mares. Shoulder bulging fat.

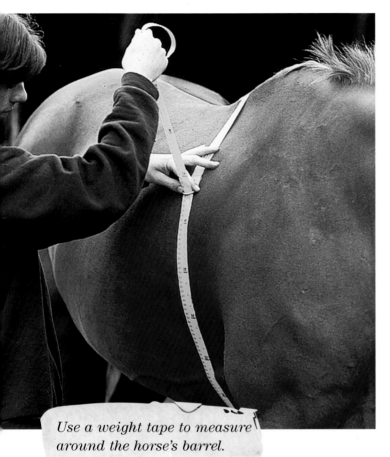

Use a weight tape to measure around the horse's barrel.

those in light work, good-quality forage may well be able to make up the total ration. As workload increases, the proportion of energy-giving concentrated feeds in the total must increase.

However, forage should never, under any circumstances, be reduced to less than 50 percent of the ration.

Most owners overestimate their horse's workload. A trail ride for an hour or so daily, with a weekly schooling session, just about qualifies as moderate work. Anything less is light work. Hard-working animals are usually serious performance athletes.

Step Four: Customizing the Ration and Meeting Special Needs

You now have established a daily total and have calculated what proportion of that must be given in forage (grass, hay, haylage, etc.). The remainder of the diet is supplied by the concentrated feed of your choice, with the type selected according to your horse's individual needs.

The ration you have calculated, based on body weight and workload, will always be a sound basis

Step Two: Calculate Basic Ration

Most horses require 2 to 2.5 percent of their body weight each day in food to maintain condition and have surplus energy for work. So, having worked out your horse's body weight, do the math to find out the weight of feed he will need daily. The appetite chart gives an approximate guide. Remember, this amount is per day, and any concentrated feed must be spread out over at least two (preferably more) meals and forage given throughout the day.

Step Three: Forage to Concentrate Ratio

Now consider what sort of work your horse does. The less work he does, the more the daily amount can be provided as bulk forage. For resting horses or

Appetite Chart

Body weight		Moderate work level: appetite=2.5% body weight	
lb	kg	lb	kg
440	200	11	5
900	400	22	10
1000	450	25	11.5
1100	500	27.5	12.5
1200	550	30	13.5
1320	600	32	14.5

Calculating Feed Rations: Forage to Concentrate Ratio

Workload	Activity level	% hay:concentrates
Maintenance	Maintaining body weight, temperature, and muscle.	100:0
	Moving about the field or quiet exercise.	90:10
Light (a)	Walking or steady trail riding 3 or 4 times a week.	85:15
Light (b)	Trail riding or short schooling sessions with some slow cantering or occasional show.	80:20
Moderate	Schooling 5–6 times a week, jumping and/or dressage with regular competition.	75:25
Hard	Affiliated eventing, driving, endurance, or hunting.	50:50
Fast	Racing.	50:50

from which to start. It may well need some fine-tuning, though, to take into account the other factors mentioned earlier. Quantity may need to be increased or decreased, the makeup of the ration altered, or the choice of concentrated feeds may need tinkering until you reach a ration that keeps your horse happy, performing well, and looking good. It is vitally important to monitor diet constantly and to be flexible if a particular formula does not seem to be working out well.

Bear in mind, for example, that your horse's diet is unlikely to stay the same all year. It will be influenced by the weather conditions and by the way you keep him. A horse who lives outside most or all of the time will get

It is only performance horses who qualify as hard-working animals.

working harder, will require more energy in the form of concentrated feed. Horses kept indoors year round must be fed hay all summer as well.

Other circumstances in which your horse may need more or less than the standard amount, or where special needs must be taken into account, include the following types of horses.

Easy and Poor Keepers: Individuals within any breed, but notoriously hairy ponies and cobs, can be exceptionally efficient food processors who appear to be able to get fat almost on fresh air. A reduction in overall quantity and restriction of grass and concentrated feed (along with regular, steady

Calculating Body Weight

Girth		Approximate body weight	
inches	cm	lb	kg
54	137	450	205
55	140	500	227
57	145	550	250
58	147	600	272
60	152	650	295
61	155	700	318
63	160	750	340
64	163	800	363
66	167	850	386
67	170	900	408
68	173	950	431
69	175	1,000	454
71	181	1,050	476
72	183	1,100	499
74	187	1,150	522
75	189	1,200	544
76	193	1,250	567
77	196	1,300	590

If your horse lives outside during the winter, his diet must be adjusted accordingly.

most or all of his needs from good pasture from May to September. In winter, he will need a diet with an emphasis on warmth, which means lots of forage in the form of hay—with extra supplied during spells of bad weather.

A horse who spends more time indoors blanketed up has less need for warmth but, if

Don't Overfeed Grains

Overfeeding grains is always going to cause problems for hairy ponies, so don't be tempted to give large quantities of these under any circumstances.

- Are you following a correct worming program. A heavy worm burden damages the gut and steals feed value from the horse.
- Is he warm enough? A cold horse uses huge amounts of calories just keeping up body temperature. Horses living out in bad weather will use up to a third more energy than those who are stabled.
- Is he happy? A tense or stressed horse will worry weight away.

Pinpointing the cause of weight loss is important because it affects how the problem is best tackled. For generally poor keepers, focus on supplying a diet that is:

- sufficient in quantity for his needs—up to 2.5 percent of body weight
- based on good-quality forage
- high in digestible fiber, protein, oils, and other sources of slow-release energy and micronutrients
- able to create and maintain a healthy gut environment through the use of forage balancers, yeast, and/or probiotics

If you suspect weight loss is due to insufficient feed for the horse's workload, provide more energy-giving feeds. Increased protein is best for metabolic problems, which will need diagnosis by a veterinarian.

exercise) is needed to keep them trim and avoid the risk of laminitis year round, but particularly from March to October.

Like some people, some horses are naturally lean, and some are particularly difficult to hold condition. Never ignore weight loss. A sudden or dramatic drop in condition for no apparent reason may indicate a problem that needs veterinary attention. If your horse seems to be eating well but still looks poor, check the following before looking at diet:

- Find out the horse's exact weight and monitor it carefully.
- Is the horse comfortable with his teeth/mouth? If he cannot chew effectively, he won't get value from his feed.

Whizz-Kids and Slowpokes: Calories not only put on weight, they provide fast-burning energy. Most horses on a high-calorie diet will become fast-ticking dynamos as surely as a child who is pumped full of chocolate and sugary soft drinks. The higher the energy

Beware of overfeeding small ponies.

Principles of Feeding

value of what you feed, the more energy your horse has to burn off. Given plenty of exercise and turnout, this is not a problem. However, give a combination of insufficient exercise and not enough turnout, it is hardly surprising that huge numbers of owners find themselves with difficulties.

Temperament will influence how calories affect your horse. Some characters are so laid back they could exist on pure carbohydrate and still need an alarm clock to wake up in the morning. Others only have to sniff a grain of cereal to turn themselves inside out. Only you know your horse, but it is always better to start off with a low-energy diet and gradually increase it, if necessary, than to create problems by overfeeding (either in quantity or by feeding the wrong type of concentrated feed). If you are having behavioral problems, take a long, hard

Winter Conditioning

For a horse who finds it difficult to hold condition over the winter, gradually replace up to half of his concentrated feed ration with a conditioning pellet or mix.

look at what you are giving your horse to eat and turn to more fiber and less carbohydrate before blaming him.

Resting or Recuperating Horses: Here, overall quantity must be maintained but concentrated feeds can be all but cut out of the diet. They can be replaced with forage to keep the system functioning

If a horse is not given sufficient exercise for his diet, he will have surplus energy, which can cause problems.

Wait an hour after feeding before asking for intensive exercise.

horse. A forage balancer, probiotic, and supplementary oils, vitamins, and minerals are all beneficial. Remember, there is no set age at which a horse becomes a senior citizen—look at him as an individual.

Fussy Feeders: Horses who are hard to tempt to eat their concentrated feed very rarely turn their noses up at grass, so the answer to a fussy feeder is to let him unwind out at pasture as much as possible and give good-quality, soaked hay when he is inside. Make concentrated feed meals small, damp, and full of tasty succulents, such as sugar beet, carrots, and apples, and add up to 10 fl oz (300 ml) of corn oil a day for extra calories if needed. A mixed feed is often more palatable than pellets. Keep trying until you find a combination that your fussy feeder likes, and make sure he's not being put off eating by any stress factors in his life.

Practical Feeding

Careful feeding is the key to keeping colic and other digestive upsets at bay. Familiarizing yourself with the feeding pattern and behavior of horses is also essential to avoid trouble on the health and safety fronts. Some of the points covered here will be familiar as golden rules of feeding. Others are simply common sense, practical moves that make life easier and safer for all concerned.

Little and Often: The horse has a small stomach and a long bowel designed for fiber not cereal. For this system to cope with concentrated feeds, cereals must be split into small meals of no more than 4 lbs (2 kg) spread throughout the day, with forage constantly available in between.

Make Changes Gradually: Efficient digestion depends on a vast army of friendly bacteria that

properly and to satisfy the horse's foraging instinct. Supplementation may be needed, and succulents will go down well.

Stallions, Brood Mares, and Young Stock: These horses all have increased protein and mineral requirements that need careful balancing. Ask your veterinarian or feed company nutritionist for advice.

Old Horses: Along with other body processes, such as repair and stress resistance, digestion becomes less efficient with age, making diligent dental care, worming, and warmth even more important. One of the main reasons for weight loss in older horses is the gradual reduction in their ability to chew properly. Help an old horse along by providing fiber in the form of soft grass hay (soaked in water) or haylage, plus chaffs or complete or high-fiber pellets softened into a mash. Use a senior mix. Alfalfa and sugar beet are both easily digested forms of quality fiber, and digestible calcium and protein are also needed in increased quantities by the older

Principles of Feeding

Winter Work Tips

- Adjusting feed ahead of work is crucial. Before days off or during cold snaps or any period when exercise is limited, reduce concentrated feed and replace it with forage to reduce the risk of metabolic upsets such as azoturia.

- Horses competing regularly or hunting over the winter will have higher energy needs, but don't pump them full of energy all week if you only go out once on the weekend.

- Winter competitions always involve a lot of hanging around in cold trailers and warm-up arenas. A low- to medium-energy feed will probably be enough for most horses. Remember to provide plenty of hay and water in the trailer.

populate the gut, breaking down fiber and helping nutrients to be absorbed. Each feedstuff requires its own unique microflora, so building up the right population takes time. Keep feeding regimes as settled as possible.

Make Water Constantly Available: The horse's body is 70 percent water, and he needs to take in around 8 gallons (37 L) a day to maintain this ratio—more with increased exercise. Exact demand will be affected by weather conditions and grass intake, but clean drinking water should be on hand at all times, including both before and after exercise.

Allow Time for Digestion Before Work: A horse feels no more comfortable doing intense, physical activity on a full stomach than we do—less so, perhaps, because his stomach is small and close to his lungs. A quiet walk will do no harm after a small meal, but before intensive exercise, allow at least an hour for digestion.

Keep Utensils Clean: Would you like to eat from the same unwashed dish every day? Neither does your horse.

Know Your Horse's Feeding Habits: Feeding behavior is very personal. For every horse that is greedy and overly enthusiastic at mealtimes, there is another that is insecure, nervous, or cautious. Take into account your horse's character when deciding where and how to feed him, giving him plenty of personal space and a quiet environment if necessary. Knowing what his normal behavior is at feed times will help you quickly spot any changes that could be early signs of something wrong.

Keep Stress Down: Emotions run high at feedtimes, so reduce the tension as much as possible by feeding all horses in a group or barn at the same, regular times each day. If one horse has to be fed at a different time, take him out of sight of the others beforehand.

Separate and Supervise: Jealousies and rivalries always surface when food is around. Accidents happen all too easily amid flying feet and flashing teeth. Each horse will feel more secure in his own space when eating – either safely in his stable, or tied up and separated by at least 15 ft (4.5 m) from any others. Horses prefer not to be hassled while they eat, but never leave them tied up to eat completely unsupervised. Also, don't leave your horse in his stable to finish his feed without seeing he has eaten it all safely. In the field, hay piles are best laid out at a minimum distance of 20 ft (6 m) apart.

Fair Shares for All: Pushy characters in a group will take more than their share if given the chance. Be observant and check that all horses are getting a full ration, changing the feeding arrangements if need be to ensure this.

When feeding hay in the field, lay out several more piles/nets than there are horses. Giving the dominant character in a group access to his feed first helps to keep him out of the picture while you sort out the rest.

Chapter Three

Routine Health Care

Although there are certain conditions that are related to the changing seasons, the overall well-being of your horse is obviously a year-round concern—the basics of good equine health care will remain the same, whatever the time of year.

In every case, prevention is indisputably better than cure, so it is important to be aware of all the circumstances that can adversely affect your horse's health.

Signs of a Healthy Horse

Every owner must be confident that she knows what to aim for in a happy, healthy horse. If you aren't sure how your horse should look and behave, it's impossible to spot the early warning signs of problems brewing.

As a responsible owner, you must get to know your horse and make yourself familiar with what is normal for him. Study his behavior. Is it usual for him to graze apart from the others? Is he characteristically irritable when his girth is tightened?

Knowing what is normal and what is abnormal for your horse, in both his attitude and appearance, is vital. It can make all the difference between eliminating a potential problem early on, or allowing it to become a serious and difficult to treat health condition.

You can tell if a horse is happy and healthy by the way he looks and moves.

Signs of a healthy horse include:
- alertness, responsiveness
- bright eyes
- good condition, relaxed manner
- shining, even coat

His vital signs should be approximately:
- 8–16 breaths per minute at rest
- 35–42 heartbeats per minute at rest
- 38°–38.5° C (99°–101.5° F) rectal temperature

Signs of an Unhealthy Horse

Treatment is often more effective in cases where trouble is spotted early on. Any deviation from the norm should cause you immediate concern. Talk to your veterinarian if you see any of these signs of physical problems or illness:
- change in amount or character of droppings (e.g., hard, diarrhea)
- change in normal behavior – lying down, dull, depressed demeanor
- dull coat, patchy hair loss, sweating without exercise, itching, or rubbing
- cough or faster at-rest breathing rate
- discharges at eyes, nose, vulva, penis
- high (or very low) resting temperature
- high resting pulse rate
- lameness
- poor appetite, or change in appetite or thirst
- reluctance to move; abnormal stance or posture
- swellings on limbs or body
- weight loss

Preventative Health Care

Good day-to-day, year-round management includes regular preventative care in four particular areas:
- vaccination program
- deworming program
- teeth rasping/floating
- foot trimming and shoeing

If done properly, attention to these four issues will not only keep your horse in shape but help prevent numerous problems.

Routine Health Care

Vaccinations

Tetanus, equine influenza, and equine herpes virus are usually preventable by regular immunization. Ignoring the need to vaccinate against tetanus is inexcusable, because horses are very susceptible to this fatal disease. Vaccination against equine influenza must be kept up-to-date for competition purposes as well as for disease prevention.

Tetanus

Tetanus is a serious, usually deadly bacterial infection. Tetanus spores live for years in soil but can enter the body through the smallest of wounds or scrapes. Horses of any age can be affected, with a gradual rigid paralysis taking over the central nervous system. Fortunately, regular vaccination with tetanus toxoid gives complete protection. The program is as follows:

• primary course: two vaccinations given 4 to 6 weeks apart
• first booster: 12 months later
• further boosters: every 1 to 3 years thereafter

Tetanus vaccination is usually incorporated into the vaccination program against equine influenza. Vets often give temporary protection with an injection of tetanus antitoxin when they attend a wounded horse with an unclear vaccination history.

Equine Influenza

Equine flu is a highly contagious respiratory virus that causes a high temperature, nasal discharge, and coughing that can prevent a horse from being worked for several weeks. The vaccination program is as follows:

• first injection: day 0
• second injection: 21–92 days after first injection
• third injection: 150–215 days after second injection
• annual boosters: not more than 365 days

Equine Herpes Virus

Equine herpes virus (EHV) can take several forms, but all lead to respiratory problems, paralysis, or may cause pregnant mares to abort their foals. Not everyone chooses to vaccinate against EHV, but it may be worth considering in high-performance horses or valuable brood mares. The program is as follows:

• vaccination against respiratory infection: boosters every 6 months
• vaccination against abortion: at 5, 7, and 9 months of pregnancy

Worm Control

Effective parasite control is a mainstay of good horse care and involves a combination of sensible pasture management and the strategic use of anthelminthic drugs. All horses will carry a certain amount of parasites, but loss of condition and weight, poor performance, diarrhea, coughing, a pot-bellied appearance, dull coat, and

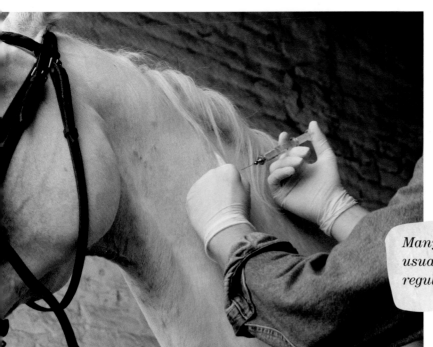

Many equine diseases are usually preventable with regular immunization.

Dewormers

There are many different dewormers available from tack shops, feed stores, and veterinary clinics. Each one contains a drug from one of the families listed below:

- ivermectin (Ivercare, Zimecterin, Rotation 1)

- moxidectin (Quest)

- benzimidazoles – fenbendazole (Panacur, Safe-Guard), oxibendazole (Equitac)

- pyrantel (Strongid P, Rotation 2, Continuex)

No single drug kills all types of worm affecting the horse, so it is important to use dewormers from the different families at the correct time of year, at the correct dose and interval, which is known as strategic dosing.

recurrent colic are serious problems that may be caused by a heavy worm burden. Young horses may also show a poor growth rate.

Types of Internal Parasite

Small Redworms (*Cyathastomes*): These worms are a particular problem because they can become encysted in the gut wall and emerge in large numbers to cause serious diarrhea and weight loss.

Large Redworms (*Strongylus*): Migrating larvae can affect the blood supply to the hindgut, causing colic.

Tapeworms (*Anoplocephala*): Heavy burdens are possibly associated with spasmodic colic.

Roundworms (*Parascaris*): Large numbers in the small intestine may cause poor health in foals.

Threadworms (*Strongyloides*): Infection can occur via the mare's milk and may cause reduced appetite and poor growth. The larval stage may migrate through lung tissue, producing a cough and nasal discharge.

Pinworms (*Oxyuris*): Itching around the anus may result in hair loss and sores around the tailbase.

Bots (*Gastrophilus*): During the summer the *Gasterophilus* fly lays oval, yellow eggs on the horse's coat, especially the limbs and flanks. The horse ingests the eggs, which hatch into larvae (bots) in the horse's stomach, where they develop and can cause internal damage.

Lungworms (*Dictyocaulus*): This is a common parasite of donkeys, which occasionally causes a chronic cough in horses.

You must use different deworming treatments depending on the time of year. Deworming treatments can be given by syringe.

Hairworms (*Trichostrongylus*): May cause weight loss and diarrhea in heavy infestations, and lack of appetite and poor growth with lower burdens.

Neck Threadworms (*Microfilariae* stage of *Onchocerca spp.*): Causes swelling followed by fibrous nodules in the ligamentous tissue of the neck and limbs.

Strategic Dosing

Check with your veterinarian before administering any medication or treatment.

- Use the correct dose. Use a weight tape to estimate the weight of your horse accurately.
- During the grazing season, use one type of dewormer for the entire grazing season (April to October). Always use the correct dosing interval for that type of dewormer:

Type of Dewormer	Dosing Interval (Weeks)
ivermectin	8–10
moxidectin	13
benzimidazole	4–6
pyrantel	4–6

- Control tapeworms using a double dose of pyrantel in the spring and fall.
- Control migrating redworms from October to December using fenbendazole, ivermectin, or moxidectin.
- Control bots acquired during the summer using ivermectin or moxidectin in December.
- Attempt to reduce numbers of encysted cyathostomes during the winter using a 5-day course of fenbendazole 10 percent or one dose of moxidectin.
- New arrivals should be dosed with a wormer and stabled for 48 hours.
- During the grazing season, dose all horses at the same time, using the same dewormer.
- Deworm foals from 6 weeks old. Read the dewormer package carefully to establish the correct dosage for a foal.

Graze sheep or cattle with horses to graze the field more evenly.

Pasture Management

The aim is to keep the pasture as clean as possible.

- Remove droppings from the field twice a week during the grazing season.
- Graze sheep or cattle with horses to graze the field more evenly.
- Rest pasture for a season or graze sheep or cattle on the pasture alternately with horses. If circumstances do not permit this, rest the pasture for at least 6 weeks, three times a year.
- Drag a chain harrow around the pasture on hot, sunny days in the summer to spread the manure so that the sun's heat kills the larvae and eggs.
- Allow 1 acre per horse to avoid overgrazing.

The Right Start

Dental Care

While the need for regular foot trimming is well recognized, dental care is all too often neglected despite being the potential source of numerous health problems, such as loss of condition, and riding difficulties, such as bit intolerance, unusual head carriage, and head shaking.

Signs associated with dental problems include:
- excessive salivation
- facial swellings
- halitosis (foul-smelling breath)
- poor appetite
- quidding (dropping half-chewed lumps of food)
- slow eating
- weight loss

Horses rarely suffer from dental decay in the way that humans do, so why the need for regular checkups? Part of the answer lies in the physiology of the mouth. Horses have six upper incisors and six lower incisors, which are used to crop grass short and close to the root. There is a gap in the teeth, conveniently placed for the bit to lie, between the incisors and the cheek teeth, which lie much farther back in the long jaw bone.

Two canine teeth (tushes) are found in the space between the incisors and the cheek teeth of the upper (maxilla) and lower (mandible) jaw of male horses and occasionally in mares. The six upper and six lower cheek teeth have hard enamel ridges that provide an efficient grinding surface to break down a fibrous diet (hay, grass, etc.). Clearly, any problems affecting the efficiency of this grinding surface will affect the horse's ability to chew and utilize feed.

Dental Problems

Dental problems tend to fall into the following categories:

Uneven Wear: Uneven wear and sharp edges can develop on the outside edges of the upper cheek teeth and cause discomfort in the mouth. This occurs to a certain extent in all horses because the lower jaw is narrower than the upper jaw, meaning that, over a period of time, uneven grinding across the tooth surface allows protruding edges to develop, which will require rasping (also known as floating). The

Horse Dentition

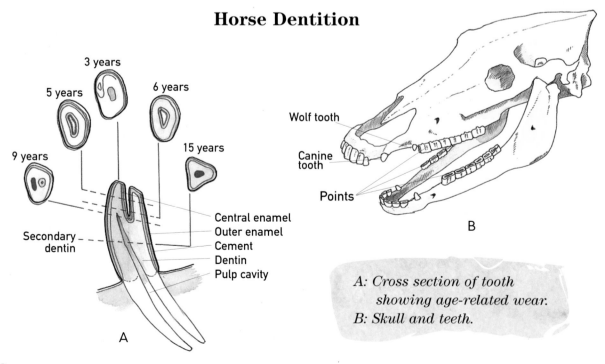

3 years
5 years
6 years
9 years
15 years

Wolf tooth
Canine tooth
Points

Secondary dentin
Central enamel
Outer enamel
Cement
Dentin
Pulp cavity

A

B

A: Cross section of tooth showing age-related wear.
B: Skull and teeth.

exact frequency will depend on the individual—some horses' teeth rarely need attention, whereas others need regular floating as frequently as twice a year. All horses should have their teeth checked at least annually.

Mouth Conformation: An individual's mouth conformation may lead to uneven wear becoming more of a problem than usual. In a parrot mouth, the upper jaw overshoots the lower jaw, resulting in sharp overgrowths (hooks) at the front of the upper row of molars and the back of the lower row.

A shear mouth has a much wider upper than lower jaw, with a steeply angled grinding surface. This leads to steep, sharp edges along the cheek sides of the upper molars and the tongue side of the lower molars. Ulcerations and lacerations often result. Normal chewing can also be difficult when a lost molar or uneven wear of the cheek teeth cause the row (arcade) of molars to vary in height.

Abscesses: Tooth root abscesses can be the result of gum disease or infection following a tooth fracture. Often, an X-ray is needed to pinpoint the affected tooth. Abscesses involving the upper teeth can cause sinusitis, facial swelling, and nasal discharge. Infected teeth usually must be removed, which, for back teeth, will probably mean a general anesthetic and oral surgery.

Wolf Teeth: Wolf teeth are small teeth found just in front of the cheek teeth, usually on the upper jaw. Not all are visible, and they are generally small and insignificant; however, if they interfere with the bit, they are often surgically removed.

With parrot mouth, the upper jaw overshoots the lower jaw.

Routine Foot Care

Five minutes of attention given to the feet each and every day will prevent many potential problems from taking hold.

Daily Care

- Pick out each hoof to remove dirt, mud, debris, and stones or soiled bedding, especially from the deep grooves to either side of the frog.
- Check the sole for bruising or penetrations.
- Check the shoe for looseness, abnormal wear, or risen clenches (nails).
- Compare the bulbs of the heel—they should be of equal size and show no signs of bruising or cuts from overreaching.
- Check the hoof wall for cracks.
- Check the coronary band for cuts or swellings.
- Avoid overuse of hoof oil, which can affect the natural moisture content of the hoof wall. If you are worried about the quality of the horn, look at

improving it through changing your horse's diet or giving dietary supplements under the guidance of your vet.

Shoeing

The exact frequency of reshoeing varies with each horse, depending on the amount of work that he does, on what kind of surface, and on the speed of growth of the feet. However, most horses need a visit from the farrier every 4 to 8 weeks.

The farrier will trim and rebalance the hoof before replacing the shoes either with the previous set or with new ones. Never get into the habit of leaving the shoes on for too long, perhaps in an attempt to save money on farrier fees—if ever there was a false economy, this is it. Failure to have a horse shod frequently enough not only means that shoes work loose and may be lost, but it significantly increases the risk of lameness as the toe grows overlong and the hoof becomes more and more unbalanced.

The Unshod Hoof

Unshod hooves require just as much careful attention as those with shoes.

• Clean them out and examine them daily.
• Carefully inspect the white line for dark areas that may lead to an infection, or small stones or gravel embedded in them.
• Have the feet trimmed and balanced by a farrier every 6 to 8 weeks.

The Older Horse

With age, the body's systems all function less effectively. The elderly horse needs special attention all through the year, especially in winter when the pressure is on.

Regular Foot Care and Vaccination: Both are just as important in older horses as any other. Don't think that because an old horse is no longer working as actively,

these crucial aspects of his health care can be reduced or neglected.

Dental Care: Chewing becomes less efficient as teeth wear down and fall out. Regular rasping/floating every 6 to 12 months will keep grinding surfaces as functional as possible. Older horses who struggle with coarse hay during the winter may need it replaced by soft meadow hay or high-fiber pellets soaked with sugar beet pulp, fed in several feeds throughout the day to keep up fiber intake.

Nutrition: Older horses often need supplemental feeding, so make use of commercial feeds aimed at seniors; these usually provide a good, basic, concentrated feed to complement good-quality grass or hay.

Soy oil, corn oil, and sunflower oil may be added gradually in small quantities; ask your vet or a nutritionist for advice. It may be well worth while to use a good multivitamin/mineral supplement. Remember that the horse should be in good physical condition going into winter.

Deworming: A less robust immune system may put the older horse at increased risk from worm-related problems, so it is vital to keep up a rigorous control program.

Parts of the Hoof

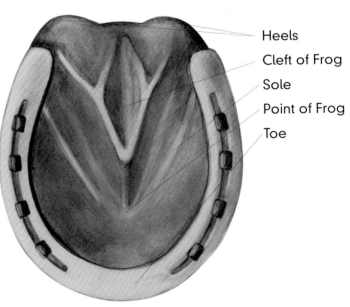

Heels

Cleft of Frog

Sole

Point of Frog

Toe

Your horse's feet must be picked out daily.

cope with minor injuries and, in the case of an emergency, to give the correct treatment until expert help is available.

First-Aid Kit

It is a good idea to keep a well-organized, clean collection of dressings, bandages, and other first-aid items in a safe place at the barn and in the trailer for use in an emergency.

A basic first-aid kit should include:
- antiseptic solution
- bandages (all types)
- cotton
- gamgee
- poultices
- scissors
- sterile wound dressings
- thermometer

Discuss your horse's foot care with your farrier.

Exercise: Try to keep up gentle, regular exercise, rather than letting an older horse languish in the field. This will help to maintain mobility and muscle tone.

Grooming: Older horses may not shed their coat as readily as younger ones, so make sure grooming is part of their daily care, especially during the spring and fall coat changes.

Arthritis: Many older horses suffer from some degree of arthritis. Your veterinarian can supply phenylbutazone to help reduce pain and keep an affected horse comfortable and mobile. Consider feeding supplements containing glucosaminoglycans, which are thought to be beneficial in keeping joints functioning.

First Aid

Accidents can happen, even for the most careful of owners. The responsible horse owner should be aware of the basic principles of first aid in order to

Horse Rescuers

Some volunteer fire departments include equine/large-animal rescue units that train rescuers to safely extricate horses from ravines, ditches, collapsed barns, overturned trailers, etc. With specially designed slings, harnesses and pulley systems, used in conjunction with tractors, cranes, and even helicopters, these equine saviors can lift horses off the ground and transport them to safety.

Many fire and police departments, search-and-rescue units, and other groups practice safe rescue and immobilization techniques with "Lucky," a life-sized equine mannequin manufactured by Rescue Critters!® Standing 15 hands tall and weighing 400 pounds (about half the weight of an average horse), Lucky has jointed, movable limbs and realistic tail and head features.

- wound ointment
- veterinarian/clinic phone number

Cuts and Wounds

Riding injuries, kicks, bites, wire wounds from fencing—wounds can happen anywhere, at any time. Your first move should always be to assess the cut or wound.

Bleeding should be controlled with pressure, using sterile or clean material applied directly over the wound or by a tourniquet between the wound and heart. Keep the horse quiet and calm in a safe environment. Severe hemorrhage from major vessels in the groin, "armpit" area, or head/neck region should be packed with clean material and pressure applied until the veterinarian arrives.

Contaminated wounds must be thoroughly cleaned and irrigated with well-diluted antibacterial solution (e.g., 0.05 percent [1:40] solution of chlorhexidine Nolvasan, 0.1 percent [1:7.5] solution povidone-iodine betadine scrub).

The depth of the cut is important. Lacerations through the full thickness of the skin or flaps will probably need suturing by a veterinarian. The position of the cut in relation to important underlying structures is also critical. Extreme care and veterinary advice is necessary for any wounds found close to joints and tendon sheaths.

Wounds associated with pain, heat, swelling, lameness, or discharge may indicate infection and should be examined by a veterinarian. It is important to make sure the horse or pony is protected against tetanus. Deep cuts to the back of the pastern and coronary band need careful management and should receive veterinary attention.

Superficial wounds may only need to be kept clean, dressed with wound ointment, protected from flies, and monitored for any sign of infection. However, veterinary advice should always be obtained if there is any doubt about how to deal with a wound.

Foot Injuries

If a horse steps on a nail, it's possible that important, sensitive structures within the hoof capsule may be penetrated, injured, or become infected. Punctures in the middle third of the sole are likely to be most serious; so if you suspect this, call your veterinarian immediately. Leave the penetrating object in position for the veterinarian to assess, providing there is no danger of it being driven deeper into the hoof.

Puncture wounds that suggest that the sole has been penetrated can be poulticed until veterinary help arrives. Bruised soles may benefit from poulticing, too.

Tendon Injuries

Swelling behind the cannon bone between the knee (or hock) and fetlock may result from a tendon injury.

These injuries are often, but not always, associated with lameness. Cold-hose the area for 30 minutes, then apply a well-padded support bandage (to the adjacent limb as well). The horse should be stall-rested until a full veterinary assessment has been made, which may involve an ultrasound scan of the tendon fibers.

NOTE: *Care should always be taken not to bandage too tightly, especially over joints.*

Dealing With a Cast Horse

When a stabled horse rolls up against a solid wall or partition so that his legs are trapped between the wall and the body, he may not be able to push himself back over. This is known as being *cast*. Some horses panic and thrash around; others lie quietly. Deeply banking the sides of the bedding against the wall may be enough to prevent the horse from getting too close to the wall.

Rolling can be discouraged by using an anti-rolling surcingle fitted over the back of the horse. A lip on the wall approximately 2 ft (0.6 m) above ground level may provide enough grip to enable the horse to push himself away from the wall.

Soft ropes looped around the legs may be the only safe way to pull the horse over and back into a position in the center of the stall, from which position he can stand. It makes safety sense to control the head with a halter and lead rope.

Superficial wounds must be kept clean.

Chapter Four

Year-Round Health Conditions

F amiliarizing yourself as much as possible with the early signs and symptoms of the common conditions that can affect a horse means a swift diagnosis can be made and treatment can get under way before things become serious.

Colic

Colic is the name given to abdominal pain in the horse. It has many different causes and can occur at any time. However, some forms of colic may be more common at certain times of the year. For example, feed-related colic may occur when a change in the feeding regime occurs (i.e., levels of hard feed increased too rapidly in winter, or sudden turnout onto lush pasture in the spring or summer).

True colic affects the digestive tract and can cause intense abdominal pain. Watch for any of the following behavioral signs that horses can show when they are experiencing a bout of colic:
- grunting, labored heavy breathing
- kicking at belly
- lack of appetite
- looking at flanks
- may lay flat out in the stall or field, reluctant to get up

- pacing around the stall, unable to settle
- pawing the ground (this may upset the bedding in a stall)
- restless, may get up and down frequently
- rolling
- some horses adopt a crouching stance, or attempt to urinate frequently
- some horses grind their teeth or yawn frequently

The veterinarian should be called immediately if colic is suspected because the horse may injure himself by violently rolling if the pain becomes severe. Some forms of colic need prompt diagnosis and referral to an equine hospital if surgery is required.

Remove water and feed, and bring the horse into a stall with deep, well-banked bedding until the veterinarian arrives. Only walk the horse if he is in danger of injuring himself by violently rolling. Take care not to place any people at risk.

The veterinarian will assess the severity of the colic by physical examination, using pulse rate, respiration rate, gut sounds, rectal examination, rectal temperature, and color of mucous membranes as indicators. Sometimes it is necessary to insert a stomach tube, perform blood tests, and obtain a sample of abdominal fluid to gain further information about the type of colic and its severity.

Types of Colic

Most types of colic respond well to intravenous injections of gut-muscle relaxants and painkillers.

Spasmodic Colic

In spasmodic colic, the pain is caused by a portion of the gut going into a spasm or cramp. The underlying cause is usually never discovered, although intestinal worms are sometimes thought to be involved.

Impaction Colic

The pelvic flexure is that part of the hindgut where the gut diameter narrows and forms a U-turn. It has a tendency to become blocked up (impacted) with food matter, and this mass can usually be felt by a veterinarian during a rectal examination.

Horses who are suddenly stabled and fed hay after being at grass (for example, stall rest following orthopedic injury or illness, such as laminitis) are the most likely candidates for impaction. Treatment often involves painkillers given intravenously, dosing with minerals via a stomach tube, and sometimes intravenous fluids.

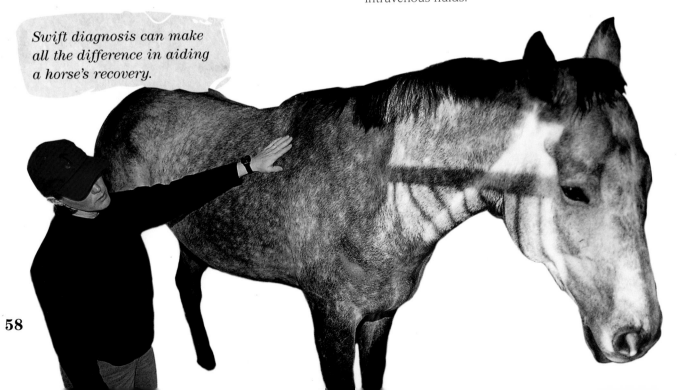

Swift diagnosis can make all the difference in aiding a horse's recovery.

Year-Round Health Conditions

Tympanitic Colic

The gut can become distended after feed has fermented excessively inside it. This can be a consequence of:
- abrupt change to a high-grain diet
- horse that breaks into the feed room
- turnout on to lush spring grass

This type of colic can be treated with gut relaxants and analgesics.

Other illnesses may be associated with colic, such as exhaustion, peritonitis, grass sickness, and enteritis.

Surgical Colic

Some causes of colic are serious and life-threatening. The gut may lose its blood supply, become strangulated, completely blocked, trapped, or twisted within the abdominal cavity and require immediate surgery at an equine hospital. Horses with this type of colic do not tend to improve much with the administration of pain-killing and gut-relaxant drugs. They often show more signs of pain, a persistently high pulse rate, gut sounds are reduced or not present at all, and peritoneal fluid often shows evidence of inflammation.

Horses with suspected surgical colic must be transported to an equine hospital as quickly as possible if they are to stand the best chance of survival. If a horse is too old for surgery, or the horse is not insured and the owner cannot afford surgery, it may be necessary to euthanize the horse to prevent further suffering.

Weight Loss

Sudden loss of condition is always a concern, made all the more worrisome because the cause is not always easy to pinpoint.

Horses may lose weight, with or without diarrhea, at any time of the year. Older horses will need extra attention to their diet, a rigorous deworming program, regular professional dental care, and blanketing up/shelter to ensure good condition throughout the year.

A tube may be used to drain fluid from the horse's stomach.

Chronic pain due to arthritis may be responsible for weight loss and can become more severe in cold, wet winter weather.

Other causes of weight loss include:
- chronic grass sickness
- chronic kidney disease
- chronic liver disease
- diarrhea
- heart disease
- inflammatory disease of the intestines
- occasionally, hormonal diseases (such as Cushing's disease in older animals)
- peritonitis (for example, from gut damage due to internal parasites, castration wounds, abdominal abscesses)
- tumors of the stomach and intestines

59

These possibilities can be investigated by a veterinarian using blood tests, peritoneal fluid analysis, feces samples, rectal examination, and biopsy techniques. Treatment and prognosis depend on the underlying cause of the weight loss. Obvious causes, such as underfeeding, incorrect work, poor worm control, and inadequate dental care must be ruled out initially.

Lymphangitis

Lymphangitis is an inflammation of the lymphatic vessels, which drain tissue fluid from the soft tissues of the limb. It can occur at any time of year, when horses are stabled or at grass. The hind limbs are more commonly affected, and the problem often affects only one side or even one limb. A high-protein diet combined with a lack of exercise is traditionally associated with this condition, which used to affect working, heavy horses on a Monday morning following a weekend of rest, thus giving rise to the name "Monday morning disease."

Watch Out!

Some conditions cause behavioral signs that can be mistaken for colic. For example, a pony with bad laminitis may lie down, be dull and depressed, and have a high respiratory and pulse rate.

It is more likely that infection (for example, a puncture wound) triggers inflammation and narrowing of the lymphatic vessels, leading to swelling and thickening, as tissue fluid accumulates in the lower limb.

Sudden-onset lameness is often the first sign noticed, followed by rapid swelling of the limb. The affected hind limb is very painful to the touch and is usually held rotated outwards with the toe pointing. An increase in temperature, heart rate, and breathing rate often occurs.

Prompt treatment is essential before inflammatory deposits, known as fibrin, form. These will make normal lymphatic drainage of the limb difficult and chronic thickening of the leg more likely. Extremely bad cases will ooze honey-like fluid through the stretched skin surface over the swollen limb.

Treatment consists of antibiotics, painkillers, and anti-inflammatory drugs combined with massage, gentle exercise, and support bandaging when stabled to encourage circulation. It is a good idea to bandage the other hind limb for support and to reduce protein levels in the feed.

Sometimes just the hock region is affected by lymphangitis, but occasionally the entire leg becomes distended. Rapid, effective treatment is required to prevent a persistent or recurrent problem.

Keep a close check on your horse's weight and condition.

Monday morning disease traditionally affects working horses.

Viral Respiratory Disease

Equine influenza virus, equine herpes virus, and equine rhinovirus are responsible for outbreaks of upper respiratory disease (coughing, wheezing, and nasal discharge) every year. Outbreaks may be more serious in a group of young, susceptible horses living in close quarters, such as 2- and 3-year-olds in training at racing barns.

Outbreaks can occur at any time of year, for example, during the summer when populations of different horses mix at shows, or during the winter when more animals are stabled together, thus increasing the spread of the infection. Stress can make individuals more vulnerable.

Infections cause poor performance, coughing, swollen glands, nasal discharge, lack of appetite, and raised temperatures. Occasionally, airway inflammation can persist after a viral infection and lead to chronic airway inflammation and chronic obstructive pulmonary disease (COPD).

Treatment is largely supportive, requiring rest in a well-ventilated area away from other animals (at least 3 weeks). Nonsteroidal anti-inflammatory drugs (NSAIDs), such as phenylbutazone, may help to reduce a high temperature, and mucolytics can help to loosen secretions. Vaccination and isolation of new arrivals at a barn are sensible measures to take to prevent the spread of infection.

Strangles

This is a nasty, highly infectious disease caused by the bacterium *Streptococcus equi*, and it can occur during the summer or winter. It causes fever, cough, excessive nasal and eye discharge, and abscesses around the lymph nodes around the throat and under the jaw. Breathing may be obstructed by very large abscesses, which often must be lanced and drained

Strangles is highly infectious and may quickly spread from horse to horse.

before antibiotics can be given. Cases should be rested and isolated where possible.

Occasionally, abscesses can spread to the abdomen, with the potential to cause weight loss, peritonitis, and colic. Some horses may shed the infectious bacteria for many weeks following infection.

Remember, though, that thick, purulent nasal discharge may also be caused by sinusitis or a tooth root abscess (although a one-sided discharge is more commonly seen in such cases).

Azoturia

This disease is also known as tying-up syndrome, Monday morning disease, or equine rhabdomyolysis syndrome. It can affect pleasure horses as well as competition horses at any time of year, although more cases are likely to be seen during the winter when horses are stabled and fed higher levels of hard feed. The exact cause is not known, but it is likely that certain factors may trigger an episode in horses who are predisposed to the condition.

During exercise, a build up of lactate occurs in the muscle due to the metabolism of glycogen stores. This results in damage to the muscle and painful cramps.

In mild cases, the rider may only notice a subtle shortening of stride length or poor performance. Moderate cases will show stiffness, reluctance to move, increased pulse and respiratory rates, and sweating.

Several muscle groups (especially in the large muscles of the quarters and the thighs) will be hard, swollen, and painful to the touch. If symptoms appear when the horse is out on a trail ride, it is best to transport him home rather than to force further walking, which will be very painful and may worsen the muscle damage.

Severe cases will even crouch, stagger, and collapse. Myoglobin (muscle pigment released from damaged muscle cells) can discolor the urine and may cause kidney damage if the horse is dehydrated. Shock can develop, occasionally with fatal consequences.

The severity of an attack of azoturia is not always obvious, and blood tests for AST and CK enzyme levels are useful to assess how long the horse will need to be rested. Mild cases may only need 3 weeks without ridden exercise, whereas severe cases may need 3 months off work. Underlying predisposing factors, such as electrolyte imbalances, viral infections, and vitamin E and selenium deficiency, may need to be investigated. Other factors, such as irregular exercise, overfeeding, and stress can also increase the risk of tying-up.

Treatment will depend on the severity of the attack and will involve a period of stall rest, followed by gentle, controlled walking exercise before AST enzyme levels are low enough to suggest the muscle has repaired sufficiently, and ridden exercise can begin again. More severely affected animals will need painkillers, fluid therapy, steroids, and sometimes sedatives.

Certain horses seem susceptible to repeated bouts of this distressing condition. These animals should be fed mainly a 100 percent forage diet if possible, with a multivitamin/mineral supplement, and additional chopped-up hay or high-fiber, low-energy pellet if required. Oil can also be introduced gradually to increase the energy content of the diet.

Choke

Choke occurs when the esophagus is blocked. The most common mistake that leads to this situation is not soaking dried sugar beet adequately before it is fed. This results in it swelling rapidly during the swallowing process when it mixes with saliva.

It is a distressing and painful condition, difficult to witness because the horse will cough and retch, often holding the head and neck in an extended position. Saliva and food material often discharge at the nostrils, and swelling can sometimes be seen on the left-hand side of the neck at the level of the obstruction. Fortunately, most cases of choke clear spontaneously within a few minutes. If there is no improvement after about 20 minutes, call the veterinarian.

Intravenous painkillers and muscle relaxants usually make the horse a lot more comfortable. In severe cases, a stomach tube is passed to the level of the obstruction and cleared with gentle lavage (water used to soften and clear the obstruction). Heavy sedation or general anesthesia is required to carry out this process safely.

If choke persists for too long, the esophageal wall may be damaged and form scar tissue. The horse may then be susceptible to recurrent episodes and must be fed sloppy, wet feed.

Although it can be distressing, choke is not usually life-threatening, and it clears spontaneously and rapidly without complications. It is more likely to occur in the winter, when more concentrated feed is fed, particularly if the horse tends to bolt food or has dental problems that prevent thorough chewing.

To avoid choke, food should be fed damp; carrots, apples, and other vegetable matter should be finely chopped; teeth should be rasped/floated regularly; and sugar beet pulp must be soaked with water for at least 24 hours before being fed.

Some horses may be subject to repeated episodes of tying-up.

Spring

The first signs of spring come as a great relief to many horse owners. March turns into April, and with that extra daylight in the evenings, they can start to reclaim some sense of normality in their lives. After-work riding is at last an option again. The fields are starting to green up, and the prospect of drier ground underfoot doesn't seem so far away. This means more turnout, less hay and concentrated feed and, best of all, less mucking out!

For the majority of horses, spring brings shifts in many aspects of their daily routine and management. Because abrupt changes and horses don't mix, any alterations to the norm must be made gradually and thought out carefully beforehand to achieve a smooth, trouble-free transition.

Chapter Five

Taking Off the Wraps

The winter seems to have dragged on interminably, and we are all desperate to get our horses out more and whip off those wrappings. For those horses who will continue to be stabled at night, swapping over to the summer routine is a relatively straightforward process of simply lengthening the time they spend out in the field as much as possible to take advantage of the lighter and warmer evenings. Those who change from being in nights to staying out all the time need a more flexible approach.

Spring weather is notoriously changeable, so don't set your plans in stone. It's no use signing away your stable in the boarding barn at the end of March only to leave your horse facing the wettest, coldest spring on record. It's best to retain the use of a stable at least until June, and preferably throughout the summer, too, for emergency use.

Pick a mild spell for your horse's first night out, and have enough bedding and hay on hand to bring your horse in again if the weather turns against you.

Good shelter in the field plus blankets, of course, can help to ease the transition. I will say again, don't be too hasty to pack away blankets on the first warm spring day because things are sure to change. Keep a

Don't be in too much of a hurry to put away winter blankets.

turnout blanket on hand until temperatures really stabilize, and check the weather forecast daily, blanketing up or not accordingly. Lightweight turnout blankets really come into their own now, giving protection from chilly winds and spring showers (which can be heavy, if short-lived) without producing a clammy coat underneath

Roughing Off

Traditionally, the process by which horses who have spent the winter working hard are transitioned gradually and turned out for the summer is known as *roughing off*. If your horse has been kept fit, mainly stabled, and on an energy-rich diet over the winter,

you must take particular care to avoid stressing his system if you plan to change over to a less intensive regimen.

This winter-to-spring transition should proceed as follows:
- gradually replace starch-based grain feeds with bulk feeds and forage
- reduce exercise slowly
- start removing layers of blanket and leaving them off altogether during the day
- have teeth checked and rasp (float) any sharp edges
- check that vaccinations are up-to-date
- book a farrier's visit to remove shoes if your horse is having a complete rest
- ensure that worming is up-to-date for all horses turned out together

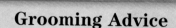

Grooming Advice

- Buy a stiff brush with a handle from a pet shop and use it to get hairs off saddle pads and blanket linings to save wear on your dandy brush. Also handy are rubber hair-removing gadgets designed for lifting dog hairs.

- Horses who are really hanging on to their full winter coats but whose work is increasing during the spring can be clipped as late as early March without this having a detrimental effect on the summer coat.

spring. Old horses, too, tend to keep their coats as a kind of adverse-weather insurance policy. The summer coat can be speeded on its way by:

- putting on extra blankets beginning around February
- energetic grooming using a rubber curry comb or grooming mitt in a circular motion to lift out the dead hair
- for stabled horses, leaving the light on longer into the evenings to fool the brain into thinking that spring has arrived early
- adding vegetable or corn oil to the feed

Remember, if you achieve a summer look by March, watch the weather and use additional blankets during cold spells.

Hair, Hair Everywhere!

Horse owners can be identified from a mile away this time of year by the innumerable horse hairs coating everything they possess (including, somehow, their clothes for the office!).

As a general rule, horses begin shedding their winter coats toward the end of March, with hair loss reaching a peak during late April and early May. The summer coat is established by early June. Shedding is triggered by the effect of lengthening days and rising temperatures on the pituitary gland at the base of the brain.

The speed with which hair is lost depends on how thick the coat was in the first place, whether the horse was clipped, what blanket was used, and prevailing weather conditions. Horses who have lived mainly in stables and have been well blanketed will not have grown thick coats, and what they have will soon come out.

Field-kept horses who have managed without blankets, on the other hand, often hang on to their wooly coats for what seems like forever, particularly during a cold

You will be amazed at how much hair your horse can shed.

Chapter Six

Spring Feeding

Feeding tends to come into focus during winter. However, it is important to bear in mind that what and how you feed your horse are crucial factors in his health and happiness year round. Given its importance, it is a surprising fact that feeding is one of those subjects that few have a sound grasp of in the horse-care business.

Among newcomers to horsekeeping, ignorance frequently means bliss. Novice owners will unquestioningly feed their horses what their previous owners did, or what their barn manager provides. At the other end of the spectrum, seasoned horsemen will, via years of experience, have arrived at a diet that they feel works for them in terms of performance and stick to it, unswayed by the influences of marketing or scientific research. There may be much that is sound in their approach, yet they are in danger of being blinded to new developments, or even ignoring some fundamental natural needs.

Somewhere between these extremes lie the vast majority of ordinary horse owners: Those who have gathered a reasonable working knowledge of feeding and want to do the best by their horse. However, many have lost confidence, overwhelmed by the plethora of products being offered at their feed suppliers and the apparent complexity of the "science" of equine nutrition.

Of course, nutrition is a science and, as such, it is complex and fascinating to learn about in depth. But it is perfectly possible to feed your horse correctly and well without getting bogged down in technicalities. The aim of the following feeding information is to arm you with the basic practical know-how you need to keep your horse in good shape 12 months a year.

Rich Pickings

More time spent out in a field full of grass that is becoming increasingly rich in carbohydrates means that, as spring gets underway, important changes are already taking place in your horse's diet, quite independently of what goes into his bucket.

This section on spring feeding will remind you how to calculate your horse's feeding needs. Now is the time for a reassessment before you make a complete change in regime. Points to keep in mind at this time of year include:

- Changes in workload: Is your horse going to be doing more work now, or less? What sort of work is it?

- How much time is he spending at grass? Spring grass is the equine equivalent of high-octane rocket fuel. It is positively loaded with calories and protein, so take this into account as you transfer from a winter to a summer diet.
- The more hours of access to good pasture, the less additional concentrated feed your horse is likely to need to fulfill his energy requirements. Two hours on rich May grass is the equivalent to two scoops of medium-energy pellets or sweet feed.
- When concentrates are dropped to below the manufacturer's recommended quantities, vitamins and minerals can be lacking, so a supplement must be given.
- Sudden alterations in diet or feeding routine are bad news for equine digestive systems. Diarrhea is common when horses go on to a richer diet with a higher moisture content, so make changes gradually, turning out for a little longer each day. Loose droppings should return to normal once the system has adjusted.

The average horse owner can easily become baffled by the science of feeding.

• Beware of laminitis. The metabolism of ponies, cobs, and other easy keepers will start responding to the increased nutritional and carbohydrate content of the grass long before you notice the pasture greening up. So don't get caught by surprise. Start controlling the concentrate and grass intake of susceptible animals by March, and then continue to keep a tight rein on it.

Left to his own devices, a horse will spend 16 to 17 hours a day grazing. This amount of time stays the same whatever the quality of the pasture. The richness of spring grass then creates a potential nightmare for horse owners in the form of laminitis. A look at the effects of laminitis will soon convince us all to take this crippling disease seriously. Many horses, and almost all ponies, simply cannot be left on good pasture all day and night without being at serious risk.

Restricting Grazing

Controlling grass intake can be approached two ways. Either the horse or pony can be taken off the grass, or the amount of grass he is allowed to eat can be restricted. Bringing the animal indoors is one option, but isolation in a stable is depressing, and the enforced idleness does nothing to help an overweight horse.

Large barns or corrals that can be shared with others are a better bet, if available. Choosing a time of the day when flies are at their worst can be an added plus here, but do remember how boring it is for horses to be confined, particularly by themselves. Always provide a little hay to pick at too. Horses should never be left without anything to eat for extended periods; 6 hours is the absolute maximum.

If removing the horse or pony from the grass is difficult, as it is for many working owners, then you must make sure that your horse has to work harder for his grass during the time he is turned out. You can achieve this by doing the following:

• Turning out on to almost-bare pasture. Your aim is

Spring grass is loaded with calories and protein.

not to starve your horse or pony, even if you do want him to lose weight. Sheep are excellent at grazing grass right down, so see if you can arrange to "borrow" some (check your fencing first!).

• Restricting him to a small area by using electric fencing, which can be moved on as the area gets grazed down.

• Using a muzzle or mouth-guard that allows the horse or pony to drink and nibble but not take large mouthfuls of grass. A few hours a day in the muzzle is enough, with no more than 12 hours total at grass. For the rest of the time, take him off the grass and allow him a little hay.

When restricting grazing areas, be tough on weeds and diligent about picking up droppings. Remember, too, that on a restricted diet the levels of essential vitamins and minerals are reduced and must be topped off by a multivitamin supplement.

For animals in regular work, a low-energy, high-fiber feed or pellet that has been nutrient-enriched (most manufacturers now produce their own version) is a solution to the problem of maintaining essential nutrient levels for easy keepers over the spring and summer.

Small ponies cannot be allowed unrestricted grazing on good pasture. One solution to controlling feeding is to keep ponies in a small paddock.

Feeding Competition Horses

For owners of competition horses, the spring months see an increase in their horse's workload as a fitness program progresses. The strategy to pursue during this time is still a diet based on forage/roughage, boosted by a low-energy concentrated feed. However, it is important to look and plan ahead for the competition season, bearing in mind:

• what the horse will be doing
• whether he gains and holds condition easily or with difficulty
• temperament
• quality of forage – grass or hay – available at this time of year
• whether a supplement is needed
• whether the horse is prone to any feeding-related conditions, for example, laminitis, tying-up, etc.

Plan ahead for the competition season and the increased workload by adjusting your horse's feeding regime accordingly.

Look back at last year's feeding regime and assess how well it worked. It is a myth that all competition horses require high levels of quick-release, starch-based energy. In common with all horses, the diet of competition horses should remain fiber-based, with starch restricted and the majority of energy provided by oils.

Although fiber is cut back as work increases, it should never fall below 50 percent of the ration even in the hardest working, top-level performers, so find ways to maximize the fiber content of the diet. Don't forget that spring grass in a good-quality pasture is positively packed with carbohydrates, with an energy content of 12 megajoules (MJ) per

2.2 lbs/1 kg of dry matter. A day's worth of lush May grass is equivalent to no less than 22 lbs/10 kg of competition feed!

The exact proportions of fiber, starch, and oil in the diet will depend on your competitive discipline and whether it requires stamina (for example, eventing, endurance) or intense bursts of power (for example, show jumping, dressage). Providing energy in the form of fiber and oil rather than carbohydrates is particularly important for highly strung and excitable horses.

Chapter Seven

Get Fit, Not Fat

Spring heralds a rest for some hard-working horses, such as hunters, who are usually roughed off for the summer months. For many competitors and serious riders, however, it's very much a case of business as usual, simply swapping indoor training and show venues for green arenas.

However, for the vast majority of leisure horses, the increased daylight signals a significant increase in exercise as owners relish making the most of brighter, milder evenings and show schedules start appearing in the mailbox.

Fitness is very much a common-sense issue. You would not expect to enter a half-marathon, or even a 2-mile fun run, without any preparation during the previous 6 months beyond walking from the front door to the car. Yet this is, in effect, what we expect of our horses if we enter, for example, a hunter pace in April, or even saddle up for a 4-hour trail ride one sunny spring morning. Remember, your horse may have spent the winter wandering around his field with maybe an hour's ride every other weekend. Demanding too much too quickly can put serious strain on your horse's limbs and body systems, and this is asking for trouble.

Spring

The time to start thinking about fitness depends on three things:
- how fit the horse is already
- what level of fitness you are aiming for
- when your horse needs to attain the required level of fitness

Humans cannot lose weight or get fit overnight, and neither can horses. Those who have been in regular work over the winter may only need their exercise levels stepped up a little over a few weeks to achieve the fitness level they require for the months ahead. Others who have had a low-key winter will require a month or more of concentrated exercise to get in shape for an active summer of rides, and perhaps, shows.

If your plans for your horse are extremely energetic or intensive (e.g., lots of cross-country, show jumping, or endurance rides), and you're starting from a very low fitness level, allow a minimum of 2 months for training—which will give you a chance to work out, too!

Fitness Schedule

Adapt this fitness schedule to fit your own situation. Semi-fit horses can come in around halfway through. Those who have had an easy winter should work through the entire program from the beginning. This schedule is based on a horse getting fit for a novice event, but you can exit whenever you feel your horse has reached the fitness level he needs for the activities you have planned.

Dressage competitors, for example, will have reached sufficient fitness for training level tests by week 5, but may wish to continue more intensive work for a few more weeks. Show jumpers will wish to concentrate on flexibility after week 6, and endurance riders on stamina. Leisure riders should focus on doing the first 5 weeks properly—after this stage, their horses should be in shape for most things expected of them.

Weeks 1 & 2

Trail Work: Start with around half an hour of trail work, and build up to about an hour a day. Keep in an active walk, but don't worry about riding in a correct outline. By the end of Week 2, short spells of trotting can be introduced.

Week 3

Trail Rides: Trail ride for an hour a day, including longer trots (tailor the amount to how your horse feels). Start encouraging him to work in an outline to develop the right muscles along his top-line and quarters. Use hills where possible.

Spring signals the start of increased work and activity. Training sessions should last no longer than 20 minutes at first.

Week 4

Start Training: Brief (about 20 minutes) training sessions can now begin 2 or 3 days a week, after a short trail ride or walk around the barn to warm up. Plan sessions beforehand, aiming to include lots of work involving curves (e.g., large circles, serpentines, etc.) and transitions. Encourage the horse to move forward from the leg into a soft, giving rein contact.
Trail Rides: At least an hour a day, shorter on training days.

Week 5

Training Steps Up: Ask more varied and demanding training questions during training sessions of up to 40 minutes by the end of the week. Introduce lungeing and/or long reining, aiming for a correct outline (15–20 minutes maximum); pole work on the lunge or ridden; and short canters.
Canter: Include short canters out on trail rides where the ground is suitable.

Weeks 6 & 7

Jumping: Introduce jumping into your horse's training sessions. Keep fences small, building up gradually to basic grids. This will all help to sharpen the horse's and rider's eye, boost confidence, and help to iron out problems. Loose jumping makes a fun, useful change.
Trail Rides: Riders focusing on competitions can start reducing trail riding time, using it for more relaxing, easy days. Eventers will need some fast work. Leisure riders can increase trail riding times to 2 or 3 hours.
Testing, Testing: By the end of week 7, you should be ready for a dressage test, a few rounds of show jumping, a hunter pace course, or training over cross-country fences.

Week 8

Go for It!: If you have followed the program correctly, and there haven't been any hiccups, you should be ready for whatever schedule you have planned.

Getting Fit

- For those horses coming into work after a winter resting at grass, start by checking feet and teeth and general tidying up: pulling manes, trimming, and, if necessary, giving a late clip. If clipping, choose a low style, leaving hair on the back—a blanket clip.

- From the start of your program, don't allow your horse to slop along on a totally loose rein—he might as well be in the field.

- Don't rush. Take your time to avoid injury and get a solid base of fitness.

- Include hills, where possible, to help get the heart, lungs, and muscles working.

- Restrict trotting to even surfaces. Never trot downhill.

- Plan work beforehand so as not to waste time, particularly when training. Stick to your plan, but allow time to work through problems.

- Keep work interesting by varying it.

- Monitor feeding to keep pace with increased energy requirements and changes in body condition and management.

- Avoid getting your horse too fit, or you may have problems. Once he has attained the required fitness level, this can be maintained with three or four rides a week if he is only going to compete on weekends. Daily turnout will keep him loose and supple.

- Get yourself fit too, or you won't be able to do your horse justice!

Chapter Eight

Spring Health Alert

As spring gets underway, be on the alert for those signs of health conditions brought on by the onset of warmer weather and lusher grass.

Laminitis

Laminitis is one of the most common of all causes of equine lameness. High levels of carbohydrate found in grass during the spring months makes this season the greatest danger period for this crippling disease. Front feet are most frequently affected because 60 percent of the horse's weight is supported by the forelimbs. However, it is possible for just one or all four feet to be affected.

What Happens During Laminitis?

The pedal bone is suspended within the horny hoof capsule by blood-filled tissues called the sensitive laminae, which, in turn, are tightly bound to the interlocking insensitive laminae on the inside of the hoof wall. Laminitis occurs when the sensitive laminae become swollen and inflamed. Pain is intense, and fluid oozes from the inflamed tissues, further weakening the bond between the pedal bone and the hoof capsule (the laminar bond).

If the laminar bond becomes weakened all the way around the hoof during an episode of laminitis, the pedal bone may begin to rotate, pulled upward from its underside by the deep digital flexor tendon that attaches at that point. An all-around weakening of the bond means that the pedal bone actually sinks within the hoof capsule, causing a depression of the coronary band. In severe cases, the bone can even sink right through the sole of the foot.

Laminitis is a management issue, and all caring horse and pony owners should know how to avoid such suffering by educating themselves about the trigger factors of the disease and by recognizing early signs so that action can be taken before irreparable damage is done.

Laminitis progresses in three distinct phases:
- **developmental:** trigger factors start chemical reactions that alter the blood flow through to the foot
- **acute:** onset of clinical signs, such as pain and displacement of the pedal bone
- **chronic:** the acute phases persist

What Causes Laminitis?

Laminitis is most commonly caused by toxins released from the overgrowth of bacteria in the fiber-processing hindgut of horses and ponies who eat either too much rich grass or concentrated feed too high in carbohydrates. The exact processes involved are still the subject of much research, but it is thought that these toxins activate enzymes in the laminae, causing the hoof to detach. Other conditions that involve the release of toxins into circulation can also cause laminitis, including retained afterbirth, colic, diarrhea, and pneumonia.

Mechanical causes can also set off a bout of laminitis, such as concussion from riding on a hard surface, or when one leg is overloaded following injury to another leg.

Hormonal imbalances, stress, and treatment with steroids have also been linked to the onset of the disease.

Signs of Laminitis

Be vigilant, because this is a condition that can creep up on the unsuspecting owner. Mild cases of laminitis may show only the subtlest of signs, such as a shortened stride length or an unwillingness to trot freely on a hard surface or to turn sharply. However, it is likely that you would still be able to feel an increased digital pulse at the coronet even at this stage.

Moderate cases may lie down more, or will have a strong digital pulse (often with a raised heart rate), shift their weight restlessly, and, not surprisingly, be reluctant to have their feet picked up.

Severe cases are extremely depressed, perhaps off their food, refuse to move, and show increased heart and breathing rates with a bounding digital pulse—drastic symptoms that can be confused with acute colic or azoturia. Where the pedal bone has sunk, you will be able to feel a depression around the coronary band. X-rays using metal markers can help to assess the degree of rotation or sinking that has taken place.

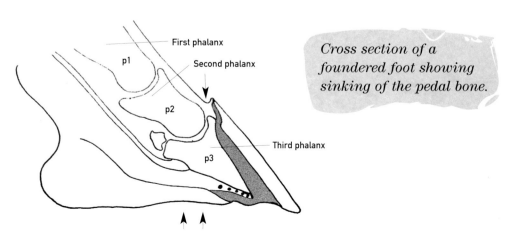

First phalanx
p1
Second phalanx
p2
Third phalanx
p3

Cross section of a foundered foot showing sinking of the pedal bone.

Take Immediate Action!

Laminitis is always an emergency, so your first action should be to call the veterinarian. As much immediate relief as possible is given through pain-killing drugs, such as phenylbutazone, sedation, and patches applied over the digital arteries to dilate the blood vessels and help restore normal circulation.

The suspected cause of the laminitis is obviously removed or treated as much as possible. The horse or pony must be removed from pasture and stall-rested on deep shavings or a sand bed, with frog supports applied by the veterinarian. Those who have been overindulging on grass must be fed only forage and high-fiber, low-carbohydrate chop. Supplements containing biotin and methionine can encourage good horn quality and help the foot to recover from its trauma.

Corrective trimming and shoeing to keep toes short and to support the frog with specialized shoes can play a vital role in preventing further rotation or sinking of the pedal bone and in restoring a normal

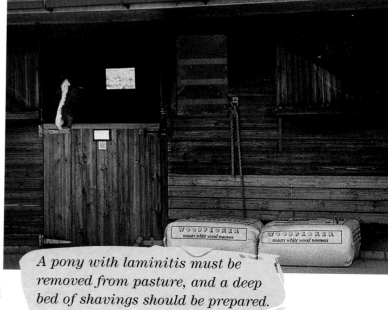

A pony with laminitis must be removed from pasture, and a deep bed of shavings should be prepared.

foot shape as the horse recovers. Be patient, though, as this may take several months.

Grass Sickness

Grass sickness is a frightening and frequently fatal condition that can strike at any time of the year, although it is most often seen during the spring and summer months, particularly between April and July.

What Causes Grass Sickness?

Despite much investigation, the cause of grass sickness is still unknown. Some researchers believe that a toxin within the grass itself is responsible, while recent evidence links the disease to high levels of cyanide found in white clover.

Horses sharing grazing may be affected by grass sickness even through the condition itself is not contagious. Other factors recognized as predisposing horses to developing the disease include stress (such as traveling, castration, mixing with a new group of horses, recent change of ownership or barn), and age (younger horses, especially those between 2 and 7 years are most commonly affected).

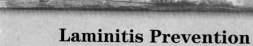

Laminitis Prevention

- Manage pasturing carefully (prevent overfeeding by using a muzzle, strip grazing, creating "starvation areas," or bringing your horse in for part of the day).

- Graze at night when fructan levels are lower to prevent a sharp increase in the toxin-producing bacteria in the hindgut.

- Feed a low-starch, high-fiber diet.

- Give steady, regular exercise.

- Have feet trimmed regularly by a good farrier.

- Avoid any sudden diet changes.

- Avoid obesity—monitor your horse's or pony's weight accurately using a weight tape.

Grass sickness may affect a number of horses who share grazing areas.

In grass sickness, damage to the nervous system controlling the gut leads to various degrees of paralysis of the digestive system. The condition has three main forms: acute, subacute, and chronic.

Acute Grass Sickness

If acute, horses suddenly show signs of severe colic, often with a sky-high pulse rate and passing little or no droppings. Swallowing is a struggle, and some horses get choke as they try to eat. Patchy sweating and muscle tremors are other possible symptoms, many of which are difficult to distinguish from a surgical form of colic.

Fluid distends the paralyzed gut, in severe cases even rupturing the stomach or overflowing out through the nostrils. As can be imagined, these horses are suffering intensely, and, as few survive more than a few days, euthanasia is usually the kindest option.

Subacute Grass Sickness

Subacute grass sickness is a similar but less severe form, with a slower onset. The horse finds it hard to swallow and can pass only a few, hard, mucus-covered droppings. Colic signs, muscle tremors, and patchy sweating are seen, along with a poor appetite and rapid weight loss.

These horses rarely survive beyond a week, and again, cases can be hard to distinguish from other causes of colic.

Chronic Grass Sickness

Developing slowly over several weeks, chronic sufferers will lose their appetite, drop weight rapidly to the point of emaciation, and show signs of mild or intermittent colic, often with drooping upper eyelids.

Chronic cases of grass sickness are the only ones for whom there is a degree of hope. With intensive nursing, those who can eat, pass droppings, and are not in too much pain may survive, although recovery will be a matter of many months and involve enormous commitment from the owner. Tasty, palatable, high-energy feeds, such as chopped vegetables, grass, and concentrates soaked in molasses must be given as part of an intensive nursing program that must also involve as much stimulation (for example, via grooming) as possible.

Sadly, no treatment is available for acute or subacute grass sickness and, until the cause is discovered, prevention is difficult, except for avoiding fields with a known history of causing the condition.

Diarrhea

Diarrhea is a symptom with a whole range of causes, from the mildly concerning to the extremely serious. Once again, careful and correct management should make it unlikely that your horse will be significantly affected.

What Causes Diarrhea?

Turning out on to lush, wet spring grass can all too often cause diarrhea in horses and ponies, but this nutritional type of diarrhea should settle quickly in most cases when good-quality hay is fed for a few days. Horses who break into a feed store or are suddenly given increased quantities of barley or wheat concentrates may similarly develop diarrhea due to excess fermentation in the hindgut.

More a cause for concern is diarrhea caused by parasitic damage to the lining of the digestive tract, a common source of the problem even in horses who are dewormed regularly. Young horses, often after the end of their second grazing season, can suddenly develop severe diarrhea and lose condition dramatically with the emergence of small redworm (*Cyathostoma*) larvae from their January to May hibernation in the gut wall.

Swelling of the sheath and belly area (ventral edema) and the lower legs is often a sign of protein loss through the damaged gut wall. Prompt dosing with the appropriate larvicidal dewormer (and sometimes steroids to reduce inflammation) is effective, although the condition can be fatal if left untreated.

Turning out onto lush spring grass can result in diarrhea.

Salmonella is a very serious bacterial cause of diarrhea that can spread rapidly to other horses and to people. Horses become very ill very quickly, run a high temperature (104°–106°F/40°–41.5°C), turn dull, and go off their food. Pulse rate increases and signs of colic are also often present. In the worst cases, the horse may die from toxic shock before he even passes any diarrhea.

In salmonella poisoning of this kind, diarrhea is very watery, often projectile, foul-smelling, and sometimes bloody. Patients must be isolated, given fluids intravenously— sometimes in addition to antibiotics—and be fed good-quality roughage. Sadly, some develop complications, such as laminitis or long-term, chronic diarrhea.

Some affected horses can continue to pass the infection for months after their own symptoms have subsided, becoming a lethal source of infection for their pasture-mates. Occasionally, horses can be passive carriers, shedding the *Salmonella* organism intermittently without showing any signs of poor health themselves. Both factors make this a tricky disease to control, no matter how conscientious owners and barns try to be.

Drug-induced diarrhea may be an unwelcome side effect of treating another condition with antibiotics, which disrupt the normal gut bacteria. In these cases, probiotics given in the feed will help to restore the normal balance. Horses and ponies on nonsteroidal anti-inflammatory drugs (NSAIDs) such as phenylbutazone ("bute") can develop diarrhea following ulceration of the gut lining.

Diarrhea may also be secondary (i.e., seen as a symptom of another condition) to hyperlipemia in fat ponies, tumors and inflammation of the gut wall, or liver disease brought on by ragwort poisoning.

Head Shaking

For a seemingly increasing number of owners, the approach of spring turns their previously steady and dependable mount into a twitching, head-tossing nightmare. Although it can appear at any time of the year, most cases of head shaking are seen during the warm spring and summer months, with signs subsiding by the fall.

Head shaking in horses is at best frustrating and at worst extremely distressing, in the most serious cases making the horse virtually impossible to ride. Affected horses may toss their heads repeatedly, often suddenly and violently throwing their head up vertically, to the side, or even round and round. Sneezing, snorting, and rubbing the muzzle and face with a foreleg or on a nearby object (sometimes causing cuts or scrapes) are all part of the horse's desperate attempts to alleviate irritation to the sensitive lining of the nose.

What Causes Head Shaking?

Identifying the cause is key to managing the condition, but finding the culprit is all too often almost impossible. The condition's seasonal pattern

Identifying the cause of irritation is key in managing head shaking.

Castration: A Job for the Spring

Fewer flies, and as such less chance of wound infection, mean that castration is a job usually scheduled for the spring or fall. It is commonly performed in the field where the horse is kept, either under sedation or a full general anesthetic.

What is involved? The procedure involves making an incision in the scrotum, one over each testicle, removing the testicle using emasculators (which cut the tissues of the spermatic cord and at the same time crush it to reduce the risk of hemorrhage). Over the next few days, the horse is given antibiotics and anti-inflammatory drugs, together with a tetanus vaccination if he is not already protected. Bathing and hosing the wound and light exercise encourages drainage and helps to reduce swelling. If the horse isn't turned out, he will need about 15 minutes trotting on the lunge three times daily.

There are times when castration is best carried out at an equine hospital. In some horses, one or both testicles are undescended (i.e., retained in the abdominal cavity). These animals, known as cryptorchids or rigs, will need more extensive, exploratory surgery. They may appear to be gelded but are capable of impregnating a mare and may show stallion-like behavior that makes them a nuisance or dangerous to handle.

Watch out for... Be alert, as complications after castration are fairly common. Bleeding often occurs, but is only serious if there is a steady stream from the wound for more than 15 minutes.

Occasionally, part of the gut can herniate through the wound site, often preceded by a long "rope" of fat. If this is going to happen, it usually occurs within a few hours of the operation. Act quickly, as emergency surgical repair is needed.

Swelling of the sheath and scrotum is usual. Reduce it with cold hosing, gentle massage, and exercise. Remember that severe swelling could be a sign of wound infection, which requires treatment with antibiotics and anti-inflammatory drugs. More serious is infection of the stump of the spermatic cord, which can lead to an abscess or the onset of peritonitis and may require surgery.

does suggest that allergic rhinitis (similar to human hay fever) could be behind some cases, the trigger being particular pollens or dust. Others cases are thought to be induced by light (known as phonetic head shaking) and these do respond to oral antihistamines.

Dental problems (e.g., sharp edges of molars, wolf teeth, abscesses, etc.) and sinus problems must be investigated with a thorough examination of the mouth and teeth, and, if necessary, an endoscopy and X-rays.

Neck and back pain, ear mites (or other foreign bodies in the ear), eye problems, discomfort from badly fitting tack or poor riding, or irritation from gnats or flies have all been suggested as causes of head shaking. Sometimes the cure for an individual may be as straightforward as a complete change of environment or buying a mesh nosenet to fit over the muzzle, providing a shield for sensitive nasal passages. Often, however, treatment is unsuccessful. Denerving the nostrils has been known to help in some cases, but is a final resort with many potential complications.

Chapter Nine

Pasture Management

P astures that have been rested over the winter will be showing spring growth by the beginning of April, but for those that have been continuously grazed, there will be plenty of work to be done. The rate of grass growth varies from season to season depending on where you live, but as soon as the ground is dry enough to allow a tractor on it, revival plans can be put into action.

If your field has come out of winter resembling a well-used soccer field, don't despair. Grass has the most incredible ability to regenerate, and you will be astounded at how quickly it starts to green over once temperatures start rising. Fields that have taken a battering will appreciate a rest now, however. Making alternative grazing arrangements for 3 to 4 weeks will allow time for fertilizer to be spread, roots to recover, and young shoots to stand a chance against the weeds. If you do not have access to a tractor and equipment, contact a professional.

Formulate a plan of action for March to May that will involve the following preparations.

Fertilizing

Unless it is going to be grazed by ponies at high risk from laminitis, a field that you intend to graze your

If your field looks like a ploughed-up soccer field after winter, do not despair! Grass has the most incredible ability to regenerate.

Apply the fertilizer during warm, damp weather when it will be readily absorbed. Use organic fertilizer if you can, although actual farmyard manure is slow to be absorbed and best applied during the damper conditions of autumn. After fertilizing, horses must be kept off the field for at least 2 weeks—longer if there has been no rain.

Chain Harrowing

Chain harrowing aerates the soil, drags out dead grass, and encourages new growth. Harrow during a sunny, rain-free spell so that the spread droppings will dry out and be exposed to sunlight, killing worm eggs and the larvae they contain.

Chain harrowing helps to aerate the soil.

horse on over the summer will need to be fertilized now. Fertilizer effectively kick-starts the healthy growth of the grass roots and plant, helping to keep out weeds. An inexpensive test will determine the levels of acidity and minerals in the soil, indicating the type of fertilizer required.

In most cases, a fertilizer including equal quantities of nitrogen, potassium, and phosphorus is suitable. Look for the label 15:15:15 or 17:17:17. Fields to be used for grazing horses don't need to be forced in the same way as those for cattle do, or where hay is being grown, so you may not need to spread at the rate suggested on the bag; applying around two 110-lb (50-kg) bags per acre is a good guideline.

Some areas may need to be reseeded.

not grass) or systemic (killing anything, including grass). If in doubt, ask for expert advice from your county agricultural agent on which product to use and how to apply it.

A large-scale problem must be dealt with by a licensed contractor because the use of certain weed killers by nonqualified persons is controlled. Sporadic growth can be tackled by spot-spraying with a suitable product.

Weed killing is not a one-time exercise, unfortunately. It must be repeated regularly throughout the summer to prevent weeds from maturing, seeding, and reappearing next year. Weather conditions need to be right (mild and free of wind, with no rain forecast that day).

Spraying is most effective when plants are growing actively, from March until June, and again in early autumn. Check the manufacturer's instructions as to when horses can be reintroduced safely after application.

Rolling

Slow rolling levels out areas that have suffered foot damage and presses the grass into contact with the soil, where it can reestablish growth more quickly. Choose the day to roll carefully; rolling wet ground will do more harm than good, but rolling when the ground is too dry is a waste of time.

Weed Killing

Weeds recover from winter much more quickly than grass. They will soon cover the bare soil in fields that have taken a battering over the previous months, unless you take action to boost grass growth. It is crucially important not to let unwanted plants get a grip—weeds don't go away when you ignore them.

The method you use depends on the extent of the difficulty. Herbicides can be either selective (attacking broad-leaved plants, such as docks and thistles, but

Reseeding

Badly poached or bare sections of the field that don't respond to your revival plan may need a complete makeover through reseeding. The same applies to areas that have been taken over by weeds. Localized patches can be a do-it-yourself job: fence off the area with electric fencing, apply weed killer, spread bare areas with seed, and roll or tread it in. For larger areas, contact your county agent for advice and help.

Tackling Drainage Problems

If you've noticed swampy areas during the winter, use the drier conditions of spring and summer as a time to remedy drainage difficulties in good time before next winter.

Chapter Ten

Spring Cleaning

Turning out our horses gives us the chance to breathe a sigh of relief, take stock, and plan a spring cleanup campaign. It is all too tempting to sit back and enjoy the warmer months before the flies come out and the heat takes over. But a thorough spring clean not only sets you up to enjoy the summer months more, it helps some of your costliest investments—the barn, equipment, blankets, and clippers—to last much longer.

It's no fun to reach September only to discover a whole list of jobs still undone that must then be fitted into shortening days with falling temperatures.

Around the Barn

It's easy to get carried away with riding and forget about spring cleaning. Be sure to do the following:

- Identify and complete any repair jobs—worn hinges, stiff bolts, doors and guttering that has unhinged or loosened, damaged panels, and raised nails, to name but a few contenders.
- Have a thorough clean up.
- Think about how things worked over the winter and make any improvements that may make life easier next year.

Spring

- Remove all bedding completely, and thoroughly scrub out all stables with a strong disinfectant.

In the Field

Assessing field conditions and attending to outdoor maintenance is also necessary:
- Check and make any repairs to fencing and gates.
- Give the water trough a good cleaning.
- Reassess how the field and gateways coped with last winter's weather. If necessary, consider options for improving drainage by fall.

Blankets

Once warmer days have finally set in and you are happy with the shade and shelter available in your field, it's safe to put winter blankets to one side for a thorough overhaul. Some saddlers now offer a blanket-cleaning service (if yours doesn't, check out ads in horse publications or search online for services in your area).

Spring Cleanup

- Make sure blankets are bone dry before packing them away for the summer, or they will become musty and moldy. Storage should be in a dry, vermin-proof environment. Blanket fabric makes great nesting material for mice!

- Avoid using ordinary detergents on anything that comes into contact with your horse's skin. Many horses are sensitive to products that human skin tolerates.

- Set aside a fine day to go through and set out the contents of the tack room. Saddle pads, bandages, cotton girths, lightweight sheets, and synthetic boots can all go in the washing machine on a cool-water setting. Leather gear will benefit from a good soaping and oiling.

At long last, you can take winter blankets to the cleaners.

This service may be a lifesaver because your horse's blankets are barely recognizable by the end of winter. For a fairly modest fee, you can hand over a torn, mud- and grease-coated rag and have it returned to you in decent condition for use in the fall.

Doing the cleaning yourself is perfectly feasible if you are on a budget. Even if the blanket will stuff into your washing machine, however (which few horse blankets do except lightweight sheets), be assured this is the fastest way possible to having a broken washing machine, clogged pipes, and a blanket that's no cleaner. It's far better to simply pick a sunny day and get going with a hose and a stiff brush.

- Lay the blanket out, lining side up, and remove as many hairs as possible from the underside.
- Thoroughly wet the blanket, which is easiest with a hose.
- Dilute the blanket cleanser, and pour it over the blanket. Now use a stiff brush to scrub all the dirt off.

- Rinse thoroughly with the hose.
- Now do the other side.
- Hang the blanket over a fence, rinse the outside again and leave it to dry.
- Once dry, apply waterproofer. Buy the correct type for the blanket fabric, applying it evenly and paying particular attention to seams.
- Once again, leave it to dry thoroughly.
- Oil any leather fittings.
- Take the blanket into a saddler's for any repairs to be done.

Clippers

Cleaning and servicing clippers at the end of a busy winter will add years to their working life. Aim to do a thorough cleaning at least once every 100 hours of use.

95

Spring

- Undo the side screws to remove the clipper head.
- Remove the blades, and brush any hair and grease from the head and gear wheel.
- Coat with new grease. Use only grease supplied or recommended by the manufacturer.
- Clean the blades with a brush or by dipping them in blade wash and drying them thoroughly. Keep blades as pairs, putting aside any pairs that have done five clips or more for sharpening.
- Remove the air filter, and brush out any hair clogged in it. Wash the filter cover in soapy water, dry, and replace.
- Now put the head back on the body of the clippers.

- Check that the plug and cord are in good order.
- Replace in the box and store in a dry place—which doesn't include a damp tack room!

Sending out your clippers for servicing every spring will ensure the first clip of next winter goes smoothly and safely. Companies that service clippers and sharpen blades can be found by contacting the manufacturers, through ads in the horse publications or online, or asking at your local agricultural merchant or tack shop.

It's all too easy to get carried away with riding and forget about spring cleaning.

Planning for Summer

March is a good time to do some forward planning for summer. Okay, so there's usually more time to play with in summer. The elements are not set against you, and there are far fewer chores to cram into the day for horses living out. On the other hand, summer does bring its own demands, especially for those who juggle horse ownership with family life, which itself picks up pace in summer months.

A Change in Routine

Questions to ask before your horse's routine changes include:

- How shall I keep my horse over the summer? Do I want him to continue coming inside at nights with hay and perhaps concentrated feed, or to be fully turned out? The answer may depend partly on:

- How much riding will I be doing over the summer, and what kind? Having reached this point in the book you will appreciate that horses are best off outside. In warmer weather, they deserve to be out in the fresh air, grazing and relaxing, and choosing their own shade, rather than standing in a stable. This applies to almost all horses—even those who need to be on a diet or kept away from flies and midges should be allowed their freedom.

It is untrue to say that you cannot compete on a horse who lives outside all the time. Busy owners whose horses work hard and compete regularly may be happier kept partly, or even mainly, stabled over the summer to retain more control over diet and fitness. But turnout for at least part of the day is still the best way to keep horses sane and ensure that they are getting sufficient intake of fiber.

- When can I make the changeover to grass? First, check the availability of the grazing you have in mind. You may have to wait until the landowner

Now is the time to plan your summer's riding activities.

feels it is dry enough or it has been rolled, harrowed, and fertilized. Is the weather suitable yet? If it's still unseasonably wet and cold, plans may have to go on hold for a few weeks.

- Can I still fit morning and evening visits in each day? "Out of the stable" must not mean "out of mind."

- Who could take over when I go away on vacation? Prepare for this now, well in advance of when you hope to travel.

Summer

Whatever summer with your horse means to you—whether it's long rides down leafy trails or poring over show schedules and practicing your braiding technique—no doubt it is more than enough reward for the endurance test that is winter horse ownership.

Even so, it would be a mistake to imagine that summer is an easy ride. Warmer, drier conditions bring their own demands on your horse's body, and keeping him happy and healthy can be quite a challenge during a long, hot summer. "Out of sight" in the field must not become "out of mind," or your horse's welfare will soon be put at risk.

For owners whose equestrian activity steps up a few gears, it is important to keep your horse's well-being the top priority at all times, whatever your riding plans and competitive ambitions.

Chapter Eleven

The Great Outdoors

*O*ver the next 4 to 6 months, your horse's field may well be his home—his living space, playground, dining area, and sleeping quarters all rolled into one. Keeping it in peak condition becomes more crucial than ever during the summer months, and nature will need a helping hand.

Pasture Management

During the winter, it is hard to believe that the grass will ever grow again, but if you have carried out all the appropriate spring pasture management tasks, your field should be facing the dry, summer months in reasonably good shape. Growth can be slow to get going during a cold spring, and grass may take time to establish itself on a pasture that has been heavily used over the winter. However, once temperatures rise, and as long as there is sufficient rain, the grass should be growing at a phenomenal rate by May, especially when fertilized.

The steps you will need to take to get the best out of your field during the summer months depend largely on how many horses (or other livestock) will be using it. The more mouths to feed, the more help the field will need to maximize growth and eating areas.

Summer Mowing

An easy way to tell if the grass needs mowing is to draw a line on your boots at about 3 inches (8 cm) above the ground.

In fields that are less intensively grazed, the problem is likely to be one of too much growth. The horses will become very selective about what they eat, leaving large areas to become overgrown and run to seed, producing open pasture that allows weeds to flourish. The field will quickly become a checkerboard of heavily grazed, short grass among areas of rank, stemmy, and unpalatable grasses—effectively reducing the available grazing area by up to a half.

Summer pasture management is all about managing these excesses and shortages, and keeping your grass as near as possible to the 3-inch (8- to 10-cm) height that horses find most inviting and palatable.

Mowing is the key strategy in dealing with fast-growing spring and summer grass. Fields are likely to need mowing every month from May until September, unless a long, dry period results in slow grass growth for a while. Mowing is crucial, not least because horses prefer eating grass leaf to fibrous stalks. By cutting the grass regularly, the plant is prevented from producing a seed head. In this way we can "fool" it into continuing to grow throughout the season, producing leaf not only upward, but also outward, to create pasture that is denser, more even, better draining, and resistant to hoof damage.

The quickest and most efficient way to keep grass under control is to use a tractor and mower, but smaller pastures can be controlled by a ride-on lawnmower.

Summer Grass Guidelines

- Aim to maintain the ideal grass height. Excess growth can be controlled bymowing, introducing more horses, and introducing other livestock (preferable, as this reduces the worm burden).
- Try to maintain a sufficient level of growth by resting the pasture and fertilizing if necessary, reducing the number of horses grazing, and restricting grazing.
- Picking up droppings is as important as ever in parasite control. Droppings soon multiply when horses are out all the time and conditions are dry. Horses will graze the field more evenly if toilet areas are cleared at least once a week. Large barns or ranches could consider investing in a pasture sweeper or organizing cleanup sessions.
- Harrowing or dragging the field occasionally during dry spells can help.
- Continue to be vigilant about weed control. Preventing weeds from seeding is crucial to staying on top of the problem.

It will not be long before you are worrying about having too much grass. If possible, graze other livestock to keep the grass down.

Making Hay

Where pasture supply outstrips demand, setting a field aside to make your own hay becomes an attractive option. It has obvious appeal in terms of budget, but remember to take into consideration the following:

- the quality of the grass—poor-quality or weed-infested grass is going to make poor-quality or weed-infested hay
- the cost of hiring someone to harvest the hay
- the stress factor of making sure it is safely harvested—particularly when relying on someone else to do the work for you
- the storage facilities available

Few people have the machinery required for hay making. Therefore, in most cases, you'll need to hire someone to do the job. Hay making is a multistage process, involving mowing, and then turning the hay three or four times so it is completely dry before baling.

Bear in mind that a farmer may be reluctant to turn up repeatedly for just a few acres' worth of hay and will inevitably put his larger customers first, which may be crucial if the weather looks at all doubtful. However, a little rain need not be a total disaster as long as the crop is turned until it has dried out again before baling.

How much hay is produced per acre will depend on the pasture quality, whether it has been fertilized, and the general growing conditions. Average production is around 100 bales per acre. Cutting in May or June, when the grass is in flower but before it seeds, produces the best-quality crop. By August, the grass will be largely fiber and seed, with very little nutritional value. Some late-cut hays will be as difficult to digest as straw.

Poisonous Plants

Spring and summer growth can reveal plants and herbs that are toxic to horses, so now is the time to make regular inspections of the field, paying particular attention to the hedges, where many species lurk. Garbage tipped over fences is another hazard to watch out for.

Horses are selective grazers. Therefore, they are less likely to be at risk from poisonous plants on well-managed, established pastures where plenty of tasty forage is available. The danger increases on poorly maintained pastures, where grass is sparse or unpalatable and weeds are allowed to flourish. In badly maintained environments, horses can be attracted to eating toxic plants (e.g., yew) that they would normally ignore.

- Many toxic plants are more palatable when they are wilting or dead. Therefore, it is best to dig them out by the roots and burn them, rather than spray them with pesticides.
- Check right into and underneath hedges, and at least a yard beyond field boundaries.

If plenty of good grass is available, horses will normally steer clear of poisonous plants.

Toxic Plants

Name	Location	Comments
Foxglove	Hedges, fields, and woodlands	Causes diarrhea, convulsions, respiratory distress, and, if consumed in large amounts, can cause death. Horses rarely eat fresh, growing foxglove, but it can be contained in hay.
Oak/acorns	Woodlands and fields	Reactions vary, but, generally speaking, acorns are more toxic than oak leaves, especially when green. Ingested, oak leaves and acorns can cause depression, convulsions, and colic.
Bracken	Hedges and fields	Field ponies can develop a taste for bracken, but eating large amounts causes staggering, fits, and eventually, death. Eating smaller amounts can cause vitamin B1 deficiency. The toxicity of bracken persists even when it is dry.
Horsetail	Anywhere where there is water	See Bracken.
Hemlock	Verges, hedges, woodlands, and fields	Hemlock is most toxic when it is fresh. It causes paralysis followed by death.
Buttercup	Fields	Buttercups are toxic in large quantities, but the irritant and unpalatable properties of this plant mean that cases of poisoning are rare. Dry buttercups are not toxic.
Nightshade	Wasteland and hedges	All plants in the nightshade family—including potatoes and tomatoes—are toxic in large quantities. Ingestion causes diarrhea, convulsions, and respiratory distress. Consumption of the roots and berries of the deadly nightshade plant can be fatal.
Laburnum	Mainly in gardens	Laburnum is highly toxic, causing hyperactivity, convulsions, colic, and diarrhea. Often, this is followed by coma then death.
Privet	Hedges	Eaten in large quantities, this plant causes convulsions and diarrhea.
Yew	Hedges and woodlands	All parts are highly toxic, causing trembling, hyperactivity, paralysis, and sudden death.

- Make doubly sure that boundaries with gardens, yards, or allotments are secure and that horses cannot reach over. Alert neighbors to the dangers of tipping grass clippings or other garden waste (such as shrub branches or rotting windfalls of apples or pears) over fences.
- Do some homework on poisonous plants so that you know what to look for.
- Many plants can cause a local, topical reaction (e.g., nettle rash). Check your horses regularly for signs.
- Break open bales of hay to check for dried plants and discard any you do not recognize.
- Fence off poisonous trees, being sure that horses cannot reach fallen seeds or fruits. Watch for twigs or branches blown down in windy weather.
- If you suspect your horse has eaten any poisonous plants, call your veterinarian immediately.
- Remember, the most common plant to poison horses is grass. Most veterinarians see more cases of laminitis in 1 month than they see genuine poisoning during their whole career.

In addition to these items, several plants may pose a danger to your horse in his home

Some field ponies develop a taste for bracken.

St. John's Wort could pose a danger for horses.

environment. Check the fields and exercise areas that your horse has access to, and, if your horse is stabled at your home, take particular care—many common garden plants and shrubs are toxic. Look out for the following, all of which are toxic to horses in varying degrees:

- Broom
- Bryony Family
- Buckthorn
- Bulbs Ofof Daffodil, Bluebell, Snowdrop
- Celandine Family
- Chickweed
- Flax
- Ground Ivy
- Guellebore
- Henbane/Cowbane
- Larkspur

- Lesser Periwinkle
- Lupin
- Magnolia
- Meadow Saffron
- Monkshood
- Poppy
- Purple Milk Vetch/Kidney Vetch
- Rhododendron
- Soapwort/Sandwort
- St. John's Wort
- Water Dropwort
- Wild Clematis (Old Man's Beard)

Coping With Heat

A horse enjoys feeling the warmth of the sun on his back, but if the temperature climbs, you must ensure that he has adequate shade and a plentiful supply of fresh water.

Providing Shade

Humans exposed to the heat of the sun with no access to shade will suffer heatstroke, dehydration, and sunburn. Horses are no different. It is essential to be aware of conditions in the field during hot days and to give horses the opportunity to cool down. Hedges, for example, can give shade in the mornings and evenings, but they offer little or no protection when the sun is at its highest and hottest.

Mature trees are always much appreciated for their shady branches, so if your field does not have any, make sure the horses have access to a run-in shelter or barn. Alternatively, bring them into a stable for the afternoon during hot weather, but bear in mind that a badly ventilated, poorly insulated stable may be worse than being outside. The best way to test it is to stand inside it yourself for 10 minutes and see how you feel. Use the facilities you have to beat the heat—

find the coolest place available and make use of it.

Just as an enclosed car can quickly become an oven in warm weather, a trailer standing in the sun at a show can be the worst place possible for a horse or pony. Park in the coolest place available, and take your horse out of the trailer if at all possible, tethering him in a cool, shady area.

Water Levels

Fresh grass is mostly water, and so one thing you will notice once grass growth really gets moving in April and May is that your horse is not drinking as much as he did during the winter months. However, this will change as the season progresses. Do not be fooled by his apparent disinterest in the trough during early spring, because from late June onwards—as the

Mature trees provide excellent shade.

A hot horse will drink a huge amount of water.

grass becomes more fibrous and the weather hotter and drier—his demand for water will increase.

A hot horse needs a huge amount of water—up to 12 gallons (40 liters) a day—and the hotter the weather, the more he will need. If water is freely available, there is no need to worry—your horse will drink enough to meet his needs. So, make sure you provide sufficient clean, fresh drinking water for all the horses in the field.

Cleaning out the trough is a weekly job during hot, sunny weather. Algae will build up quickly (especially in the old, enamel tubs popularly recycled as troughs). Check water levels daily, making sure automatic-filling troughs are working properly, and topping off other water containers as necessary.

Securing buckets in an old tire will prevent them from being accidentally knocked over and leaving the horses without water.

Remember, natural sources of water frequently dry up to nothing during the summer months. At best, they become stagnant. A stream that can be relied on throughout the winter is unlikely to provide sufficient clean water throughout the summer months, and you will need to make alternative arrangements.

Summer Nuisances

Summer sees a plethora of insects and parasites emerging to irritate our horses, some of which can cause significant problems. As with most things, prevention is better than cure, and there are many things you can do to lessen summer nuisances.

Flies

Make the most of riding during the spring months, because by June the flies have usually arrived in force and are here to stay until the end of September at the earliest. If flies are a nuisance to riders, you can only imagine what misery they cause to horses—particularly those out in the sun for long, hot days at a time.

House Flies

Small, black house flies are the annoying ones that hover around the face and under the belly, attracted to moist areas, such as watery eyes or the blood of a wound. There, their activity (feeding, drinking, and laying eggs) causes irritation, further discharge, and often infection. The stable fly is related to the common house fly. It flourishes in dirty barnyards and causes small, itchy, painful lumps with a central crust on the legs and body.

Horse Flies

Large, distinctive, orange-backed horse flies appear from June onward. They prefer warm, sultry days

Horses can be plagued by flies in the summer months.

and bright sunlight. These will land anywhere on the body to bite and feed, causing painful lumps or elongated welts that can easily become infected.

Gnats

Gnat bites can provoke the extreme allergic reaction known as sweet itch, with biting concentrated around the mane, tail, and back. Swarms can be seen hovering at dawn and dusk on still days.

Bot Flies

The bot fly is easily spotted by the long, egg-laying tube that dangles from its body. Bot flies are public enemy number one when it comes to large flies. Not only do they give as painful a bite as the infamous horse fly, but the tiny eggs that bots lay in clusters on the skin of the lower legs and neck are a potential cause of severe internal damage. Licked off the skin by the horse, the eggs hatch inside the digestive system, where the larvae feed before emerging in droppings during winter.

Many horses learn to recognize the characteristic buzz of the dark, furry bot fly and will start to display restless behavior when bots are buzzing around them. Bot flies are around from mid-summer onward and are impossible for pasture-kept horses to avoid.

Their white eggs are horrendously sticky and hard to remove without also removing the hair to which they are attached. The best methods of removal are plucking or scraping with a rough anti-bot block, available from saddlers. Do this daily—one bot fly can lay 300 eggs in an hour!

Internal damage caused by the ingestion of bot eggs can be prevented by deworming with a product containing ivermectin (e.g., Ivercare) or moxidectin (e.g., Quest) at the end of the summer and again during winter.

Fly Prevention

An individual horse's response to fly bites can vary hugely. Some horses hardly seem to sport so much as a single bite all season, whereas others can be tortured by flies and covered in lumps. Moist, exposed areas (such as eyes, udders, and sheaths) are the most vulnerable and so need to be kept scrupulously clean in summer. Any wounds should be bathed and dried frequently.

Keeping flies away from horses is far easier said than done, but far more options are available today than in the past. Listed in the following is the arsenal of weapons available to us in the anti-fly battle. You may well want to make use of a combination to attack on several fronts. However, you can also help your

A fly fringe is an inexpensive way of coping with fly or insect problems.

horse by taking some sensible precautions:
- provide shady areas in the field
- pick up droppings frequently
- keep muck heaps compact and sited well away from the field and stables
- provide a friend, so your horse can share "fly-swishing" duties
- bring your horse indoors during the hottest parts of the day
- think hard before roaching a mane, as a horse's mane and tail are his only built-in defense against flies

Fly Fringes/Masks

Fringes and masks are inexpensive and useful aids to keeping flies away from vulnerable eyes.

A fly fringe requires a halter, which should be made from leather and have a quick-release clip and breakaway headpiece for safety. Choose a fringe with sewn loops rather than Velcro, as Velcro attachments soon clog up with grass and dirt. Make sure the fringe sits comfortably, with no pressure on the base of the ears, and also ensure that the head collar halter fits snugly but not too tightly. Net fly masks can include ear covers, which can be very useful for horses who are particularly sensitive in this area.

Both fringes and masks require regular checking as they are easily dislodged if the horse rubs his ears or face. A horse with a fringe or net across his eyes, or with a fly trapped inside the face net or mask, will soon become distressed.

Nose Nets

Many owners of horses who head shake have long been aware of the benefits offered by a fine mesh or muslin nose net to filter out dust, pollen, and midges from the sensitive muzzle area. However, bear in mind that these cannot be used in dressage competitions affiliated with the United States Dressage Federation.

Anti-Fly Sheets

Another recent innovation in the battle against flies is the all-over, breathable mesh summer sheet, designed to keep flies off the skin. Anti-fly sheets can bring great relief to horses particularly prone or sensitive to fly bites.

A fly mask also covers the ears.

Types of Repellents

Water-based repellent sprays are the best choice for covering large areas, but keep handy wipes or roll-ons for use at shows. Powders and oil-based gels evaporate less quickly than other types of product, as well as being particularly useful for horses who dislike sprays. Apply gels with a cloth or, for particularly sensitive areas such as the face, use your fingers (remember to wash your hands afterward).

Most sheets are designed to keep the horse cool and to dry quickly after rain. Commercially produced anti-fly sheets come in two types:

• general-purpose sheets: these improve comfort for all horses at grass by protecting the horse from large biting flies

• anti-gnat sheets: these are available as different brands, but they are all custom-made to cover every inch of the body, preventing even the most intrepid gnat from getting a mouthful

As a cheaper alternative to commercially produced anti-fly sheets, you can adapt a simple cotton sheet. However, remember to remove the sheet if it becomes wet.

Fly Repellents

Unfortunately, fly repellents seem to be much less effective on horses than on other livestock. However, this does not prevent horse owners from spending large sums of money on them in the hope of bringing their horses some relief and to keep flies at bay during dressage tests, show classes, and jumping rounds.

Whatever form of fly repellent you use, it must be used in the right way to maximize its effectiveness:

• Perform a patch test before widespread use because

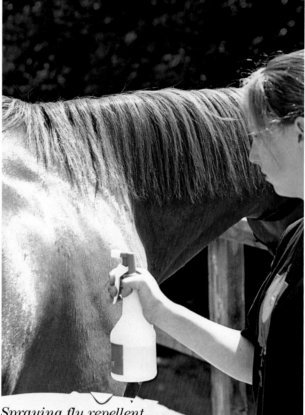

Spraying fly repellent on your horse offers some relief.

certain ingredients can cause skin irritation in some animals (placing a blanket on the horse after applying repellent may also provoke a reaction).

• Follow dilution and application instructions carefully.

• Take care when applying repellent around the eyes and nose, and avoid sensitive areas.

• Reapply as often as the manufacturer's maximum frequency recommendation allows (sweat, rain, and evaporation all reduce effectiveness).

• Purchase products containing diethyltoluamide (DEET), pyrethrum, or permethrin, which kill insects on contact.

• Applying petroleum jelly around the eyes, nostrils, and inside the ears will help to form a barrier, preventing flies from landing and biting.

• Spray the walls of stables and field shelters (which may require a different product), hang up flypapers, and install a fan to create air movement. Make sure flypapers and fans are safely out of the horse's reach. Remember, you tend to get what you pay for, and more expensive, well-known brands are often the most effective.

• Dust even the smallest wounds immediately with a wound powder containing fly-repellent properties, clean it off and reapply it twice a day.

• Benzyl benzoate (available from your veterinarian) applied to cracked or inflamed skin is an effective soother and fly repellent.

• Tags designed for use on cattle can be attached to a halter at the cheek or poll, or braided into the mane.

• Always bathe a sweaty horse using a shampoo with fly-repellent ingredients (e.g., tea tree oil).

Recently introduced and fast becoming very popular are the new, spot-on fly repellents, which seem to be more effective. Spot-on repellent usually comes in liquid form, and they are administered from a plastic vial in much the same way as the spot-on flea treatments used on domestic cats and dogs. The liquid is absorbed into the horse's body and repels flies for approximately 2 weeks.

Some owners have their own favorite natural fly-repellent "recipes," the most popular ingredients being the oils of citronella, lavender, rosemary, thyme, geranium, eucalyptus, tea tree, lime, and juniper berry. These natural ingredients are now being more widely used in commercial preparations, but should never be applied undiluted. Feeding garlic also has its supporters because it is thought to be excreted through the skin and off-putting to flies.

Ticks

Ticks can cause real problems (commonly in the United States, but not so much elsewhere). Once the tick's jaws are locked into the horse's skin, it will not let go. Never attempt to remove a tick simply by

Applying petroleum jelly forms a barrier so that flies do not land and bite.

pulling it because, although the body will come off, the mouthparts will be left behind and can cause infection. Ticks can be effectively removed by using a purpose-made tick remover (following the manufacturer's instructions). You can also use tweezers, making sure you grip the mouthparts so that the whole tick is removed (there is a special knack to this technique, so it is best not to attempt it unless you know what you are doing). Alternatively, remove the tick by forcing its mouth open, either by soaking it in oil (so it cannot breathe) or "doping" it by using cotton soaked in fly repellent.

Chapter Twelve

Summer Feeding

*H*aving worked out what you will be doing with your horse over the spring and summer, you should, by now, have made the gradual change to your horse's feeding regime. During May to June, it is worth reviewing your program and making any changes you feel are necessary, whatever your horse's workload.

Look back at the advice given for spring feeding, remembering to keep up the proportions of fiber in the diet. Continuing to turn your horse out for part of the day will help to maintain fiber intake, as well as keeping him level-headed and relaxed. Reassess feeding needs as the summer season progresses (see Principles of Feeding). Bear in mind that it is far too easy to blame the feed when things go wrong. Instead, you should look at all the other management and training factors that may be involved.

Feeding for Competition

Showing enthusiasts must be especially vigilant that their attempts to have their superstars look well fed and healthy do not result in laminitis. Nutrition can also affect the horse's behavior and the quality of his coat, as well as his overall shape and size. Supplements promising a coat so shiny that you

The nutrient value of grass will decrease from the end of June onward.

calorie feeds; otherwise stick to low-energy, high-fiber feeds, giving supplements if necessary. Deficiencies of vitamin A and the minerals zinc and copper are sometimes associated with a poor skin and coat. These can be boosted with a suitable additive. However, a cup of corn oil each day, split into several feeds, will also help to improve the "bloom" on some coats.

Above all, remember, the shiniest of coats are achieved in well-cared-for horses who are groomed regularly. Natural shine is produced by naturally occurring oils (sebum) that line each coat hair. Regular grooming keeps hairs dust-free and encourages the production of sebum—so there's no replacing good old elbow grease!

could see your face in it line the shelves; but remember, beauty comes from within.

A well-balanced, nutritionally sound diet, combined with the right amount of exercise to boost circulation, will produce a glossy, healthy coat. Indeed, achieving a lovely sheen on the coat using these natural methods is far better—you have the knowledge that your horse is just as healthy on the inside as he appears to be on the outside.

Your horse's summer diet should consist of a high-quality feed sufficient for his workload. It should be based on fiber, with some—not too much—high-starch conditioning feeds. Only use concentrated feeds specifically for showing if you know your horse's temperament can take high-

Grazing

Weather conditions will largely determine the role that grass continues to play in your horse's diet over the summer. Damp, mild weather will allow grass to continue to grow, especially if it is regularly mowed, so continue to control intake if necessary.

The energy and nutrient content of grass will decrease from the end of June onward, but drier conditions will accelerate this reduction. If a prolonged dry spell sets in, pastures will soon begin to yellow and will provide little nutrition. In these conditions, supplementing the diet with hay or a little high-fiber concentrated feed may well be necessary, especially for horses being regularly ridden, but even for relatively inactive horses.

Dieting

Many an owner will be taken by surprise by the amount of weight his horse or pony has put on

Summer Feeding

during May and June, particularly those with draft blood. Even if your horse goes into spring looking as if he could do with some filling out, once grass growth really takes off, weight increase can become a problem very quickly—even the sparsest pastures will be packed with calories at this time of year. High protein levels (about 4.5 percent) are also part of the problem, because horses convert excess protein to energy and store excess energy as fat.

Check weight regularly, using a weight tape or by condition scoring. A quick guideline is given by the ribs, which you should be able to feel, but not see. If you have to push into your horse's skin to feel his ribs, he is overweight.

Managing the overweight horse is difficult, partly because it is difficult for us—as caring owners—to deprive our horses of their main

pastime and source of enjoyment! However, remember that fat horses are not healthy horses. Excess weight limits performance, places greater demand on the organs and body systems, increases the stress on the limbs, and reduces resistance to disease.

To take control of your horse's weight management, you will need to be cruel to be kind. It is far safer to slightly underfeed a horse than to overfeed him. Start by limiting grass intake, because grass alone is perfectly capable of making a horse obese.

• Never starve your horse. Depriving him of feed may result in colic, liver damage, and kidney damage because the horse simply holds on to the nutrients he has by excreting less. Starvation is also cruel and totally unnecessary. The key to successful weight loss is to reduce the nutritional value of your horse's food, rather than the quantity. This way, his appetite and his need to feed remain satisfied.

Work off calories by stepping up exercise.

- Allow 7 to 10 days to make changes in diet, however small. Rapid changes can cause digestion problems.
- During mealtimes, separate your overweight horse so he cannot finish his own bucket and immediately raid another horse's food.
- Find out your horse's ideal body weight, and plan a gradual reduction in calories to reach this target. Aim to feed fewer calories in such a manner that your horse will not realize he is eating less. Check progress with regular weigh-ins, and adjust feed as necessary.
- Rather than the usual 2 to 2.5 percent of body weight that feed intake is based on, make it 1.5 to 2 percent, depending on how much weight must be lost. Remember, this will affect the ratio of hard feed to forage.
- Weigh feeds accurately—do not guess.
- Limit or exclude concentrated feeds. Many horses can work quite hard from a grass/forage diet alone. When concentrated feeds are necessary, use feeds as high in fiber and as low in energy as possible.

- If forage only is fed, dilute the energy levels by mixing it with low-energy fiber sources. For example, hay can be mixed with a little oat straw.
- Maintain vitamin and mineral levels using a supplement, forage balancer, or nutrient-enriched high-fiber feed.
- Decrease feed before decreasing work.
- Increase exercise—work uses up calories and, when your horse is working, he's not eating (or thinking about eating)! Obese horses should begin with slow walking only, but make each ride count by making him use himself properly. Use more calories by substituting training for trail rides.
- Be patient. Fat does not disappear quickly (as we all know). Taking things slowly will ensure weight loss is not accompanied by stress, either mental or physical.

Buying Hay

During the summer, you should start to make preparations for fall and winter feeding. If you have a suitable, dry, vermin-free storage space, hay is far cheaper to buy direct from the farmer off the field as soon as it has been harvested. Depending on the weather, farmers will be producing hay from the end of May onward, so make your contacts in plenty

In most cases, hay is cheaper to buy direct from the farmer off the field.

of time, or look out for ads. Most will deliver for an extra fee if transport is a problem.

Be fussy about the quality of the hay you purchase, and do not always opt for so-called bargains. Using a supplier you can trust means he will back you up if there is any subsequent problem. However you purchase your hay, always check the quality first-hand before okaying a delivery and price.

Hay is normally sold in square or round bales. Ask the farmer for the biggest bales he can provide. Big loads are more economical, and they store better—the more hay is handled, the quicker it deteriorates.

Feed Quality

- Get into the habit of checking feed labels to compare the calorie levels. These will be measured in megajoules (MJ) per kg of dry matter. Multiply the MJ value by 2.2 to work out the calorific content in pounds (lb).

- Feeds and supplements deteriorate more rapidly in hot weather, so keep them cool to keep them fresh. An old fridge in the tack room may be useful at this time of year.

Check out the quality of hay before purchase.

Hay Varieties

Numerous choices of hay are available, the main varieties being timothy (a very stalky hay), alfalfa (a protein-rich hay), clover, and grass hay. Most farmers plant mixtures in their fields, so you may well be offered a hay mixture, such as a bale of alfalfa-and-grass hay. The advantage of having so many different types of hay from which to choose is that it allows you to manage your horse's protein and fiber levels more effectively.

Chapter Thirteen

Summer Grooming

*I*t is much easier to keep your horse looking handsome once he has finally shed the last vestiges of his winter woollies. Warmer weather usually means a shining, short-haired summer coat. Grooming remains as important as ever throughout the summer months, however. If you are going to cultivate a show-stopping gleam, keep your horse's skin healthy and help him to fight off flies.

You can get to work with a vengeance using a body brush now, as even nonstabled horses living outdoors do not need the same quantity of natural, insulating grease as they did during the winter. Brushing plays a large part in creating a glossy coat because it stimulates sebum production, keeps off dust, and gets the circulation going. So, even if your horse looks clean or if you are short on time, allow 10 minutes for a thorough body brush before each ride.

Eyes and nostrils suffer from dust in dry spells, so daily sponging with cool, clean water will be much appreciated, as well as help to deter flies and infection. Udders need a regular wipe, and sheaths benefit from a refreshing cleanup, too.

Bath Time

We humans feel a whole lot better after a shower when we've been exercising, and the same applies to our horses. A regular bath helps to maintain skin and coat condition, as well as refreshing your horse after a workout or a long ride. As long as you bathe only on mild, still days, your horse should not become chilled.

- Prepare a bucket of warm water, a sponge, a water brush, and some horse shampoo. Only use shampoo designed for equestrian use—allergic reactions to human products are common.
- Dilute the shampoo as directed, and apply the soapy water all over the horse, scrubbing at greasy areas (such as under the saddle) with the water brush.
- Wipe gently around the face with the wrung-out sponge, taking care not to get soap in the eyes.
- Massage shampoo directly into the mane, getting right to the roots.
- Use the water brush to work shampoo into the legs, particularly white areas. For safety's sake, crouch instead of kneeling.
- Dunk the tail into the bucket, using the water brush to scrub soapy water well into the dock area. Stand slightly to the side for this.
- Use a hose to rinse the whole body thoroughly. Some horses are alarmed by hoses, so take care and go steady. Would you like it if someone turned on a hose and squirted it directly at you? Check that you have removed all the suds by rubbing the hair backwards and forwards.
- Use a sweat scraper to remove excess water, going with the lie of the coat.
- Comb through the mane to remove knots. A little baby oil or detangling product will help.
- Rinse out the tail in a bucket of clean water. If your horse does not object, hold the tail below the bone and spin it, so that it dries more quickly.
- A quiet walk in the sun will help your horse to dry off. Once the coat is dry, a flick over with a clean body brush will remove water marks and bring out the shine.

Cooling Clips

Some older horses and many furry ponies believe in being prepared! They begin growing their winter coat as early as the beginning of August. If temperatures are high, and you have a busy schedule planned, clipping will keep them cool and will not harm later regrowth. A persistently long, curly coat can be a sign of Cushing's disease and needs investigation by a veterinarian.

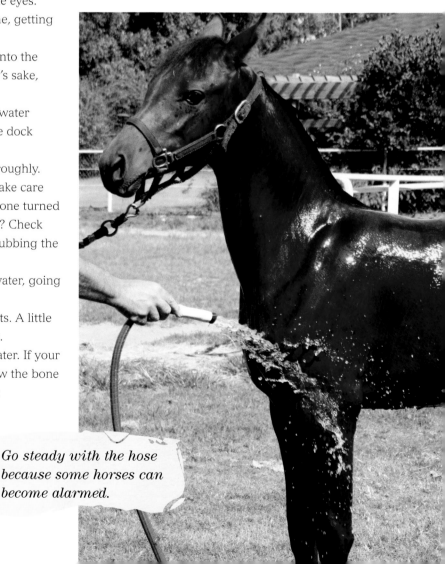

Go steady with the hose because some horses can become alarmed.

Daily Grooming

Summer is the time to get to work with a body brush.

Your horse will appreciate daily sponging of the eyes and nostrils in hot weather.

Bathing Your Horse

Don't forget to rinse hard to reach areas.

Work shampoo well into the coat.

Use a sweat scraper to get rid of excess water.

Braiding Techniques

Braiding techniques can play tricks on the eyes. A few extra braids on a short-necked horse create the illusion of more length. For a long neck, use fewer braids. Chunky horses look better with a smaller number of chunkier braids. Finer bred animals look good with smaller braids and more of them.

Show Preparations

Showing is all about showing off—and why not, when the sun is out and your horse is feeling and looking good? Whether you plan to tackle a show class, dressage test, or a round of jumping, presenting yourself and your horse to look your polished best is part of the challenge of the day, and a major fun factor in summer horse ownership.

Here are some tips on finishing touches that will give you that winning edge.

- Check rules about clipping and trimming before you get snipping. Some shows disqualify certain clipping styles. Aim for a smart and tidy appearance, with a braided mane and tail.
- Pull the mane to reduce its length and thickness ready for braiding. About 4 inches (10 cm) is a good length. Take only a few hairs at a time to avoid creating soreness, choosing a warm day when the pores are open. Never cut the mane.
- Hairs can be carefully pulled from the sides of the top of the tail. Horses who

live out are better left with full tails that are braided. Cutting across the bottom of the tail creates a neat, straight edge. Ask a friend to place an arm under the tail at the dock and cut across at hock level.

- Quarter marks can make the quarters look more powerful and improve the look of a low-set tail carriage. Dampen the coat slightly, then use a small comb to make diamond patterns, or use a brush to create "shark's teeth."
- Trim heels and chins for a more streamlined look, although remember that cutting off muzzle whiskers is unfair and unnecessary.
- Oil your horse's feet before entering the ring. A small amount of petroleum jelly around the eyes and nostrils gives emphasis and deters flies.

When showing, present yourself and your horse to look your polished best.

Manes

- Comb hair and dampen slightly. Divide into even sections using rubber bands.

- Starting at the top of the neck, take the first bunch of hair. Separate into three equal strands. Begin to braid, lifting the bunch slightly away from the crest. Braid to the end, keeping an even, firm tension.

- If using a needle and thread, loop the thread around the end of the braid to secure it. Push the needle up from underneath, near the crest, to create a loop. Fold as many times as necessary to make a neat "button," stitching through from the underside to secure.

- If using rubber bands, use one to finish off each braid. Double up the braid to create a "button" and secure with more bands until tight. Use bands of a color that blends with the hair.

Comb through the mane and dampen it slightly.

Braid to the end, securing with a needle and thread or a rubber band.

Double up the plait, and then secure it with thread or a rubber band.

Tails

- You will need a full, unpulled tail with at least 3 months' growth at the top.

- Standing slightly to one side (for safety), dampen the hair at the dock.

- Take three thin bunches of long hair from the top of the tail. Take either one from the middle and one from each side, or two from one side and one from the other.

- Braid down the center of the tail, taking a few hairs from each side in turn and incorporating them. Work down to three-quarters of the length of the bone, then finish braiding the hairs already in the bunch.

- Secure the end with thread or a rubber band. Loop it back underneath itself and sew firmly into position.

Braid down the center of the tail.

Secure the end with thread or a rubber band, and then loop the braid back underneath itself.

Chapter Fourteen

Summer Health Alert

Summer may be the easiest time of the year when it comes to looking after your horse, but careful owners can never afford to relax. Heat and dry conditions during the warmer months of the year make horses susceptible to a number of problems that can cause concern.

Heatstroke

Heatstroke is most likely to happen to unfit horses or ponies during hot, humid weather, after or during high-intensity, fast, strenuous work at a competition.

The horse may pull up or finish in distress, gasping for air, often with a high pulse rate and rectal temperature above 104°F (40°C). The horse is usually reluctant to move, may be wobbly on his legs, and may show signs of colic.

Cool the horse as quickly as possible by applying cold (39°–50°F/ 4°–10°C) water all over the body, especially the hindquarters. Gradually remove tack and move the horse into a cool, shady, breezy area if possible. Encourage the horse to drink oral electrolytes if possible.

Skin Conditions

Sunburn

We all know how sore even the slightest touch of sunburn can be after we've overdone our exposure on a bright, cloudless day. It's all too easy to forget that many horses have areas of unpigmented skin that are just as sensitive to the sun as our own. The nose and muzzle of white-faced horses and ponies frequently become inflamed, sore, and crusty during prolonged spells of intense sunshine.

Uncomplicated sunburn is easily prevented in exactly the same way as we should sensibly protect our own skin—by applying a high-protection-factor sunscreen frequently to the areas affected, or by keeping the horse out of direct sun (for example, stabling during the day).

Photosensitization

Not all soreness and blistering on the muzzle area is due to sunburn. Horses may eat plants, such as St. John's Wort, which contain photodynamic agents that react with sunlight in unpigmented or lightly pigmented (white) areas of skin. This is more likely to happen during the summer, when horses are turned out in bright, sunny weather and are free to pick at a variety of plant species in hedges and ditches.

Although inflammation and crusting is confined to the white or pink skin, in severe cases skin in these parts may peel off completely. The horse must then be kept out of the sunlight altogether until the skin has totally healed; any bacterial infection that may have set in must be treated with antibiotics.

Photosensitization can also occur in horses with liver disease, so always contact your veterinarian if you are worried about lesions on you horse's unpigmented skin. She will then arrange blood tests to check liver function.

Warts

Young horses (usually between 6 months and 4 years) are readily infected by the equine papilloma virus, resulting in batches of small pink or grey warts spreading over the muzzle, lips, and face. Occasionally, the lower limbs and genital areas can be affected too, but there is no need for treatment. The warts tend not to cause any problems and will eventually drop off of their own accord within 2 or 3 months.

Because groups of youngsters are often affected after being turned out for their first or second grazing season, you may have heard these warts referred to as grass warts. Other types of wart, known as aural warts, are flat areas of pink/grey skin proliferating over the insides of the ears. Again, these rarely cause problems and are best left alone.

Sarcoids

Sarcoids are skin tumors, which, although a long-term problem for affected horses and ponies, do become more noticeable during the summer months when the coat is short and sleek. They are hairless growths that may be flat, warty, or nodular in appearance or sometimes a mixture of these

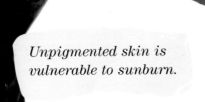

Unpigmented skin is vulnerable to sunburn.

types, and may also be ulcerative (that is, oozing blood and serum).

Sarcoids can appear anywhere on the body and, although unsightly, often pose few problems. Difficulties can arise when the growth appears in a position that interferes with tack or perhaps with the horse's movement. Some sarcoids appear and then never change, whereas others grow rapidly and ulcerate alarmingly. The way in which a particular one is treated will depend on its type and position, and may involve surgery, cryosurgery (freezing), cytotoxic cream, or vaccination. Their unpredictability means repeat treatments are often necessary.

Insect Bites

Flying insects that bite and sting are magnetized to sweaty horses on sultry summer days, quickly making them not only hot but bothered, too. Foot stamping, tail switching, head tossing, nervousness, and restlessness are all signs of irritation and distress from flies and their bites, which can be extremely painful and cause localized swelling and nodules.

Reduce your horse's distress by incorporating as many anti-fly measures as you can into your summer management routine, especially on those hot and humid days that bring insects out in droves:
- apply fly repellent frequently and generously
- use a comfortable, well-fitting fly fringe or mask to protect the eyes and/or nose (but check it regularly)
- fit your horse with a lightweight turnout sheet
- stable your horse during the worst heat of the day
- keep your horse's environment, both in the field and stable, as clean and dropping-free as possible

Collagen Granulomas

Owners are frequently mystified by the appearance of these small, firm but nonpainful nosodes on the face and body (especially the saddle area) during the spring and summer. It is thought that they are also signs of an allergy to insect bites.

Usually, the overlying skin is normal, but hardening of the core of the nodule can cause some inflammation and create a nuisance when the lumps

Youngsters may be affected by the equine papilloma virus, which heals on its own and rarely causes serious problems.

appear right where the panels of the saddle would rest. Unfortunately, they are often persistent, and a good-quality saddle pad or numnah is going to be needed to give sufficient protection from pressure if the horse is to be ridden. Sometimes treatment is attempted by surgical removal or anti-inflammatory injections into the nodules, but most mild cases eventually subside on their own in due course.

Saddle Sores and Girth Galls

Pressure, sweat, and dirt in the coat or on the girth or saddle pad can lead to thickening and inflammation

Ill-fitting tack rubbing on a thin summer coat can quickly lead to saddle sores.

and a painful area of skin known as a saddle sore or, in the girth area, a girth gall. Of course, this can happen at any time of the year, although sweating under the tack during summer activities (when the coat is thin and the skin is more exposed) makes sores more of a problem during the warmer months—just when poor performance and a nasty sore requiring weeks off work are least welcome!

Antibiotics and anti-inflammatory drugs may be needed, but usually rest, protecting the affected area, and applying topical antibiotic/anti-inflammatory ointment is sufficient to encourage healing.

Saddles must be correctly fitted and checked for fit regularly because horses frequently change shape as they mature, or when they are given different work or a different feeding regime. Saddle pads and girths must be washed regularly (or cleaned, in the case of leather girths) to remove dirt and dried sweat.

Melanoma

Melanomas are tumors commonly seen in older gray horses. They are usually found around the anus and

under the tail, although the salivary glands at the side of the head where the neck meets the jaw (the parotid area), within the colored part of the eye (the iris), and the third eyelid are other susceptible sites. Occasionally, the growths can occur as solitary skin masses anywhere on the body. As a general rule, melanomas are usually benign and are rarely treated.

Urticaria

Wheals, or hives, are flat-topped skin swellings that leave a marked depression or pit when pressed firmly by the finger. They tend not to be itchy or hairless, but may merge together to form larger, unsightly swellings, often on the body and/or flanks.

Such swellings are usually signs of an allergic reaction, so check the horse's recent exposure to:
• drugs (for example, penicillin or phenylbutazone)
• a different feed (especially a grain)
• insect bites
• contact with an irritant (for example, a shampoo or other preparation, perhaps one not specifically designed for horses)

In some cases, the underlying cause can never be pinpointed because the reaction can just as easily occur hours or minutes after contact with an allergen. Most cases respond well to steroid injections, however, although recurrent ones may need more investigation.

What Happens With Sweet Itch?

As the name suggests, affected horses or ponies become extremely itchy, switching their tails in irritation, rubbing aggressively, and becoming increasingly restless in their frustration and discomfort. With the gnats biting most actively along the line of the back, the base of the tail, back, withers, neck, and face cause the most intense rubbing, leading not only to hair loss but progressively to thickening and crusting of the skin and even, in severe cases, open sores. The constant irritation and distress will cause some horses to lose weight. In those cases in which the sensitivity is to insects that tend to bite the underside, similar itching and skin changes are seen under the belly area.

Preventing Sweet Itch

With midges everywhere in summer, managing a horse or pony with sweet itch can be almost as frustrating for the owner as it is for the animal. Lotions and potions abound, but there is no doubt that the only effective way to control the condition is to prevent the horse from coming into contact with gnats and other pesky flies—keep the midges from biting, and there will be no allergic reaction. Not an easy task, but a concentrated effort will pay off with a relieved and very grateful horse:

• stable at dawn and dusk when gnats are most active
• apply copious amounts of powerful fly repellents, such as citronella, pyrethroids, and benzyl benzoate
• graze away from water, ditches, and hedges
• buy a well-fitting whole-body fly sheet and hood, and make sure the horse or pony wears it at all times when turned out (and, if necessary, when ridden)

Soothing shampoos and creams may help heal traumatized skin. In particular cases, oral steroid tablets may be prescribed to reduce intense itching and inflammation, but these can carry the risk of inducing laminitis in susceptible ponies.

Diarrhea

Diarrhea seen in foals and weanlings in late summer can be due to damage to the lining of the digestive tract as parasitic larvae burrow into the gut wall to start their hibernation period. Older horses can be affected too, despite regular deworming, because levels of these encysted larvae can build up over many grazing seasons, and no drug can reliably kill them off completely. Intermittent diarrhea, colic, or simply weight loss and edema (fluid buildup in the

lower limbs and under the belly) are signs to look for in the mature horse.

Poisoning from toxic plants, such as rhododendron, is another cause of diarrhea in late summer (or winter) when grazing is limited.

Eye Conditions
Conjunctivitis

In this common summer eye problem, the delicate pink membrane under the eyelid becomes red and inflamed. A watery or thick yellow/green discharge comes from the eye, which can become sore and swollen where the horse has tried to rub it. It has a range of causes:

• viral (for example, equine influenza or equine herpes)
• bacterial
• fungal
• allergic (for example, to pollens) or irritant (from smoke, dust, or pollution)

Flies are clearly public enemy number one in all summer eye problems, spreading infection rapidly around the herd. Careful cleaning and topical ointments from your veterinarian applied several times daily for at least a week are usually needed to

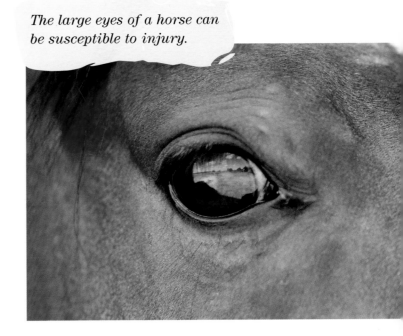

The large eyes of a horse can be susceptible to injury.

clear bacterial or viral infection. The vet will also want to examine the eye carefully for any cuts, foreign bodies, or marks on the cornea, because it is important not to mistake a more serious problem that may need immediate veterinary attention.

Tear Overflow

The tears that lubricate the surface of the eye are drained from inside the lower eyelids through the skull to the nostrils via the naso-lacrimal ducts. Sometimes these ducts become blocked, and tears overflow on to the face, making the eye look as if it is discharging.

The duct can be flushed by the veterinarian using a catheter inserted into it at the nostril end, but it is important to investigate the underlying cause of the blockage, which may be tooth or sinus problems, traumas, or tumors.

Fencing and hedging are typical sources of trauma in the field.

Trauma

Horses have the largest eyes of all mammals relative to their size, and set as they are quite prominently on the side of the head, the eyes are very susceptible to direct trauma damage. Foals, with their uninhibited curiosity, combined with a less brisk withdrawal (menace) response than adult horses, are particularly at risk.

Fencing and hedging are typical sources of trauma in the field, and in the stable the culprit is generally a hayrack or other fitting. Traveling or competing are other times when the horse, under stress, is more likely to suffer an eye injury.

Any cuts or grazes in the eyelid region need careful assessment and veterinary attention because the wrong course of action could lead to permanent deformity of the eyelids, affecting tear production and proper protection of the eye.

Significant lacerations (that is, through the full thickness of the skin) will need stitching (suturing) by your vet. Always clean grazes near the eye very carefully, using sterilized water that won't irritate the eye if it accidentally runs into it. Any marked swelling, bony damage, or suspected injuries deeper into the eye must be assessed by a veterinarian.

Foreign Bodies

Splinters of wood, grass seeds, pieces of hay, and even sizeable twigs are among the many foreign bodies that horses can manage to get embedded in their eyelids or conjunctival membranes. At times, these can be tiny and hard to spot, but the sudden onset of pain, inflammation, discharge, a closed eye, or hypersensitivity to having the eye touched should ring alarm bells.

A veterinarian will need to locate and remove the foreign body carefully, often using anesthetic eye drops, sedation, and nerve blocks, checking at the same time for other possible damage (such as corneal ulcers) or secondary infection. Deeper objects, which penetrate the cornea or globe of the eye, will be more difficult to treat and can involve serious complications, such as permanent scarring or even loss of the eye. Foreign bodies and trauma are often responsible for causing corneal ulcers.

Corneal Ulcers

The cornea, the delicate, glassy front surface of the eye, is a common area for equine eye problems. Any damage or disruption to the surface cells here creates a shallow pit on the eye surface, often causing surrounding corneal cells to swell, giving the eye a bluish, cloudy appearance.

Some ulcers are obvious, showing up clearly as a white/yellow opaque area. Others need to be located using fluorescein dye, which stains the ulcerated area bright green. Corneal ulcers are painful, and, not surprisingly, the horse will hold the eye partially closed, and it will appear red and watery due to increased tear production.

Treatment involves the veterinarian removing any underlying cause (such as a foreign body), and applying antibiotic ointment frequently to treat any infection and help lubricate the surface of the eye. Painkillers can help to make the eye more comfortable.

Some corneal ulcers improve rapidly, whereas others seem inexplicably slow to heal; so begin treatment promptly and make sure that progress is regularly monitored. The ulcer may heal leaving a pale, white scar on the cornea, but it rarely affects the horse's vision.

Uveitis

The intense sunlight of the summer months can frequently bring on an episode of this common but potentially serious eye condition in horses with a history of the disease. It is thought that uveitis can become a serious recurrent problem when it is described as periodic ophthalmia, moon blindness, or equine recurrent uveitis, a condition that vets will fail a horse for during a prepurchase examination.

Summer Foot and Leg Problems

The temptation to set out on our horses and enjoy a lovely prolonged spell of dry, sunny weather, or the urge to put long weeks of training into practice in the arena can often blind us to the trauma that hard ground can cause throughout the whole equine musculoskeletal system, particularly the area where their suspension is most intensely focused—the foot.

Concussion

Overdoing fast work on hard surfaces does not only lead to bruising of the sole, but occasionally to a traumatic form of laminitis. Joints will also come under stress, putting the horse at risk of developing bursal enlargements and causing stiffness in older, arthritic animals.

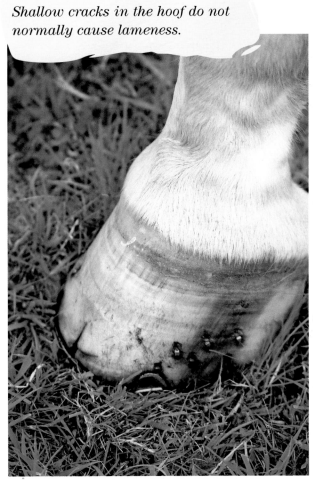

Shallow cracks in the hoof do not normally cause lameness.

These kinds of problems are best tackled with common sense—rest, a sensible exercise regime, and regular attention from the farrier to make sure the foot is properly balanced.

Cracks in the Hoof

Cracks that appear at the coronary band are known as sand cracks or quarter cracks. Those originating at the weight-bearing surface are called grass/toe cracks.

If your horse is prone to cracked feet, check carefully through the list of possible causes, which includes:

- hoof imbalance due to poor or too infrequent trimming and shoeing, leading to abnormal loading of the hoof wall
- overfrequent shoeing, creating weaknesses in the hoof wall from multiple nail holes
- poor nutrition, leading to weak horn quality
- injury to the coronary band, resulting in a weak or deformed hoof wall
- dry conditions, which reduce the natural moisture content of the hoof, making it brittle

Shallow cracks don't usually cause lameness because they do not involve any sensitive tissues. Deeper cracks, however, or those on the side of the hoof or heel, can cause lameness problems, particularly if infection sets in.

Treatment depends on the depth and position of the crack. Corrective trimming/shoeing may be enough for shallow cracks. Infected cracks must be cleaned out and treated with an antibacterial or antifungal solution such as Povidine-iodine. Severe infections may mean the crack must be opened up so it can be thoroughly cleaned. The hoof wall might need to be stabilized with special bar shoes and clips fitted to either side of the crack, which is filled in once any infection is cleared using hoof repair material.

It may take many months for the crack to finally grow out, but in the meantime it's important to improve horn quality by adding supplements to the feed that contain biotin and methionine.

Corns and Bruised Soles

Corns and bruising to the sole are two other year-round conditions exacerbated by more frequent work on hard, leg-jarring ground.

What Is a Corn?

Any increased pressure on the tissues of the heel can predispose a horse to corns—bruising and hemorrhaging in the sole at the angle of the wall and the bar that is known as the seat of the corn. The vet or farrier will often detect sensitivity using hoof testers directly over the point where a red discoloration of the horn is found once the shoe is taken off and the area explored with a paring knife.

Corns can be caused by poor shoeing (too tight at the heels or shoes too small for the foot) or shoes left on too long (so the hoof growth pulls the shoe forward and allows it to embed itself in the seat of the corn). However, an abnormal gait, poor conformation, flat soles, or an unbalanced foot with long toes and low heels can also predispose a horse to recurrent problems.

Coping With Corns

Corns can lead to varying degrees of lameness—from barely noticeable to severe—but it is always worse on hard

Special shoes, such as these aluminum eggbar shoes, give added protection to the navicular bone and its associated structures.

ground and when turning. The shoe will need to be removed, the foot poulticed for 2 to 3 days, and the horse rested until he is sound. Seated-out shoes that are concave on the surface against the foot in the area of the corn can help to support and protect this vulnerable spot, but really, a well-fitting standard shoe should be all that is needed.

When a corn becomes infected and develops into an abscess, it must be drained.

Bruising

Horses who have large, flat feet, thin soles, or have suffered in the past from laminitis are most prone to bruising of the sole, with trauma from a rock or stone causing red discoloration and soreness that is the telltale sign of hemorrhaging. If the bruise is deep, the red sole may not be seen until it grows out; but, as with corns, be vigilant because the bruised area may easily develop into an abscess.

Rest the horse and poultice the affected foot for 2 to 3 days. Paring away superficial layers of horn over the bruise can sometimes help to relieve some of the pressure. Where bruising is a recurrent problem, think about offering extra protection by having the farrier fit wide-webbed shoes or protective pads. Most importantly, avoid riding over rough and hard ground.

Tendonitis

Tendon injuries are frequently seen during the summer months because performance horses are asked to stretch their physique to its limits during the competition season, often on less-than-perfect surfaces.

Overextension of the fetlock, used during fast work, can lead to tearing and damage to the collagen fibers in the body of the deep flexor tendons and/or superficial digital flexor tendons behind the cannon bone. Immediately suspect tendon trouble if the horse is lame and heat, pain, and swelling is present in that area.

Hard, sun-baked ground can cause concussion injuries.

Stall rest will be needed in the case of tendonitis.

Initially, treatment involves stall rest, cold hosing, and then support bandaging and anti-inflammatory medication. Ultrasound scanning 7 to 10 days after the injury will help to assess the extent of the damage and monitor repair. Unfortunately, healing is slow, but controlled exercise is usually beneficial. Occasionally, surgery is needed to split and drain the tendon.

Suspensory Ligament Desmitis

The suspensory ligament, situated between the cannon bone and the deep digital flexor tendon, is another tissue susceptible to trauma from overexertion. The area usually swells, but the horse is not always lame, and the strain may become chronic, producing a niggling, intermittent lameness. Quite commonly, the associated splint bone on the affected leg can fracture. Treatment is the same as for tendonitis.

Splints

The inner splint bones of the forelimbs are most commonly affected by trauma. A kick in the field can fracture this narrow, fragile bone. Repetitive concussion on hard ground or from overloading an unbalanced limb results in the tearing of the ligament that connects the splint bone to the cannon bone. Either can produce the firm, painful swelling over the splint bone known as splints.

Rest and anti-inflammatory drugs help the bony reaction to settle, usually within 6 to 12 weeks.

Navicular Disease

Hard summer ground will also affect horses who suffer from navicular disease, a condition in which this small but crucial bone in the foot begins to degenerate, causing lameness and a stilted, "pottery" gait. Both forefeet are often affected, most commonly in horses between the ages of 4 and 9.

Nerve blocks and X-rays will be needed before other causes of foot pain can be ruled out, but once a definite diagnosis is made, specialized shoeing can help to support the heel area. Drugs are used to increase the blood supply to the affected tissues and to help with pain and inflammation. Removing a section of the palmar digital nerve that provides sensation to the heel area has helped in some cases, but carries its own risks and potential complications.

Degenerative Joint Disease

Wear and tear on the joints will affect different horses at different ages, with conformation and workload obviously being important variables. But as inflammation within the one or more affected joints increases, the result will be pain and lameness. At the outer edges of the joints, bony overgrowth or narrowed joint spaces can sometimes be seen on X-rays.

Local anesthetic injected into the joint is often the best way to isolate the source of pain and unsoundness. Arthroscopy (key-hole surgery) under general anesthetic then allows the vet to get a good look at what is going on inside the joint and flush out any damaging products that are contributing to the inflammation.

Rest, anti-inflammatory drugs, joint medication, and dietary supplements containing glucosamine may help to control the rate at which the condition progresses.

Social and Sexual Behavior

For horses living a natural life, the urge to reproduce is quite a preoccupation. However, as owners of domestic horses, we tend to take little interest in our horses' sex lives until sexual behavior becomes an inconvenience—when the barn owner is reluctant to turn out a mare with geldings, or during the spring and summer months when her regular season can turn a normally sweet-tempered and amenable mare into an irritable and distracted ride.

Mares are seasonal breeders and are only sexually active from the spring through to fall.

During this time, the mare will have estrus cycles that last about 21 days and are controlled by hormones. Only during 4 or 5 days of this cycle will she be receptive, raising her tail to "wink" her vulva and urinate frequently, showing more than usual interest in male horses, and possibly even attempting to jump out to go in search of a likely mate. For their part, geldings will tend to show interest in an in-estrus mare despite being castrated, leading to fighting and competition within their social group. For this reason, it makes sense to separate mares and geldings with strong, safe fencing during this period.

Some geldings may show signs of sexual behavior, such as mounting, and if these are found to be rigs, can prove a nuisance when turned out with mares. More frequent comings and goings during the spring and summer months can also unsettle an established social group, and introductions must be made slowly and carefully to avoid unnecessary injuries from fighting.

It is advisable to keep in-season mares away from geldings.

Chapter Fifteen

Summer Riding

*I*t's the time of the year we've all been waiting for—the days are warm and long, and we can truly make the most of our horses. However, summer riding is not always a picnic. The majority of horses are better adapted for colder climates than they are for warm ones.

Hot-blooded breeds, such as Arabs and Thoroughbreds, are better able to cope with heat than those with pony and draft blood, but most domestic horses are generally unhappy in hot temperatures. Left to their own devices, all would seek rest and shade during the warmest parts of the day. Any observant owner will confirm that horses like their "siestas" when the weather is hot, becoming more active in the mornings and evenings.

This sensible behavior is designed to keep horses from overheating. Yet, unfortunately, it is at odds with what we tend to expect of our horses during the summer months. Most owners have planned a busy program of activities (whatever the expected weather) involving strenuous exertion during the hottest part of the day, when horses would prefer to take it easy. In addition, transportation to and from competition venues usually means a long journey in a hot and stuffy horse trailer.

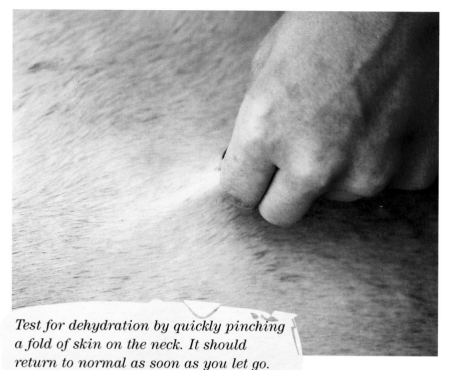

Test for dehydration by quickly pinching a fold of skin on the neck. It should return to normal as soon as you let go. If it takes time to smooth out, the horse may be dehydrated.

stress. When a horse becomes heat stressed, he loses his ability to control his body temperature and, instead of cooling down, he becomes hotter and hotter, begins panting like a dog, and the situation worsens further. Heat stress can be fatal if the horse is not cooled down immediately.

Dehydration is not a problem exclusive to high-performance horses—veterinarians regularly see cases of heat-stressed horses and ponies that have been stood or ridden in the sun all day at local shows. Always be acutely aware of your horse's water intake on hot or humid days when he is expected to be active.

Horses can be their own worst enemies in hot conditions, too. Their incredible willingness to work hard for us means they can frequently go far beyond what is good for them. As caring owners, it is our responsibility to be aware of the welfare issues involved in summer riding, which do not stop at keeping cool. Hard ground, brittle hooves, flies, and insects are just some of the other concerns that caring owners must put before their own enjoyment.

Avoid dehydration by:
- limiting fast work on hot and humid days
- offering water little and often (approximately half a bucket several times throughout the day), keeping tabs on how much is actually drunk (water passes quickly from the stomach, so it is quite safe for a horse to drink up to 15 minutes before the most strenuous of exercise)
- on trail rides, allowing the horse to drink whenever he has the chance, avoiding fast work for five minutes afterward

Dehydration

Water loss from the body rockets with higher temperatures and increased work because the body attempts to maximize heat loss by sweating. As sweat is excreted, fluid-borne minerals, such as potassium, sodium chloride, magnesium, and calcium (together known as electrolytes), are also lost. Once the body starts to struggle with the imbalance and deficiencies this can cause, the result is increasing fatigue and muscle weakness, which, if ignored, can lead to heat

Electrolytes

Electrolytes cannot be stored in the body, so there is no point in giving them before work. Add electrolytes to feed or water after exercise, making sure they are contained in something familiar that the horse will not refuse.

- offering water or small, wet feeds during long journeys
- providing a cool, shady place for the horse to rest in
- allowing the horse to cool off properly after strenuous exercise, and by adding electrolytes to his water

Take plenty of water with you when traveling to shows—at least a 6-gallon (23-liter) container per horse. Small amounts of water are perfectly safe to give before competition, and water should always be offered after exertion. Again, a little at a time is the best policy, and drinking water should never be icy cold. Nervous tension combined with a strange environment may put off some horses from drinking during shows, so be aware of this, and, if necessary, offer a small amount of wet feed instead. For those suspicious of "strange" water, take plenty from home, or add a small amount of molasses to the bucket.

Supplementation with powders or syrups containing concentrated electrolytes allows the body to maintain the correct balance of minerals. Therefore, supplementation use is something that all owners should be informed about. Supplements should be a routine ingredient in the feeding package of the working or performance horse. However, they are not always necessary for all horses in hot weather because a balanced diet should replace missing minerals satisfactorily. A simple option is to add a small amount (e.g., a teaspoon) of ordinary salt to the feed once a day. Avoid larger amounts, which will only increase thirst.

Cooling Off

Proper cooling off helps the body systems return to normal more quickly after strenuous exercise; this process is crucial to avoid heat stress and dehydration. If the weather is hot or humid, allow time to cool off and wash down your horse following an excursion—even after a relatively short summer trail ride. Not only is sweat nearly impossible to remove once dry, but it also leaves the horse feeling uncomfortable, as well as doing his coat and skin no good. Turning out your horse when he is damp with sweat is also an open invitation to flies.

The following cooling method has been devised following extensive research into heat stress in competition horses:

- Begin cooling off your horse immediately after exercise, in a shady spot if possible.
- Wash him down with cool water to take away excess heat. Cover the whole body with water, including areas where the major blood vessels lie

Sponge your horse down with cool water after strenuous exercise.

(e.g., neck, chest and belly, and the large muscle masses of the quarters).

- If exercise has been strenuous, cool for 20 to 30 seconds, then walk the horse around for a further 20 to 30 seconds, and then cool again. This helps to keep the circulation going.
- Keep up the cooling/walking sequence. After 15 minutes of cooling, check that the horse's temperature, pulse, and respiration rates are falling. Cooling can be stopped when the rectal temperature is less than 100°–102°F (38°–39°C). You should also stop cooling if the horse's skin feels cool after walking, his respiration rate falls under 30 breaths per minute, or if the horse starts to shiver.
- Offer small amounts of tepid water for your horse to drink.
- Avoid applying cold, wet towels or bags of ice to the horse's skin.

Hard Ground

It takes only a few days of sunshine for the ground to become surprisingly hard in the summer. Hard ground poses problems for horses, whose suspension systems are designed to work best on a firm but yielding surface. The particular problems associated with hard ground are jarring of the muscles and skeleton and the strain placed on a horse's joints when the ground offers no grip or is uneven.

Jarring

Despite the horse's built-in shock-absorption system, the leg can only take so much concussion. Impact is absorbed by the sole of the foot, tendons, ligaments, and joints. The strain taken by these—when an average-sized horse lands over a jump—is the equivalent of dropping 880 to 1,100 lbs (400–500 kg) from a height of 11 to 12 feet (3.3–3.6 m).

When there is no give in the ground, the shock impact is transferred to the foot, then travels up through the legs into the body and spine. The effects of jarring are not just felt by the feet, but can also lead to leg and spinal problems.

Do not make the mistake of thinking that high-quality shoes can help to overcome the problem, because shoes *prevent* the foot from expanding to absorb concussion.

Lack of Grip

On a training surface or on reasonably soft ground, the terrain dents a little as each foot lands, helping the horse to grip the surface, particularly on corners and landings. Hard ground offers little or no grip, effectively becoming a skating rink and placing the horse at risk of injury.

Jarring is a risk when horses are ridden on hard ground.

Uneven Ground

When dry weather follows a period of rain, ground that has been churned up by feet can harden into solid ruts and bumps that twist the feet and joints each time they come down.

Consequences

Pounding on hard ground causes trouble all the way up the shock-absorption system. Overloading means something has to give. Frequently, it is the flexor tendons, which support the leg and connect the muscles of the forearm with the lower limb and foot. This can result in bowed tendons. The joints of the lower leg also are vulnerable; these can become filled with fluid, leading to windgalls or, in the longer term, to arthritis.

Further down at the foot, only the sole, frog, and heel cushion the bone from the hard ground. Not surprisingly then, the feet suffer most from too much contact with solid ground. The consequences can range from short-term bruising or, over a longer period, repeated jarring can cause inflammation of the bone and other chronic conditions, such as pedalosteitis or navicular and degenerative joint disease. Traumatic concussion is also a cause of laminitis.

Conformation plays its part, too. Flat feet and poorly shaped limbs are less efficient shock absorbers, making these horses perform less well on hard ground. Inconsistency in riding conditions (ground that can be rock hard one day, or in one particular area, and soft and deep in another) makes matters worse.

Shock Tactics

If at all possible, avoid exercising when the ground is hard. For some reason, riders who would never dream of jumping or galloping on the road can be seen competing and training for hours on end on paddocks that are, in effect, just as hard as concrete.

You can soften the blow of hard ground by doing the following:

A horse's legs take the full force of impact on landing.

- Reduce work and avoid concussive activities (e.g., jumping, fast work). Do not risk long-term injury for the sake of one class or show.
- Search out better ground, either for trail riding or competing. Contact show and event secretaries to ask about the state of the ground and what, if anything, is being done to improve it in the arena and warmup areas. There is no shame in withdrawing if your horse's safety is at risk. Walk jumping courses carefully to pick a route across the best ground.
- Have your horse shod regularly and well. A well-balanced foot lands evenly, distributing the effects of concussion more evenly up the leg.
- Reduce the likelihood of knocks and twists by using boots and bandages when exercise cannot be avoided.

Horses on Hard Ground

Watch out for tell-tale signs that show your horse is unhappy about working on hard ground:

- shortened strides, particularly around corners
- frequent changes of leg/diagonal
- loss of balance
- going on the forehand
- reluctance to move on freely
- refusing, or knocking down, more jumps than usual
- shifting weight from leg to leg when standing
- general body language (e.g., tail-swishing, or holding back the ears)
- tightness in the back, or a dislike of girth being done up
- lack of impulsion
- bucking, or other signs of "grumpiness" or resistance.

- Know your horse's legs inside out, so that you can spot any new lumps or bumps immediately.
- Do not allow your horse to become overweight.
- Fit your horse with appropriate studs.
- Consider having your farrier fit foot cushions during prolonged dry spells. These are pads of leather, rubber, or plastic, placed between the foot and the shoe for extra shock absorption. One disadvantage is that pads tend to compress with wear, which results in shoes becoming loose prematurely. This can allow moisture to build up underneath, which can lead to thrush and horn infections.
- When ground conditions are difficult, do not wait too long between shoeings. A new set of shoes can give a horse as much confidence as an old, worn pair with studs.

Summer Feet

Brittle feet are a common problem during the summer months, particularly when the ground is hard. The horn that makes up the wall and sole of a horse's feet is like ultra-tough skin. A living tissue, just like ordinary skin, the horn needs the correct amount of moisture to remain healthy. Too much, and the horn becomes soft, weak, and misshapen. Too little, and the walls and soles of the feet begin to shrink and become brittle, vulnerable to the damage from concussion that inevitably comes with hard ground and dry conditions.

Cracks and splits in the feet can cause lameness and loose shoes, as well as allowing bacteria to enter the foot. There are no easy answers, and certainly no quick fix. Poor foot quality owes as much to general health as it does to environmental conditions, so:

- Have feet regularly and well shod (or trimmed).

Hooves should be trimmed on a regular basis.

- Feed a well-balanced diet and consider an additive to promote healthy horn growth from the coronet. Remember, it will take a full year for any dietary changes to affect horn quality throughout the whole foot. Additives containing biotin, zinc, and methionine have been identified as helping promote healthy horn; however, in the overall picture of a well-balanced diet, these form only a very small part.

- Foot dressings can seal in moisture, but they can also keep out moisture and oxygen. Consequently, they are not recommended by some foot-care experts. Use dressings on horses with brittle feet in dry conditions only, and be wary of products designed to harden feet because these may serve only to further reduce their shock-absorbing ability. Oils and grease certainly cannot improve existing horn quality.

Summer Riding Ideas

Summer is not all about shows. Try some of the following ideas to get out and about with your horse.

Beach Rides

If you live within striking distance of the coast, get together with some friends and share transport to the nearest beach. Check tide times with the local governmental agency to make sure you'll be welcome and safe. Go steady, as footing can change—barely-wet sand is best. Watch for other beach users, and take care going for a swim. Synthetic tack copes better with a salt-water dousing than leather gear.

Horse Vacations

Why not take your horse on vacation with you? Many instructional centers offer weekend or week-long breaks for owners wanting to bring their own horse for some intensive but enjoyable tuition. Alternatively, check out those providing long-distance trail-riding routes and accommodation, and explore some of the country's most beautiful areas together.

Make use of the summer months to get in as much riding as possible.

Picnic Rides

Use the long summer days to go on an extra-long trail ride with friends, stopping for a picnic lunch en route. You'll need a little forward planning to choose a route with somewhere safe and shady to tie the horses. Carry snacks in a saddlebag, or get a friend to deliver lunch to a prearranged spot.

Charity Fun Rides

Have fun and raise money for a good cause, riding across land often closed to the public at other times. Make sure your horse is fit enough to go the distance, however.

Studs

Studs are invaluable aids to jumping or working fast on slippery ground. They provide a horse with extra grip and, therefore, extra confidence. Ground conditions can be notoriously variable and change rapidly, so it is important to know how to use and fit different types of studs, especially if you compete. Slippery, dangerous surfaces are produced just as easily by dry, unyielding ground as they are by wet, muddy conditions or frost.

- Your farrier will put stud holes into your horse's shoes. For general purposes, a hole on each branch of each hind shoe is sufficient.

- Two small studs on each foot create a better balance than one on the outer branch, as is often seen. Regular competitors may want stud holes on the front shoes, too.

- Buy a selection of screw-in studs for different conditions. Pointed studs are used when the ground is dry and hard. Square, blunted studs work best in soft, wet conditions.

- Before fitting, clean out the stud hole thoroughly, and screw a T-tap or safety spin tap into the hole to clean the thread.

- Screw the stud in carefully to avoid cross-threading it, then tighten it using a small wrench or T-tap.

- Avoid walking on paved surfaces when the horse is wearing studs. Never allow your horse to travel with studs in.

- After finishing your class, unscrew the stud and fill the hole with a plug of cotton wool (cotton) or rubber.

- Borium (a hard metal) is an alternative to studs. Dots of borium are welded to the branches of the rear hooves for permanent traction. Borium studs are suitable for trail riding, lower level eventing, and jumping.

Learning Lessons

Book a course of regular lessons to give your skills a boost and to help you come to grips with any ongoing training hiccups. Keep an eye out for clinics and lecture demonstrations at equestrian centers and riding clubs.

Try Something New

Summer is the in-season for most equestrian sports, so there is no better time to become involved with something new. Find a sport you think you'll enjoy, join the sport's organizational body, and get involved. Whether it is western riding, polo, polocross, or dressage, try something new! Even if you do not want to compete in a serious fashion, most local shows have something for everyone, whatever their age or ability. Try it, just for the fun of it—you may discover a wonderful new hobby.

Summer Safety

As a general rule, better conditions mean safer summer trail rides. However, remember that sunshine brings its own hazards:
- When planning a longer ride, always tell someone where you intend to go and give an estimated return time. Take a cell phone if possible.
- Watch out for extra vehicles on the roads, especially on weekends and holidays.

Be aware of the dangers of bright sun, particularly when it is low in the sky, during late afternoon and early evening. A driver can be surprised turning a corner into blinding light, and fail to see a horse and rider because of the glare. Wear high-visibility clothing whenever you are riding and take extra care when the sun is low.

Vacations

It makes double sense for horse owners to take vacations during the summer, not only because of the better weather, but also because the less chaotic summer lifestyle makes it easier to hand over horse-care duties to a qualified handler.

Making Arrangements

The arrangements you make for your horse's care while you are away depend largely on the kind of living arrangements you have set up for him. Points to bear in mind include:

- Plan well in advance—remember that helpers take holidays too!
- Try to minimize changes to your horse's routine and environment. Taking your horse to another barn should only be a last resort, because even temporary changes can be far more upsetting to a horse than we realize. It is better to find someone to care for him in his usual home.
- Make sure the person you have in mind to help is reliable and up to the job. He or she must be able to visit at least twice a day.
- Give your helper a thorough briefing on all the tasks to be carried out in your absence.
- Leave contact numbers for yourself, the veterinarian, the farrier, and the insurance company. It is also a good idea to leave contact details for an experienced horse owner/handler, to whom your helper can turn for any other type of help.
- Have the farrier check your horse's feet before you go away so there is less chance for trouble caused by loose or lost shoes.

Take your vacations in the summer when horse management is at its easiest.

Fall

Every year, around the beginning of September, the light evenings get noticeably shorter. It always seems so unjust that the best of the long days come early in the summer, often before the weather has settled and become reliable. Then, just as summer hits its stride—and often with plenty of running still left—opportunities for riding are limited again by the shorter evenings, reminding us that winter will soon be on its way.

For horse owners, fall is always all too brief. One minute it's August, with the show season in full swing, plenty of sweltering days, and fields that look yellow and dry. The next, we are pulling on the rubber boots, bringing in the horses, and preparing for the long haul ahead.

That only leaves the 6 weeks or so during September and early October to enjoy seeing our horses still relaxing out in the field and riding out on mild fall days with no pestering flies and softer ground beneath our horses' feet.

Chapter Sixteen

Changing Routines

The key to a smooth and trouble-free change from a summer to fall routine is to maintain an "easy-does-it" approach. Risks of digestive upsets and other health problems increase during these transitional months, usually because owners try to make changes too quickly, not giving their horse's system sufficient time to adjust.

Be Flexible

Fall weather, like that of spring, is so variable that it's far better to think flexibly and keep an open mind about when to clip, when to put on your horse's blankets, and when to start bringing him in. If the days are still mild and reasonably dry, there's no point in rushing to stable him at night and curtailing his time out in the field—the winter's going to be long enough.

Much depends on the activities you have planned for the coming months. Those who are aiming to maintain, or step up, their horse's current workload will be keen to clip and get their horse inside more in order to monitor fitness and condition more closely. If you have a target date in mind, then you may want to bring your horse in at night from, say, the beginning of September.

Will you be keeping your horse at the same workload, or is it time to start easing off for winter?

For many though, fall brings a gradual wind-down in action. There is then certainly no rush—allow your horse to make the most of the relatively mild weather and fall flush of grass while he can, and allow yourself an extended break from mucking out.

Whichever the case, if your winter regime is going to include stabling at night, make the transition gradually. The shortening evenings do tend to mean this happens naturally, as we bring our horses in for the night earlier and earlier over the weeks of September.

Chapter Seventeen

Fall Feeding

ransitioning from a summer to winter diet is the major change that affects our horses in the fall. Even coming inside at night, rather than staying out, has a major impact on the horse's diet and digestion. And we all know how sensitive that digestion is—transitions must be handled tactfully. A sure way to guarantee colic is to fix a day when your horse must go from living out 24 hours a day on a diet of all—or almost all—grass, to coming inside, eating hay, and being given large concentrated feeds morning and evening.

Your feed strategy from this point on will depend on the riding you plan to do over the winter; whether your horse will be living in, out, or on a combined regime; the quality of your hay; and the condition your horse is in right now.

Maintaining Condition

Early October can see horses lose condition quickly because grass quality suddenly drops off. It is far better to be prepared for this and to help your horse go into winter looking well, rather than to hang on to a summer feeding regime too long when he needs more help.

Fall

- Make increases gradually. Increase the concentrated ration progressively, and only if the horse's workload requires it. Horses in light to medium work can get most, if not all, of their nutritional needs from forage (grass and hay) during the fall months.
- Monitor grass quality. Watch your horse's pasture quality because it will have a significant effect on his overall diet. Depending on local weather, fall pastures might either be green and lush looking or already a bare mud patch.

Grass will keep growing as long as temperatures stay above 41°F (5°C), although growth is slower than in spring. A well greened-up field will still provide a fair amount of energy and nutrients. In fact, owners of laminitis-prone animals must be careful not to be caught off guard by this fall flush. By the middle of October, however, even green-looking grass won't contain enough goodness to sustain a horse, especially if grazing is limited.

If the weather has been wet, some pasture will already be suffering poaching, which damages grass and reduces grazing areas. For those whose pasture is already suffering, start feeding hay early in the field. You will also need to supply concentrated feed much sooner to keep up nutrient levels so that your horse doesn't go into winter looking lean.

The only individuals who seem perfectly happy in a muddy field, with the minimum of supplementary feeding, are hardy ponies whose appetites gradually decrease during fall to 75 percent

Monitor grass quality so that your horse does not lose condition if grazing starts to deteriorate.

Fall Feeding

of the summer levels. Designed to thrive on the poorest forage, this type of pony stocks up on calories during the summer to use when needed over the winter. Hay is all he will need, although a high-fiber concentrated feed and vitamin supplement may be needed to maintain micronutrient levels. Even in the wettest fall (and winter) weather, don't be tempted to cheer a soggy, shaggy pony up with scoops of concentrated feeds like sweet feeds or pellets.

Go into winter in good condition. Use condition scoring to keep a watchful eye on your horse's shape over the fall weeks. If he is lacking condition now, things certainly aren't going to improve as the weather and the quality of grass deteriorate, unless you take action. Offer as much hay as your horse wants in order to provide warmth and to fill him up. Increase concentrated feeds over several days to make up the shortfall if pasture quality is poor. Consider using an energy- and protein-rich feed for up to 50 percent of the ration, and you should see a difference within a few weeks.

Hardy ponies will stock up on calories during the summer months.

Chapter Eighteen

Clipping

Winter coats start appearing as early as August and as late as October, depending on your individual horse and his breeding, the way he lives, and whether or not you have blanketed up early, discouraging the growth of his own natural weather protection. By the end of October, however, coats are growing with a vengeance, and the time has come to make a decision on clipping.

Rather than deciding when to clip, the prime question is whether to clip at all. A horse's winter coat is very effective at the job it is designed for—insulation. The very qualities that help the coat to keep warmth in become a real hindrance to a horse expected to work hard during the winter months—especially very hairy ponies and cobs—because the body produces vast amounts of additional heat during intensive exercise.

When heat produced by the muscles cannot pass freely into the air, the body temperature rises, stressing the entire system. Ultimately, continually getting hot and bothered in this way causes loss of condition. A sweaty, thick-coated horse is also difficult to clean without washing and hard to dry without chilling. By clipping away part or all of the hair, he can be kept at a comfortable, constant temperature without all this additional hassle.

To Clip or Not to Clip

Having said that clipping is the way to reconcile work with woolliness, it is not automatically what all horses want or need. A clipped horse may look smarter and be easier to work and to keep clean, but deciding whether or not to clip means assessing whether the benefits of keeping his hair on outweigh the disadvantages of removing it.

Taking away the natural protection of his home-grown coat means you must replace that warmth by providing more feed and blankets. Many horses do not work hard enough in winter to justify a clip. If your horse lives fully or mainly out, and only gets ridden for a few hours on weekends from October to March, it makes far more sense to leave him with his cozy coat for the other 160+ hours a week

that he really needs it. All you need to do is allow for a little extra drying-off time after rides.

Old horses, in particular, are less efficient at keeping warm and are unlikely to be working hard enough to require much clipping. In these cases, a tidy-up and trim is perfectly adequate.

If you decide a clip would be beneficial, give careful thought to how much hair really needs to come off. Again, put the horse's practical needs first. Too many horses are left shivering under inadequate blankets, or look ribby by November, largely because their owner fancied showing off with a flashy hunter clip when a bottom-warming chaser or trace clip would have been more than enough for the work they were doing.

As a general rule, take the minimum amount of coat off that you think you need to, especially after December, when the hair is not growing fast. It's always possible to take more hair away—putting it back on is more of a problem! Remember, the quarters need the most protection because horses turn their backs to the weather. Excessive sweating occurs at the neck, the breast, and around the tops of the legs.

Choosing a Clip
Neck and Belly

Hair removed: Broad strip from under the gullet, chest, and belly, and, if possible, inside the tops of the hind legs.

Suitable for: A minimal clip, perfect for keeping horses with long coats cooler when ridden, but having no ill effect on animals living out, even permanently, provided they have a good blanket with plenty of depth to it, and shelter.

The decision to clip or not depends entirely on how much work you plan to do with your horse.

Do not deprive your horse of his coat if he is going to be living out all winter.

Chaser or Irish Clip

Hair removed: From the gullet (the whole or lower half of the head can also be included) midway along the neck to the shoulder, tapering to the flank. Hair is left on the upper half of the body, the quarters, and the legs.

Suitable for: An all-purpose clip ideal for horses doing light work. Again, the horse can live out with adequate blanketing and shelter.

Trace Clip

Hair removed: Head, gullet, neck, and legs as in a chaser clip, but continues along the side of the body

in a straight line to the buttocks. Back of the buttocks up to the dock is usually removed. Termed high, medium, or low according to the level of the line.

Suitable for: Horses doing medium to hard work, stabled at night. Low trace clipped horses can live out, but make sure blankets are deep and extend well back to protect the quarters. A neck cover may be needed for longer periods of turnout.

Blanket Clip

Hair removed: Head, neck, and belly completely clipped out, leaving hair on the legs and on the top half of the body from the withers back (as if the horse is wearing a short blanket). Back of the buttocks to the dock also removed.

Suitable for: Horses doing medium to hard work stabled at night. Blankets for outdoor wear must be heavier weight and must be deep and long enough. Neck cover is advisable for longer turnout periods.

Hunter Clip

Hair removed: All except for legs and saddle patch.

Suitable for: Horses doing hard work only, stabled at night. Horse can be turned out with blanket and neck cover—heavy-duty for those outside for longer periods.

How to Clip

Clipping is potentially alarming to a horse and involves a powerful piece of electrical equipment. For these reasons, clipping is one of those horse-care jobs that is best left to an expert, particularly where young or nervous horses are concerned.

To gain some clipping experience, ask someone knowledgeable to demonstrate what is involved, and practice on a quiet horse. Horses and electricity are not a good mix—safety is paramount.

Before Beginning

Check your equipment. Ensure that:

• blades are sharp and you have a spare set

• wire and plug are in good condition

• clippers have been regularly serviced and are oiled

Choice of Clips

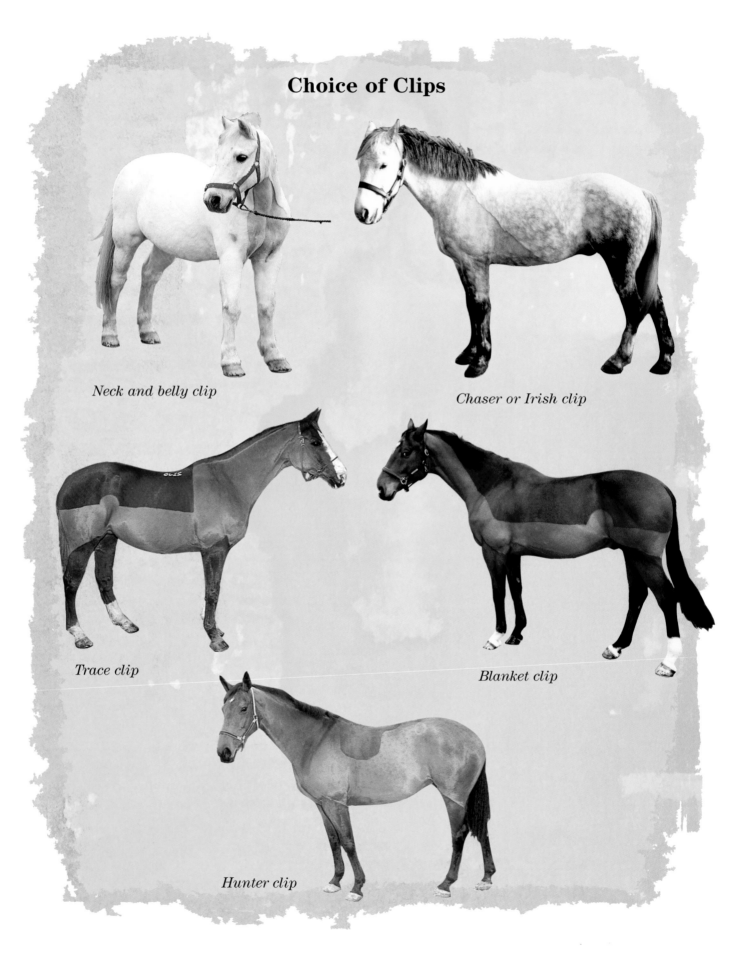

Neck and belly clip

Chaser or Irish clip

Trace clip

Blanket clip

Hunter clip

Clipping

- you are using a circuit breaker
- tension is correct

  Wear the right gear:
- tough, rubber-soled footwear
- overalls (clipped hair gets everywhere!)
- a riding helmet helps to keep hair (human and horse) out of the eyes, as well as provides protection when clipping a difficult horse
- keep long hair tied back

  Prepare the horse:
- brush off all mud and dried sweat; dirt will make clipping more difficult and uncomfortable and may damage the blades
- have the tail bandaged (except for neck/belly or chaser clips)
- tie your horse up in a dry, nonslip area that can be easily cleaned afterward (not a stable with its bed down)
- give a haynet
- have blankets available
- mark the line of the clip using chalk (a length of string helps measure an equal distance down each side)

Time spent acclimatizing your horse to the clippers is a worthwhile investment.

When You Are Ready

- Take your time. This is not a job that can be rushed.
- Run the clippers for a few minutes to accustom the horse to the sound, and check they are working correctly. Rest them on your hand on the horse's side, so that he feels the vibration.
- Place the blades gently but firmly against the skin on a large, flat area, such as the side.
- Take long, sweeping strokes against the lie of the hair.
- Adjust direction to remove hair over any whorls.
- Keep pressure even, or some of the coat will be left behind.
- Avoid getting carried away and then having to take off more than you intended in order to get a good line or to even up lines on opposite sides of the horse.
- A tidier look is achieved by following the lines of muscle where possible—for example, at the tops of

the legs and along the neck. Form a "V" shape at the backs of the hind legs.
- Stretch areas of loose skin to prevent them from being nicked. Have help on hand to lift and pull the forelegs forward to remove hair behind the elbows.
- Take care around sensitive areas, such as under the belly.
- Ask a helper to hold up a leg while you work here, if necessary.
- Reassure the horse as you work. Stop frequently to re-oil, to let the blades cool, and to clean the blades and filters. Sweep up clipped hair while you wait.
- The head is often a sensitive area, so clip it before the horse is bored and fed up. Smaller, quieter, battery-powered clippers are useful for tricky areas like the head.
- Removing all the hair neatly from the head is difficult and time-consuming. Most horses look perfectly acceptable with hair taken below a line

Clipping Tips

- There's no reason you have to stick to the same clip all season. Be adaptable according to your horse's needs. It may be suitable to take hair off in October when the coat is growing fast and your horse is still doing a fair bit of work. In December, you may choose to take a lower line, going back to a fuller clip as spring approaches.

- Your horse's type or breeding and management regime determine how quickly his coat grows in the fall. Workload also influences when you do the first clip, which might be as early as the end of September or as late as November.

- The thickness of the coat can also be controlled to a degree by starting to blanket early in the fall and, as the days shorten, leaving the light on in the stable into the evenings to "fool" the body into thinking the days are not shortening. By November, the coat is usually as full as it is going to get.

- The fastest months for growth are early winter, when you may need to re-clip within 3 to 4 weeks to maintain the ultimate "tidy" look.

- Clipping through to early March won't hurt the summer coat and will give you, and your horse, a helping hand in shifting the redundant winter woollies. Alternatively, keep the horse warm and increase his exposure to light to help the winter coat on its way. Watch for late frosts and typically erratic spring weather though, and be prepared with the right blankets.

- Choose a mild day, avoiding rain or windy weather unless you can clip indoors.

- Legs should never be clipped unless the horse is not going to spend any time, all winter, in either muddy or wet conditions.

Always clip against the lie of the hair.

Lift and pull the foreleg forward to remove hair behind the elbows.

Be careful in sensitive areas, such as under the belly.

The head can be a difficult area to clip.

Stop frequently to re-oil the clippers.

Clipping

from the corner of the lips to the ears. Muzzle hairs or hairs inside the ears should never be clipped.

- In a trace or blanket clip, a small arc is often clipped at the flanks.
- In a hunter clip, a small "V" is left at the dock.

When You Have Finished

- In good light, check to ensure no patches have been missed.
- Brush the horse over with a body brush and wipe with a damp cloth to remove loose hairs.
- Blanket as necessary.
- Clean the clippers and put them away.

Clipper Anxiety

Most horses accept clipping quite happily if they are introduced sensitively to it, and if they are always clipped with care. Youngsters and first-timers must be acclimatized by standing near other quiet horses who are being clipped so that they get used to the sound. Then, gradually let the horse get used to the feel of the clippers against his skin. Allow plenty of time, stay calm, and give lots of reassurance.

Horses who have developed a clipper phobia must be taken back to basics and treated in the same way as a first-timer. Make sure you have help on hand, but avoid excessive restraining or putting pressure on a frightened horse. Try to find out whether it is the noise he dislikes, the vibration, or perhaps restraint or a past fright that has caused the problem. Sometimes playing music or putting cotton wool in the ears can help. In the short term, it is better to use sedation than to force a battle. To get long-term acceptance, gain his trust.

Many horses tolerate their bodies being clipped, but become anxious or awkward if you try to clip around the head. Again, time, patience, and persistence will usually win out. If your horse will accept a twitch, this may be necessary for the few minutes it takes to clip the cheeks and jaw line safely.

Blanketing

Once hair has been removed by clipping, blankets are needed to replace warmth and insulation. As in spring, a lightweight turnout blanket comes into its own in the fall, enabling you to avoid a more heavy-duty blanket until the temperatures really start falling, a time when your horse will really appreciate its extra protection.

Don't be too hasty to blanket up on mild, dry fall days though, when a partly clipped horse will appreciate the sunlight on his back.

Once hair has been clipped, blankets are needed for warmth and insulation.

Chapter Nineteen

Fall Health Alert

s in spring, fall is a season when it's crucial to be flexible, taking each day as it comes. Depending on the temperature, summer conditions may persist into the fall. On the other hand, winter problems could crop up much sooner than expected. Be vigilant during this season, which frequently features warm days and cold nights, so you can spot any signs of trouble at an early stage.

Laminitis Check

Don't be fooled into thinking that laminitis is purely a spring and summer problem. The risk remains well into the fall. Chilly nights and sunny days boost the fructan content of the grass. Fructans are the villains in laminitis. These carbohydrates produce lactic acid as they ferment in the horse's hindgut. This lactic acid is thought to activate metalloproteinase (MMP) enzymes that cause the disruption to the attachments of the laminae in the hoof, leading to pain, inflammation, and separation of these interlocking tissues: laminitis.

Frosty grass can also contain higher fructan levels, putting horses and ponies susceptible to laminitis at even greater risk. Therefore, delay turning

Be on your guard for laminitis striking in the fall.

Healthy Hooves

Regardless of the season, your horse's hooves need to be in top shape. A healthy hoof should have smooth, uncracked walls, a thick, concave sole, and broad, fleshy-looking heels and frog. Like your fingernails, hooves should contain enough moisture to be resistant to chipping and cracking, but not so much that they're soft and mushy.

You can do several things to promote healthy hooves:

- Pick out your horse's hooves daily, removing dirt, manure, rocks, gravel, etc.

- Keep his stall as clean, dry, and well bedded as possible. Moist, dirty stalls are hotbeds for hoof-damaging bacteria.

- If possible, limit turn-out and exercise when conditions are extremely wet or muddy.

- Avoid frequent bathing (which can dry hooves out) or, if you must bathe, apply a hoof-moisturizing product beforehand, then dry the hooves and lower legs well with a towel afterward.

- Schedule regular farrier (blacksmith) visits every four to six weeks. In between visits, consult him or her about any unusual changes in the hooves---cracks, bruises, loose shoes, etc.

out until later in the morning when the frost has gone and the grass is able to grow, converting the fructans into sugar.

In addition, grass stems are packed with fructans, a point to remember for owners considering turning their laminitis-prone horse or pony to graze on a field of stubble, inadvertently thinking that the stalky leftovers can do little harm.

Chapter Twenty

Planning Ahead for Winter

During September and October, it is a good idea to make your plans for the winter to ensure a smooth transition from summer to winter routines. It's all too easy to be so determined to cling to the last vestiges of summer that we end up leaving things to the last minute, in a kind of denial that winter is actually going to happen.

Begin by making a checklist of those tasks to be tackled in the fall that will transition you smoothly into winter. Next, give yourself a deadline to have made your management decisions and to have everything in place. The occasional Indian summer cannot be relied on, and a wet, cold fall that catches you unprepared can be a significant setback for your horse, just when he needs building up for the tough months ahead.

Matters to Consider

The experienced owner learns to plan ahead for winter to give his horse the best possible care for the months that lie ahead.

Whether October means clipping and polishing for a season full of activity or simply battening down the hatches to survive the mud and hairy coats until spring, this month does signal the start of a 6-month

Short on Transport?

Unless you have the facilities to keep a horse at home, travel issues loom large in your decisions. Can you get to your horse twice daily if he is relying solely on you? How much traveling time can you spare? What happens if you hit travel problems?

What you can do:

- find a suitable barn within walking or cycling distance

- see if it may be possible to keep your horse at home

- opt for a barn with another owner who lives close to you

- make sure youngsters helping out make their parents fully aware of the commitment involved

labor of love for the dedicated horse owner. Hence the knowing look in the eyes of the experienced owner as an unsuspecting rookie arrives at the barn to face their first winter!

Learning by experience is as much a part of horse owning as it is in acquiring any new skill. Hardened campaigners will look back to last year and remember many a lesson learned and a dozen things they are going to do differently this time around to make life easier.

You may well find that you adjust your routine and your way of working as the months go by. However, it is worth spending time now—before the cold sets in and it's pitch black by late afternoon—to take a really good look at the system you have in mind and see how it will bear up in the months ahead.

Advance planning keeps stress to a minimum for both you and your horse. It could also save some very expensive, time-consuming mistakes just when you could least do with extra work or worry. Don't wait

until you think your horse is starting to feel the cold nights before thinking about how and where your horse can be stabled.

Equally, don't presume that, just because you rented a stable at a particular boarding yard last year, the owner will have a stable ready and waiting at a moment's notice. It is also inadvisable to assume that when you call a hay supplier in November, he's going to have plenty of good stuff left.

A well thought out ground plan will at least help get you off to a good start, along with a workable system already in place. Once you have a realistic idea of what you can achieve, then you can start to prioritize your jobs and work out the best way of using every precious minute of time.

Fall Checklist

Consider these issues when preparing for winter:
- stabling and grazing
- hay supply
- diet
- bedding supply
- routine
- backup help
- health care (teeth rasping, worming, vaccinations)

Choosing a Management System

During the summer months, when costs and chores are at a minimum, it is easy to forget how the demands of complete responsibility for a horse in winter can take over a huge chunk of your life. It is important not to underestimate seemingly small details, such as where your horse lives and the help and facilities available because these can suddenly take on huge significance when every minute counts.

Take time out, by the end of September at the latest, to consider the following:
- what your horse's winter management needs are going to be
- how you are going to supply them (accounting for all your commitments)
- exactly what you want to achieve with your horse this winter

Put pen to paper (or finger to keyboard) to create a checklist of needs tailored to your individual horse and personal circumstances.

What Your Horse Needs

First, think about what your horse needs from the management system you are planning. To be happy and healthy, your horse needs to be able to act like a horse. However you choose to keep him during the winter, it must take into account your horse's priorities and be able to provide for them adequately.

Every horse should be allowed access to loose exercise, the company of other horses, and a suitable diet. These needs apply to every equine, from the family Shetland to the professional show jumper.

You will then need to look at your horse's specific requirements during the winter months.

Workload

The more ridden exercise your horse gets each day, the more your regime can be based on stabling. This will mean that fitness, condition, and performance can be more easily monitored. However, do be realistic about how much riding you are likely to do, especially during December and January. Fully stabling a horse puts him under great physical and mental pressure. Whatever their workload, all horses should have time at liberty every day.

Age

Older horses feel the cold more and have less efficient digestion, so access to a stable at nights helps them to save energy and retain condition.

Type

This is less of an issue than many owners are led to believe. Given adequate shelter, weather protection, and feeding, even Thoroughbreds and Arabs can

Short on Time or Backup?

If you anticipate having problems looking after your horse in the winter, a number of options are worth considering.

What you can do:

- Go for part, working, or full board.

- Consider sharing your horse. Potential sharers can be found by asking around or advertising. Make sure you work out arrangements carefully and make a binding contract. Sharing works best between people whose different lifestyles mean that the demands on the horse and the responsibility of care duties can be spread fairly throughout the week.

- Opt for a do-it-yourself boarding barn, where people help each other out on a fixed schedule. Discuss with your boss at work whether any flexibility in your hours is permissible.

- Recruit a reliable helper, either paid (if money allows) or a volunteer keen to get experience, perhaps in return for some riding. Professional freelance help can usually be found, at a price, for anything from routine duties to extras such as clipping or exercise. Research a few numbers to contact if the need arises.

- Be choosy, particularly with volunteer helpers. After all, this person will have your horse's welfare in his hands. Put time aside for supervision at first. An enthusiastic adult is often best. Children can be eager to help, but having to be on hand to oversee things tends to defeat the objective. In addition, youngsters often rely on parents for transport and may only want to show up on weekends when you least need help.

- Help can be found by checking out the small ads in equine publications, online, or on your local saddlery/feed merchant/vet's notice board. You can also place a "Help Wanted" ad yourself. Specify the experience you require, plus age limits, and what help you need (e.g., mucking out, catching/feeding, riding).

- Start coaching a (willing!) friend or partner who is available at those times when you're busy.

thrive outside 24 hours a day during a chilly winter. Clipped horses can also live out, although obviously the more coat is taken off, the greater their blanketing requirements.

Health Issues

Individuals may have health care issues that your management system must allow for. For example, dust-sensitive horses require the maximum time possible outdoors, whereas others prone to mud fever need the opportunity to dry out away from wet ground conditions on a regular basis.

Individual Preferences

There is no point battling against character. Try to settle on a regime that everyone is happy with. If your horse is one of those characters who simply cannot tolerate enclosure within the four walls of a stable, then work with this rather than fighting against him, and find a way of letting him live outside.

Likewise, you may (rarely, but it happens!) come across the type who mopes all day by the field gate longing to come inside. In this case, think of other ways to provide loose exercise (after investigating reasons why turnout isn't the relaxing time for him that it ought to be).

Your Needs

Having taken into account what makes a good care plan for your horse, give some thought to the issues you face.

The more flexibility you have time-wise, the more options you have, because you can take on all or most management chores yourself. The less time you can commit to, the more help you will need from other people.

While it is possible to juggle some horse care jobs to suit the time you are available, others must be done at certain hours of the day. How flexible can you be? Don't forget that your boss and/or your family needs you, too. Realistically, can you take care of your horse morning and evening every day? Can you only manage certain mornings and/or evenings, or you are only available on weekends?

The amount of riding you hope to do will also affect your timetable. Winter plans that include competing or fox hunting, for example, mean exercise time must be built into the scenario. The more time your horse is stabled, the more important ridden exercise becomes. With access to unlimited turnout, you can afford to be more flexible and less ambitious about riding plans.

Time available for riding will be influenced by:

- how long your horse has to spend confined to the stable
- what you intend to do with him (i.e., how fit he needs to be)
- special needs (e.g., older horses are best kept in light work to counter the effects of stiffening, etc.)

Remember, you must see your horse twice a day.

Chapter Twenty-One

Counting the Cost

No matter how you approach it, winter horsekeeping is never going to fit into the inexpensive category. Even a hairy horse out in the field day and night, without a saddle on his back from October to March, still needs quality hay, supplementary feeding, regular deworming, and visits from the farrier. And that's the economy version!

When you are making your plans in the fall, make sure you can keep your horse in the manner he deserves all winter long, without the risk of facing a financial crisis at a time when it may be impossible to make alternative arrangements. Obviously, no one can account for a sudden loss of income but, even so, it's worth adding a backup plan into your calculations.

It is difficult to generalize about costs, which vary enormously from area to area and according to exactly what it is you are buying or paying for. A little local research should arm you with the precise figures you need. Those with a computer at home certainly have no excuse, as a spreadsheet will even do the sums for you.

Variable Costs

Not all the costs listed under "other expenses" may be applicable to your situation. However, it is important not to calculate your budget so tightly that there is absolutely no room to maneuver when an unexpected crisis hits, or nothing is left for treats like lessons or hiring an indoor arena every once in a while.

Insurance is another case in point. As premiums creep steadily upward, mainly in response to rising veterinary fees, it is tempting to leave those few hundred dollars in your pocket. But when a single bout of colic or a tangle with the fence could lead to surgery costing five or even ten times that annual premium, ignoring insurance is potentially a huge mistake. Unless you can afford to write off the value of your horse should the worst happen or sign a check without taking out another mortgage, find an affordable premium and buy yourself some peace of mind.

Many people find it works best to set up a separate bank account for their horse expenses, which makes it far easier to keep track of how much is being spent and on what.

Saving Money

Ideas for budgets that will boost the health of your bank balance without affecting the health of your horse can be found all the way through this book. However, some extra budget-busting ground rules could go a long way.

Shop Around

The equestrian marketplace becomes more competitive every day. Horse owners now have a massive, bewildering choice of all kinds of goods and services. There is more than enough opportunity to compare prices and root out the best deal.

In addition to the traditional saddlery shop and feed supplier, the smart owner can now search out competitive rates on anything from a foot pick to a hay rack in equestrian newspapers and magazines (local and national), ads, and mail-order catalogs, or on the Internet, which has opened up a whole new world of money-saving possibilities.

Of course, there are a few golden rules when bargain hunting. Among the most crucial are:

- Always compare like with like.
- Read the small print (particularly where insurance policies and credit agreements are concerned).
- Out-and-out bargains are few and far between, so be wary of apparently amazing discounts.
- Quality is generally (although not always) reflected in price. Don't compromise on anything that directly affects your horse's health (for example, hay, feed, bedding, and care). Remember that gear is going to get some serious wear and tear, so be sure it's built to last.

Buy in Bulk

Many horse necessities, including hay, bedding, and feed, can be bought at substantial discounts if you order in bulk. Hay is also cheaper to purchase off the field, direct from the farmer, if you have a way of transporting and storing it.

If you board your horse, you may be able to take advantage of the owner's hay supply.

Winter Essentials: Budgeting Costs

Consider the following essential care needs when preparing your winter budget and calculate the approximate costs for the following:

Boarding Fees

- home
- DIY field-kept only
- DIY field/stable
- partial board
- working
- full care

Forage

Allow 3 bales (small pony) to 10+ bales (hunter, mainly stabled)

- cost per bale depending on quality and quantity
- large round bales of hay

Concentrated Feed

Number of bags required (depends on individual diet needs)

- pellets
- sweet feed
- sugar beet pulp
- alfalfa cubes
- oats
- bran
- supplements/additives as required

Bedding

Required unless the horse is on field-care only. Exact amount varies according to stable size, bale size, and time spent inside. Price varies according to quantity supplied. Account for three to five established bales to start off bed.

- straw: 4-5 bales
- shavings: 2-4 bales
- rubber matting requires 1 bale bedding per week

Routine Health Care

Shoeing

Required every 6 to 8 weeks
- new set
- removes
- trim only

Deworming

- $1/2$ (small pony)—$1^1/_2$ (large hunter) syringes of paste required every 6 to 8 weeks

Teeth Rasping

- Once every 6 to 12 months

Vaccinations

- cost per vaccination

Other Expenses

Travel

- transport costs to and from yard for regular care
- transport costs for travel to competitions/lessons
- trailer/truck maintenance
- trailer/truck insurance

Insurance

- for basic package, including veterinarian's fees but excluding loss of use

Equipment

- as required (compare prices in local outlets and mail order)

Emergency Veterinarian's Fees

- if insured, account for policy excess amount $80+ per claim
- if uninsured, budget for emergency expenses up to $5,000+

Repairs

- to saddlery, equipment, and fencing, as required

Lessons

- per lesson fees

This is one area where sharing a yard with other owners comes in handy because you may be able to organize a bulk delivery, taking advantage of the reduced costs per bale/bag.

One word of warning on storage, though: Feed does not keep forever, so avoid buying more than you can easily get through before the "use by" date printed on the bag. The entire load must be kept in a dry, vermin-proof place. Likewise, hay and straw must be properly stored in a dry area. If storage space is limited, bulk buying may not be viable except for nonperishable or wrapped products, such as shavings.

Coordinate

When shoeing, vaccinations, and teeth rasping are due, ask around to see if anyone else can split the cost of the farrier or veterinarian's visit. A notice pinned up at the yard could alert other owners to opportunities to share costs in this way. Likewise, see who else may be interested in sharing a lesson or hiring training facilities.

Buy In-House

Take advantage of the yard's own supply of hay, bedding, and/or feed, if it is cost-effective and suits your requirements—you will be saving on transport as well as time and effort. Don't just assume it offers good value, though. Check yard prices against outside products of the same quality and quantity. Don't accept being forced to use inferior stuff, and maybe even be charged more for the privilege than you might pay elsewhere.

Buy Second-Hand

Bargains can be picked up on all kinds of used gear, from yard equipment to tack and blankets. If your tack shop doesn't have a second-hand section, then scan its bulletin board and the classified ads in local papers and national equestrian magazines.

Start up a bulletin board at the yard for owners to sell or swap unwanted items, or share the cost of new tools and other gear. See if your local riding club will hold a "barn sale," or organize one yourself!

Saving Time

With some imagination, there are likely to be various ways to fit the winter care your horse needs into your lifestyle. Some owners will find it easier than others, but whatever your situation, where there's a will, there's always a way. It all comes down to planning ahead and settling on a good routine.

Half the battle is in prioritizing your jobs, and much of this depends on the system of management you have chosen. For example, some tasks are vitally important to do first thing in the morning for a horse who is going to be in most of the day. But you may find that these jobs can often be left until evening if your horse is being turned out and won't be back in

Try to plan a winter routine that will suit you and your horse.

his stable before dinnertime. Again, certain chores are quickest and easiest to do in daylight; with others it makes little difference whether it's dark or light.

Before looking at how everything can be fit into the time slots available, determine what flexibility may exist within the various daily chores that the do-it-yourself or home-based owner must somehow squeeze in. Figuring this all out in advance makes it easier to see where opportunities for saving time exist, presuming you are in charge.

Feeding Schedule

Planning a diet is discussed elsewhere, but as far as routine goes, feeding little and often and providing plenty of hay are the two rules around which your time plan must revolve.

Whether your horse lives out, mainly in, or half-and-half, your aim is to imitate nature's way as much as possible, keeping the stomach at least part full for the majority of your horse's day and night. In the field, this is easy to achieve (presuming sufficient grazing is available for all the occupants) because your horse is eating almost continuously.

The provision of additional hay in winter provides the goodness lacking in the grass, as well as added bulk where grass is limited or particularly poor.

Whenever your horse is indoors, he must have hay constantly available to replicate his situation in nature. So, stage one is to figure out how you are going to supply this. Is one hay net or rack enough to last the whole time your horse is indoors (whether that be during the day or the night)? In addition to keeping his stomach and his urge to chew satisfied, hay also provides an entertaining diversion for the stabled horse. Therefore, it is crucial that it is not all eaten within a few hours.

What kind and how much concentrated feed you give will depend on workload and many other factors, but this will also need to be provided little and often, whether a horse is kept in a field or is stabled.

Gone are the days of the old horse-care manuals that presumed owners (or their grooms!) were on the yard from 6 a.m. to 10 p.m., ready to provide four or

Whenever your horse is indoors, he must have hay constantly available to replicate his situation in nature.

five small meals at regular intervals. That is simply not the case for 99 percent of us today; however, two visits per day are an absolute minimum just to cover feed times, not to mention other duties.

Working owners generally find morning and early evening feed times must suffice. When possible, however, the total daily ration should be split three or more ways, adding lunch and dinnertime meals. Again, this is particularly important to the horse forced to spend long periods inside because it helps to relieve boredom and break up his day.

Fitting feed times in with riding times, you also must remember that a horse must have time to digest his meal before exercise. If the meal was relatively small, and you were only planning a half-hour slow trail ride, then there is no need to get overly concerned about this. But do allow at least an hour between feeding and exercise if a more strenuous workout is expected.

Feeding Related Chores

Other feeding-related chores for which to set aside time include soaking hay, filling hay nets/racks, dishing up feeds, cleaning buckets, and advance preparation of feeds where necessary (e.g., soaking sugar beet). When hay is being soaked, give thought to filling and emptying the water container. This is quite time-consuming, but it is possible to get other things done while this is going on.

Optimum soaking time is no longer than 30 minutes, so it makes sense to make this one of your first jobs on arrival. You can then soak and drain a bale before leaving, ready to feed immediately or later. If you can't hang around while the hay drains, is there someone who can? Leaving it soaking too long is highly detrimental to the hay quality—leaving it all day is certainly not an option. If time is at a premium, small quantities of hay can be steamed instead.

When time is particularly tight in the mornings, it may help to make up feeds the previous night so that they are ready for feeding the next day. Avoid adding vitamin supplements until just before feeding because these deteriorate rapidly in contact with air. Damp ingredients must also be added at the last minute. Buckets should be carefully covered if left overnight or they will provide a welcome meal for resident rats and mice.

Saving a few seconds by putting the evening feed in the stable later at night for the horse to come into is not such a smart idea. It takes a matter of days for your previously polite animal to learn to barge into his stable like a bulldozer once he knows dinner's ready and waiting there. Hay, however, can be prepared (even a whole week's supply of hay nets if you have enough, and if you have time on the weekend to make them up). The only qualification to this concerns soaked hay: If it is allowed to dry out before feeding, there was no point to soaking it in the first place.

Leaving the horse to finish his feed completely unsupervised is another no-no. The accidents that can happen are not worth contemplating, so organize your chores so that you can be busy around the barn while he finishes up. Avoid rushing or harassing him to eat up quickly (would you appreciate being hurried over your dinner?), and take the bucket away when he has finished, checking everything has been eaten up as you would expect.

Mucking Out

The horse owner's most hated chore must be the daily grind of mucking out—unless you have managed to off-load this one onto your yard proprietor or an unsuspecting helper! During the winter, most owners would agree it feels like 10 hours are spent picking up manure for every one spent in the saddle.

That said, everyone soon finds their own system for speeding up the process. A stable that takes you 40 minutes to do in October will be whistled through

You will save time if you store mucking out tools near the stable.

Counting the Cost

in 10 minutes by December—mucking out is definitely an art in which practice makes perfect.

In terms of routine, here are some time-saving tips:

- Have the right tools for the job. These include as big a wheelbarrow as you can afford, a large but lightweight shovel, a purpose-designed lightweight stable pitchfork or shavings pitchfork depending on bedding used, a tough yard broom, and a muck bucket (plastic laundry baskets do the job just fine).
- Store tools tidily but nearby.
- Pick up droppings whenever possible. If the horse is inside during the day, picking up droppings as they appear, before they become squashed or scattered, helps save time and bedding. Don't get hung up on unearthing every little ball if you are pushed for

time though. It is far more important to dig out wet areas than to pick up every dried piece of dropping.

- Choose the right bedding. It takes significantly longer to do a good job cleaning out a straw bed (and disposing of the dirty bedding) than one with a shavings or natural fiber base.
- Consider a deep or semi-deep litter system. Those in a rush in the mornings can save time on weekdays by only picking up droppings and the worst of the soiled patches, adding a fresh layer of bedding on top. An hour or so can then be set aside on the weekend for a thorough cleanout.
- Consider rubber matting—it's undoubtedly the ultimate in time-saving bedding systems, although it does have its disadvantages.
- Time the mucking out to suit you. There is no law to say mucking out must be done in the mornings. Perhaps it suits your day better to muck out fully in the evening—if you can face it after work. Even if your horse is not being turned out straight away in the morning, as long as you clean out his feet, pick up the droppings, and tidy the bedding, he won't suffer. Mucking out is certainly one of those jobs that can be done while it's dark outside (as long as there's a light in the stable, of course).

Whatever bedding material you use, the one thing that won't save you time or money is to skimp on it. A thin bed is harder to muck out, uncomfortable and cold for your horse, and puts him at risk of endless bumps and scrapes to the knees and hocks and of becoming cast.

It is also unfair to leave the bed banked up around the sides to air out if your horse is going to be standing in for long periods. Many horses refuse to urinate on a hard floor—imagine how you would feel if denied access to a bathroom for most of the day! Airing out the center of the floor and digging out of the sides can both be left until more time is available on weekends.

Much as you want to make the most of time while your horse is eating, it is also not safe to muck out around your poor horse while he is having his breakfast (or dinner). In addition intruding on one of the highlights of his day, it is extremely unhygienic for him to have to stand and eat amid clouds of ammonia and bacteria. It is also impossible for you to do a decent job with a horse in the stable; so, if you want to use this time to clean the stable, make sure he has another dry and sheltered area in which to have his meal in peace.

Finally, don't forget to include picking up droppings in the field or corral on your list of tasks. Depending on the size of the area, this could be a daily or weekly chore.

Grooming

Horse mastership "bibles" would have us all putting our backs into grooming our horses for at least an hour a day—enough to scare off even the most dedicated part-time owner. While this might be ideal for a fully stabled horse being produced for top-flight performance or regular hard work such as hunting, it is a relief to know that the everyday horse will live even if he never sets eyes on a dandy brush. In fact, too much enthusiasm here can do more harm than good.

Neglecting grooming completely is not sensible, either, no matter how pressed for time you are. Grooming is about more than cleaning off areas where the tack or blankets might rub. It is important because it maintains the skin and coat in good condition by stimulating the blood supply, clearing away dried scurf, and toning the muscles. It also provides a daily opportunity to check your horse over closely for signs of general well-being (or otherwise), and to spot any problems or trouble brewing.

Horses kept wholly or partly outside do not need to be groomed as thoroughly as those spending more time stabled because the oils in their coat need to stay there for all-weather protection. Time saved by not body-brushing is often spent drying and brushing off mud to make them comfortable and half-respectable to ride, however! This is where blanket accessories like hoods and neck covers come in handy.

Those horses on restricted turnout may coat themselves in less mud, but the appearance of cleanliness can be deceptive. Lack of natural exercise and less exposure to fresh air and sunlight means lots more elbow grease is required to stimulate their circulation and keep the coat healthy.

Grooming Checklist

You will soon work out the average time to allow each day for grooming. Estimate a total of at least 10 minutes on busy weekdays, with longer sessions on weekends.

Daily cleaning duties that simply cannot be neglected are picking out the feet (morning and evening) and sponging the eyes, nose, and dock (particularly where horses are confined to dusty stables). Washing the horse's whole body is not a wise idea during the colder months, especially for the owner on the go, who is unlikely to have the time to hang around for several hours supervising the horse as he dries off without chilling.

Wiping or washing limited areas, such as the saddle area, is possible if excess water is well scraped off and the horse has a modern breathable blanket that wicks away moisture.

Leg washing is a topic open to debate. Suffice it to say that if you decide to wash or hose off muddy legs, make sure you leave sufficient time to see they are dried thoroughly afterward. It's worth keeping a supply of dry towels at the yard for this purpose. Regardless of whether mud fever and cracked heels are a problem, you should allow time to clean and inspect legs regularly. This means washing the legs, or leaving mud to dry overnight while the horse is in, then brushing it off carefully. This routine care is an important part of preventing and treating both mud fever and cracked heels.

If grooming time is limited:

- Make sure your horse gets lots of turnout time.
- Make time to do the essentials (above).
- Before exercise, clean areas where the tack and boots go, but don't waste precious minutes fussing about the odd bit of bedding in the tail.
- Spend time cleaning your horse in the evening, so that making him presentable before a morning ride is much quicker.
- Make sure your horse is getting a balanced diet with sufficient vitamin and mineral intake. If in doubt, give a multivitamin supplement or, if you are worried about skin and coat condition, give a supplement aimed at improving these.

The amount of grooming needed depends on how much time your horse spends stabled.

Setting a Schedule:
Approximate Time Allowance per Horse

Feeding

- Dishing up feed (per horse): 2 mins

- Supervising eating: 20 mins

- Cleaning bucket and putting away: 2 mins

- Hay soaking (up to 2 horses) Putting hay in (and time to fill water container): 2 mins

- Soaking time: 30 mins

- Draining time: 10+ mins

- Filling hay rack: 4 mins

- Filling/tying up haynet: 6 mins

- Filling water bucket: 3 mins

- Feeding hay in field: 10+ mins

Mucking Out

- Getting out and putting away tools: 2 mins

- Full muck-out (depending on skill and size of stable): 15-25 mins

- Replacing bedding after full muck-out: 5 mins

- Cleaning up/disposing of muck: 5 mins

- Skipping out only (semi and deep litter): 5-10 mins

- Adding bedding: 2 mins

- Picking up droppings outdoors (depending on area): 10-30 mins

Grooming

Horse kept out for all or most of the time:

- Nonexercise day: 5 mins

- Pre-exercise: 10+ mins (depending on the mud layer!)

Horse stabled for most or all of the time:

- Every day: 25+ mins

- Leg washing/drying: 20+ mins

- Washing, e.g. after exercise: 10 mins (if a suitable rug is available for drying): 30 mins (if the horse has to be dry before the blanket can go back on): 10 mins

General Handling

- Checking over: 2 mins

- Changing rugs: 4 mins

- Turning out: 2+ mins

- Bringing in:1 min (standing by the gate)

- General to-ing and fro-ing around yard: 5+ mins

- Weekday field checks: 5 mins

- Weekend field checks: 10+ mins

Exercise

- Tacking up: 10 mins

- Exercise for horse mainly or fully stabled: 2 hours minimum

- Exercise for horse partly or fully out: as required

- Untacking: 5 mins

- Cooling/drying off: see Grooming, above

Counting the Cost

Handling

When planning a routine, it is easy to forget those other little jobs that all take time, such as catching and bringing in, turning out, changing and readjusting blankets, and simply hiking across the yard. Precious minutes can be saved if:

• stables are located alongside the pasture
• paddocks are split into reasonable sizes, rather than one 40-acre field (with the tastiest grass and best shelter at the far end)
• fields aren't allowed to become swamps
• gates are easy to open and close even on a windy day

Checks that should be done each day, at least briefly, include a quick scan of the fencing and water supply and a check for dangerous litter or garbage in the field. More thorough investigations of the fence line, poisonous plants, and other hazards can be done on weekends.

The winter-hardened, experienced owner will also have chosen blankets carefully for ease of use. But, even if you are using a dual-purpose outdoor/indoor blanket, or your horse lives out permanently, the blanket will still need to be removed, shaken out, and replaced twice daily.

You will work out how to minimize effort and maximize your time as you go along, but these suggestions will make a difference:

• Always put things away neatly in the same place so that they are always there ready for the next time you need them.
• Fold blankets up neatly and ready to go, including a spare turnout blanket to replace one that has gotten soaked through or damaged.
• Make every trip across the yard count (e.g., as you take the empty hay net over to the hay storage area, carry the water bucket over at the same time and start it filling while you prepare the net).

Exercise

Last but not least, fit in the best bit—riding. The time required to set aside for this depends on:

• how much turnout time your horse enjoys
• how fit you want him to be (for example, what you expect him to be up to doing on weekends)
• how much riding time you want over the winter months

Exercise is a vital part of your horse's routine during any season.

As has already been stressed, it is up to you to maximize the time your horse spends outside his stable in every way you can. If circumstances mean turnout is limited, you must take this responsibility upon yourself and get him out by exercising him by other means, such as spending time grazing him in-hand.

Time-out opportunities should, as far as possible, be spread throughout the day to ward off boredom and stiffness. For example, a short morning ride could be followed by 20 minutes of in-hand grazing or lungeing at lunchtime, followed by another short ride in the evening.

Time-Out Alternatives

Exercise need not necessarily mean riding, of course; alternatives exist that may be easier at certain times (e.g., when it is dark) and will give variety. Exercise ideas are discussed in more detail later, but look upon ridden exercise as the next best thing (from your horse's point of view) to time at liberty. Loose training, lungeing, long reining, and in-hand work should be extras, rather than mainstays, of a daily exercise program for the stabled or mainly stabled horse.

Spending day in and day out trapped in a small room for 23 1/2 hours with only half an hour running around in circles on the end of a rope sounds more like a prison regime than a routine devised by a caring horse owner.

For owners whose horses do get turned out for a decent amount of time every day, the amount of riding can be a matter of personal preference. However, it should be enough to build and maintain the level of fitness demanded by your equestrian interests. If it is not possible to ride during the week, your horse's weekend activities must be tailored to his reduced fitness. Bear in mind, too, that it is much easier (and better for the horse) to keep him semi-fit all year than to let fitness go down and then build it up again from scratch.

The time of day you do your exercising will be dictated by what time and facilities you have available. For those working regular office hours without the bonus of an indoor arena or floodlit ring, weekday exercise will be confined to the unsociable hours before 9 a.m.

Routine planning must take into account tack-up time beforehand, untacking afterward, cooling/drying off (if necessary), and blanketing. Using an exercise sheet in wet weather can literally save hours on drying. But, however pushed you are on exercise time, allow for the extra few minutes needed to put on the right gear correctly. This goes for whatever you are doing, whether it's putting on boots for lungeing or high-visibility fluorescent gear for trail rides in gloomy weather.

It is up to you to maximize the time your horse spends outside his stable in every way you can.

Work and Home Commitments

Of course, for most of us, horses are not the only thing in our lives. The well-organized owner's schedule also must account for getting up and out to work, getting two-legged dependents up and out to school, or even both (yes, it can be done). Those with families may also have to pick up from school at the end of the afternoon, and they will almost certainly be required to produce a meal at an hour approximately around dinnertime as opposed to 8:30 p.m.!

The challenge for any worker is to arrive at the office without anyone suspecting you have already been up for 3 hours shoveling horse manure. Tips include:

- Having your office clothes ready to change into in the tackroom, office bathroom, or on the train if you don't have time to go home before work.
- Having your work clothes on underneath old horse gear or a coverall. The downside here is that rather crumpled and grubby feeling—and that the boss is sure to be the one to point out that wisp of straw stuck in your hair!
- Keeping a pair of rubber boots, waterproof coveralls, and a coat in the car for quick dashes to the yard. Gloves will keep hands and fingernails reasonably clean.
- Squashed and windswept hairdos are an unavoidable consequence of your Jekyll and Hyde lifestyle, so opt for an easily revivable style!

Suggested Daily Winter Routines

Use these plans as guidelines for drawing up your own routine, which can be adapted to suit your situation and account for any jobs a yard owner might help with.

Field-Kept Horse

AM

- 5 mins: Arrive. Get tack and grooming kit ready.
- 5 mins: Catch horse, tie up.
- 20 mins: Remove turnout blanket and put somewhere dry, brush horse and tack up if riding. Adjust blankets, check over, pick out feet, and feed if not riding.
- 45 mins: Ride.
- 25 mins+: Untack. Dry off if wet. Replace blanket. Feed – while eating, put out hay and collect gear.
- 5 mins: Turnout.

TOTAL: 1 hour (+ 45 mins if riding)

PM

- 10 mins: Arrive. Catch horse.
- 5 mins: Remove and replace blankets. Pick out feet. Check over.
- 20 mins+: Feed. While eating, put out hay, check field.
- 5 mins: Turnout.

TOTAL: 40 mins

A well-planned routine makes all the difference.

Horse In at Night, Out During Day

AM

- 20 mins: Arrive. Tie up and check over. Brush off and pick out feet. Tack up if riding.
- 45 mins: Ride.
- 15 mins: Untack. Groom if time. Put on turnout blanket.
- 25 mins: Feed. While eating, collect mucking out kit, muck out, and add fresh bedding, hay, and water.
- 10 mins: Check field. Put out hay. Turn out.

TOTAL: 55 mins (+ 1 hour if riding)

PM

- 10 mins: Arrive. Catch horse.
- 20 mins: Tie up and check over. Remove and replace blanket. Pick out feet
- Groom if not done in morning.
- 20 mins+: Feed – while eating, fill haynets and water buckets for the morning.

TOTAL: 50 mins+

Late Evening (if possible)

- 15 mins: Check, pick out stable, give more hay/water if necessary.

TOTAL: 15 mins

Horse Turned Out for Less Than Three Hours a Day

AM

- 5 mins: Arrive. Tie up and check over.
- 15 mins: Pick out feet. Remove blankets. Brush off. Tack up.
- 60-90 mins: Ride.
- 20 mins: Untack. Groom. Replace blankets.
- 20 mins+: Feed – while eating, collect mucking out kit, muck out, add fresh bedding, put up haynet and refill buckets.
- 5 mins: Put horse back in stable and put away gear.

TOTAL: 2 hours 5 mins-2 hours 35 mins

Lunchtime

- 10 mins: Arrive. Check over. Pick out stable.
- 60 mins: Tack up. Exercise. Untack.
- 20 mins+: Feed while eating, give more hay and water.

TOTAL: 30 mins (+ 1 hour extra if riding or exercising horse)

PM

- 15 mins+: Arrive. Tie up and check over. Groom if not done in the morning. Pick out feet. Remove and replace blanket.
- 20 mins+: Feed – while eating, replace haynet, refill buckets, prepare haynet/feeds for morning.
- 10 mins: Pick out stable and tidy bed.

TOTAL: 45 mins+

Late Evening (if possible)

- Check. Give more hay/water if necessary. Give dinner.

TOTAL: 20 mins

Weekend Chores

Some jobs can certainly be left until the end of the weekend – though beware of piling these chores up until they take up the entire two days.

- 30 mins: Picking up droppings in larger-size field – small turnout areas should be done daily (allow time as necessary).
- 5 mins: Cleaning buckets.
- 30 mins: Thorough grooming (unless field-kept).
- 30 mins: Proper muck-out if using semi-deep litter system.
- 20 mins: Cleaning tack.

TOTAL: 1hour 55 mins

A turnout blanket will be needed during the day. The stable blanket must be removed after riding.

Winter

Few horse owners look forward to winter, when the workload increases and the opportunities to ride become increasingly limited. However, with good planning and management, you can make the best of this time of the year so that you do not spend hours mucking out, without time left to enjoy your horse.

Remember, your horse is an individual. Be flexible in your approach. If the feeding, exercise, or stable routine you have worked out does not suit him, think again! It is your responsibility to provide the best possible care for your horse during the winter months so that he will be in tip-top condition when spring comes around again.

Chapter Twenty-Two

Living In

For all horses, except those living permanently out at grass, winter involves spending a certain amount of time inside a stable. Horses are adaptable creatures and, as stabling becomes a part of their lives beginning at an early age, most learn to settle and accept a certain amount of confinement. Some even seem to come to like it, particularly if their stable offers a comfortable refuge from bad weather or stresses such as work or bullying companions.

With correct feeding (a constant supply of roughage as they would have at pasture) and daily opportunity for movement (ideally, including plenty at liberty), partly stabling your horse over the winter is a compromise system of management that suits many owners. It can also offer the best of both worlds to a horse. Stabling at night provides extra warmth and comfort for a clipped or finely bred horse, allows greater control over feeding and fitness for hard-working or performance horses, and is convenient for busy owners trying to fit exercise into a tight winter schedule.

Access to some sort of accommodation should always be on standby, even for field-kept horses. You never know when illness or injury could strike, requiring your horse to be brought indoors for awhile.

That said, as we have already seen, being kept indoors is an artificial way of life for a horse. Despite the arguments that exist for stabling, the fact remains that, in a stable a horse is effectively a prisoner, completely at our mercy and dependent on us to provide for his every need. Poor accommodation, excessive confinement, and a lack of understanding of his needs can lead to all kinds of problems and important welfare issues.

Given that horses are designed for the great outdoors, how can we make indoor living comfortable, nonstressful (on body and mind), and generally more equine-friendly? The answer is: In many ways. Most of these alternatives are simple, not necessarily expensive, and require only creativity, common sense, and the will to see life through a horse's eyes.

Housing for Horses

There are as many options on horse housing as there are yards. From the traditional square stable to the American yard system with its rows of stalls under one roof, to converted farm buildings, to a covered yard system where horses mingle together, each type of accommodation has its advocates. But how does each measure up against a horse's wish list?

Size

Traditional handbooks on stable management talk about minimum dimensions of 12 ft x 1 2ft (3.6 m x 3.6 m) for a horse, and 10 ft x 10 ft (3 m x 3 m) for a pony. Most standard prefabricated stables are made to these sizes, with a height to the eaves of 8 ft (2.4 m) or even less. However, these measurements don't even approach the horse's own "personal space" requirement, let alone give a leeway for safety. If a horse decides to go up on his hind legs, he can easily reach over 10 ft 6 in (3.15 m).

Stand inside a stable of this size, and you soon realize just how claustrophobic and stuffy it is. Imagine then a horse in there, barely able to turn around or lie down, his head half way or more to the ceiling. It is only then that you start appreciating

There are many benefits to stabling a horse, but they are mostly for the owner.

what it must be like for a large animal who needs freedom of movement and company to feel secure.

The rule on stables is: The bigger the better. Those "traditional" measurements should be considered an absolute minimum and, even then, view a stable of this size as temporary rather than permanent accommodation—in other words, somewhere your horse spends only a small part of his day. The "increased warmth" argument for smaller stables is nonsense, easily countered by adding blankets and putting down a thick, cozy bed, and is far outweighed by the benefits of greater area to move around in and improved ventilation.

Ventilation

Horses need head space, not only for safety reasons and to counter claustrophobia, but also to create a

Living In

sufficient volume of air so that they are not breathing in an atmosphere that is stale, contaminated by ammonia, and full of dust and spores from bedding. Respiratory disease is a condition of the stabled horse, and the more fresh air a horse gets, the better chance you will have of preventing it.

In addition to ensuring ceilings are sufficiently high (a minimum of 11 ft [3.3 m] with a minimum pitch of 15 degrees), ventilation sources should be improved as much as possible. Avoid creating drafts, but remember you do need air flow. One opening alone (such as a top stable door) or two openings on the same wall (such as a door and window) will have little beneficial effect.

What you are aiming to create is a gentle cross-flow of air above the horse's head height, using some form of ventilation on all four walls. As long as sufficient openings are high enough, cool air will enter at door level, be warmed by the horse and rise up through roof vents, creating a gentle and regular exchange of air. The flow of air must not be too aggressive, or the horse will have no choice but to stand in a permanent draft.

Depending on the building construction and design, use a combination of roof or side-wall ventilation:

- Roof ventilation: Either via open ridge vents with hoods, louvering, or windows (both of which are more effective and safer placed in a roof); hopper vents should always open inward and direct air upward.
- Side-wall ventilation: Preferably on the opposite wall to the door, either by a window or more easily and safely via louvers, or even by removing a few bricks/planks.

Yard-type, multistall complexes may appear to provide plenty of air space, but ventilation can be a real problem, especially if there is only one door to the outside that is frequently closed. The thick atmosphere that can build up is ideal for the spread of disease between horses housed together in this way. Electric air extraction systems offer a pricey

solution, but a far better solution is to design the building giving each horse a window (or even a door) to the open air.

The air quality in a stable is easily tested—simply walk straight in and take a deep breath. If you wouldn't like to spend time in there, don't ask your horse to! Any hint of ammonia or stuffiness means the bedding must be kept cleaner and/or more fresh air must be supplied.

While discussing ventilation, it is worth a reminder that the top doors of stables should never be shut—a practice that still goes on at nights in some traditionally run yards. When the cold wind is blowing, put on an extra blanket, make sure your horse has enough space to stand and eat out of the direct line of the wind or rain, and he will hardly notice it. Keeping him in the dark with no source of fresh air is both unfair and extremely unhealthy.

The stable must be as spacious as possible. Good ventilation is a must.

View

Instinct tells a horse that, when he has an all-around view of his surroundings, his chances of detecting and escaping threat are much better. And (surprise!) research has recently confirmed that horses kept in stables in which there was more than one "outlook" on the world were more relaxed and less prone to suffer from behavioral abnormalities than those in a conventional-style stable with one split door and a dusty, barred window.

It was also found that the best scenario was to provide see-through facilities on all four walls of a stable, with at least one, preferably two, views of the outside world.

Again, be wary of creating a through-draft, and think creatively about how to give your horse at least a choice of vista, particularly if he spends long periods inside. Think too, about the view from his stable and how it fits his personality. Most horses appreciate the stimulus of plenty of activity to help stave off boredom. However, be sensitive to the touchy horse who would rather not have someone peering in over his door every few minutes, or one who gets easily upset or overly stimulated by constant activity outside (it may be, of course, he wishes he was out there too!).

Yard-type stabling has obvious advantages in terms of view over a stable with one door that faces out on a yard, but be aware of the advantage of having at least one high, solid wall. Some horses can feel constantly threatened if surrounded by others on all sides and unable to move right away.

Contact

It should also have come as no shock to researchers to have discovered that horses are more content when stabled, not only within sight and hearing distance, but also in touch contact with their own kind.

Being able to see other horses in the barn area is crucial, but by itself is not enough to recreate the feeling of security in a herd situation. By making sure every stable allows its inmate the chance to see, smell, and touch at least one other horse, we not only give reassurance but also the entertainment of social contact, which goes a long way toward keeping boredom at bay.

This is easily enough done using a grille to provide a "chat hole" in dividing walls, although reducing walls to chest height (at least 5 ft/1.5 m) and leaving the remaining height open or grilled is even better.

Yards score highly in this respect, but care always must be taken about who is neighbors with who. In any kind of housing, a horse stabled next to one he dislikes or who bullies him is never going to relax, particularly if his stable is not large enough for him to keep his distance. Watch reactions carefully to judge whether neighbors are getting along, and move occupants around until everyone is content. Housing friends in adjacent stables obviously has a calming influence. And, if space is

Horses like to see what is going on around them.

A horse is miserable unless he is in contact with other horses.

sufficient, give thought to the possibility of putting pair-bonded horses in together. Unconventional maybe, but why not?

The logical next step from sharing is, of course, the yarded enclosure, which is undoubtedly the most horse-friendly way of keeping horses under cover—especially if it opens out on to pasture to allow horses total freedom of access to either shelter or the outdoors. This system presents many benefits to the horse and few inconveniences to humans. Although a close eye must be kept on individuals to make sure each one's needs are met and that group members are compatible, communal feeding and bedding facilities mean economies can be made in virtually every aspect of horsekeeping—not least in labor and time. And the horses are happy too!

For some reason, because we ourselves like the privacy of our own bedrooms, we assume horses are the same. Yet segregating them into individual cells, where movement, contact, and fresh air are all so limited, is one of the biggest mistakes we have made in horse care. Housing systems that allow ad lib

space and contact provide a far better quality of life. So, if your horse is housed at all in winter—whether a little or a lot—do all you can to get that housing as near as possible to his ideal environment.

Bedding Systems

Before looking at bedding and mucking out, it is worth giving some thought to the good, bad, and ugly with regard to stable floors.

If you are planning to build a stable, or have any control over the design of your horse's accommodations, a floor made of free-draining material is infinitely preferable. This can be created by digging out the floor area, filling it with any hard, inert waste material that can be used as a fill and topped with graded stone or gravel, then smoothing it off loosely with a thick layer of coarse asphalt. Alternatively, bricks can be laid edgeways on a similar gravel base.

Whatever the stable floor is made from, the ill-effects of odors and ammonia can be minimized by using one of the granular stable deodorants now available on the market before laying down a bed. These products absorb wetness and fumes and improve stable hygiene, and they undoubtedly help. However, a bulk application of cat litter is probably cheaper and as effective. No amount of deodorizing can make up for a dirty bed, however.

Whatever bedding material you use, and however you manage it, your aim is to provide a bed that is:

- warm
- comfortable and encourages the horse to lie down and to urinate
- clean
- conducive to a hygienic and dust-free environment

When looking at options, keep all these criteria in mind, as well as considering what best suits your own budget and time schedule.

Daily Muck Out or Deep Litter?

Beds can be cleaned out daily in their entirety, or they can be managed on a deep or semi-deep litter system. A deep litter system is one in which droppings and wet patches only are cleared, new bedding spread on top, and the whole bed is given a thorough clean at weekends (or, in the case of really deep litter, every few months).

Deep litter is obviously an attractive method for busy owners in winter, but to do it properly without compromising your horse's health may not necessarily be as straightforward as it seems. Once any bedding becomes saturated with urine and compacted, spores flourish, and it will give off strong fumes, both of which will irritate the horse's respiratory tract.

For this reason, deep or semi-deep litter can only be considered in a big stable that has extremely good ventilation and very effective drainage. It is unsuitable for most individual stables, where a daily muck out is far healthier. Without great care to keep the sides of the bed dry, deep litter will also quickly rot the sides of a wooden stable.

All beds must be kept well topped off with fresh bedding to create a deep, dry, and clean layer for the horse to stand and lie down on. And, in the case of deep litter, to seal in the wet bed below. Certain materials suit a semi-deep litter system better than others. Like straw, paper quickly becomes a soggy, spore-filled mass if left too long. Overall, shavings or hemp best suit semi-deep or deep littering.

Choosing Bedding

Almost as much choice in bedding for horses is available as there is feedstuffs. This is mostly good news for the horse because every owner now has easy access to a range of dust-free bedding materials.

Straw

Straw is the traditional bedding, bought in bales directly from the farmer or feed merchant. It is still

Deep litter can only be used in big stables with good ventilation.

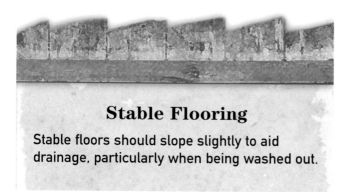

Stable Flooring

Stable floors should slope slightly to aid drainage, particularly when being washed out.

widely used and has a lot going for it in terms of absorbency, drainage, comfort, value, and, ultimately, as useful compost. But if you are thinking of using straw, or your barn only provides it, keep three facts in mind:

• All unprocessed straw is full of dust. However clean a bale looks, it will already contain mold spores, even before it becomes soiled in the stable.

• Straw is edible, and if your horse finds it more palatable than the hay on offer, it will be difficult to stop him tucking into his bed.

• Mucking out an average stable properly on a daily basis will use almost a bale of straw a day and create large quantities of waste. Therefore, you may not save on cost choosing this option over other materials, beyond the initial laying of the bed.

For the difference in price, the guarantee of an improvement in the air quality, the reduction of the risk of respiratory disease, ability to control your horse's fiber intake, and great savings in labor and time, it is well worth considering one of the following low-dust bedding alternatives.

Dust-Extracted Straw

This has all the advantages of straw without the dust. It is available in wrapped bales that can be stored outside. It is usually chopped short, so it is better for lame or convalescent horses than long-stalked straw.

Shavings

This type of bedding is absorbent, easy to manage, suitable for all systems, easy to store, and inedible. It is pricey for daily muck outs, but very cost-effective for semi- and deep litter systems. It is slow to rot down. Choose a recognized product—cheap or free shavings from the local sawmill are not only a chore to bag, but may contain foreign bodies or be chemically treated and full of sawdust (which is, as described, dust).

Shredded Paper

Paper is as absorbent and easily stored as shavings, and often slightly cheaper. Disadvantages are that it is not so well suited to deep litter, it is very heavy when wet, and it blows around everywhere when dry.

Hemp and Flax

Two relative newcomers to the market, hemp and flax are now becoming increasingly popular. They are expensive per bale, but once a bed is laid, an average stable needs a bale or less a week for topping off. Both are absorbent, hygienic, easy to store and handle, and inedible. Find out how to manage the bed at its optimum from the manufacturer's instructions.

Straw is a traditional bedding, but problems with dust should be considered. A bed made of shavings is expensive to set up, but easy to maintain.

Rubber Matting—
A Revolutionary Idea?

Rubber matting for stables, another recent advance in horse care, is advertised widely throughout the equestrian press. Designs vary, and most suppliers acknowledge that the use of a little bedding spread on top of it is advisable, although some barns do use matting without any additional bedding material.

When kept scrupulously clean, lifted, and disinfected regularly underneath, rubber matting is certainly hygienic. It is also dust-free, saves mucking-out time, and, after the initial laying cost, allows for big savings on bedding.

From a personal point of view (which I am sure coincides with a horse's), I think matting is dreadful. Despite the promoters' insistence on its warmth and anti-concussive properties, surely no slab of smooth rubber can replace the comfort and reassurance of a deep, well-kept bed. Which would you prefer in your bedroom? I have certainly yet to see a relaxed horse enjoying a snooze on his rubber mat.

Bed Eating

Few horses won't at least try a sample of their straw bed. Many greedy guts, of course, get stuck on it unashamedly. How much of a problem is this? The answer is probably not as much as you think.

Horses in hard work do need their fiber intake controlled and, in this case, it makes sense to change to an inedible type of bedding, such as shavings or paper, which will also reduce dust as well. For most others, the relatively small amount of straw eaten is unlikely to have any adverse effects—it is, after all, only another source of fiber, albeit of little nutritional value.

If you are worried about your horse overindulging, try to provide better quality hay, or

If your horse samples his straw bed too often, consider changing bedding materials.

change your bedding material. It is not a good idea to spray any sort of chemicals over the bed that your horse has to lie on and breathe near.

Mucking Out Tips

Get the right tools for the job:
- big wheelbarrow
- stable fork
- pitchfork (straw)
- shavings fork (shavings/hemp/paper)
- muck bucket (plastic laundry baskets are ideal)
- shovel
- barn brush

Any bed will stay cleaner if you pick out droppings as often as possible, preferably before they get squashed into the bed.

Technique

Take the horse out of the stable, either to turn out or tie up outside—you cannot muck out safely around a horse. Also remove and empty water buckets.

Living In

Deep Litter: Use a stable fork to remove droppings and the worst wet patches. Avoid disturbing the bottom layer. Pull clean bedding from the sides down into the center, and add fresh bedding on top. Dig out all wet patches on weekends, adding plenty of fresh bedding piled high at the sides to act as your bedding stash over the next week.

Complete Clean-Out: Remove obvious droppings piles first using a pitchfork. Now clear a corner ready for dirty bedding and one for clean. Start digging! Separate the clean bedding from the dirty, which is usually concentrated in one or two central areas. Fork the dirty bedding into the wheelbarrow. Sweep the exposed floor. Spread the clean bedding back down as a base layer, then add some fresh on top.

- A skimpy bed is not economical: It will get dirtier quicker, and there is a risk of endless knocks and scrapes. Test whether the bed is clean, and see if you have been generous enough with the fresh bedding by kneeling down. If your knees get damp or dirty, add more. As a rough guide, bedding must be about 1 ft (30 cm) deep.
- Leaving the bedding off the floor to air out the stall is okay if the horse is being turned out, but it is unfair to expect a horse to stand for any length of time on a cold, bare floor.
- Create banks of bedding around the walls to help block drafts and prevent the horse from getting itself cast (unable to get up). Don't forget to shift these regularly for a thorough clean out, though.
- Allow at least 20 minutes for any dust to settle before putting the horse back inside, together with his refilled water bucket.
- Empty the wheelbarrow of dirty bedding onto the muck heap. If it's windy, stop bedding from blowing around by covering the barrow with an old sack or elastic-trimmed plastic cover.
- Sweep up and put tools away, propping the wheelbarrow upright against a wall to help deter rusting. It only takes a minute.

Pick out droppings as often as possible.

Where There's Muck...

Here are some suggestions for proper mucking out "etiquette":

- Muck heaps attract flies and are packed with mold spores. Site them well away and downwind from stables and feed and bedding stores.
- It's a chore when you are short of time, but try to keep a neat, rubbish-free heap—it rots quicker, holds more, is easier to remove, and looks like far less of an eye-sore than a sprawling muck mountain.
- Put dirty bedding well on top, and stamp it down to compress the heap and help it rot more quickly.
- Don't upset neighbors by letting a muck heap build up too high.

Disposal ideas include selling or giving muck away by the bag to local gardeners (try advertising to spread the word); spreading it on your fields (after a

201

minimum of 6 months' rotting); or offering it to local farmers or mushroom growers. In barns tight on space, renting a disposal unit is expensive but convenient.

Indoor Wear

What clothing does your horse need when he is inside? If he is unclipped, the answer may well be none. It all depends on the thickness of his coat and, to some extent, the size of his stable. If the area is big enough to allow plenty of movement, then the unclipped horse's skin and coat will be all the healthier for not wearing a blanket.

Clipped horses and those kept in small individual stables without much opportunity to move about to keep themselves warm will need the help of a blanket when inside.

There was a time when indoor wear for horses consisted of either a posh wool day blanket or a night-time canvas blanket with any number of lighter blankets underneath, depending on the weather. These were all fastened in place around the middle by a gut-and-spine-crunching roller. Thankfully, these are items now largely consigned to the history books, along with the numerous spinal injuries, sores, and accidents that resulted from badly fitted rollers and backward-slipping blankets.

Today, like us, our horses can snuggle up inside a cozy but lightweight comforter for the night. Their version is easy to put on, fastened with broad belly surcingles or leg straps to avoid pressure, and washable in the machine. Now that's what you call progress!

Making the Choice

As with outdoor blankets, a huge choice of stable blankets is available, in every price range. And, once again, as a general rule, you get what you pay for. Cheap blankets will be relatively thin, although they may be sufficient to help out a hairy pony or cob, or as an extra layer under another blanket during cold spells. On the other hand, an ultra-high-performance, top-of-the-line blanket would toast an unclipped or

partly clipped animal who may be far more comfortable in a well-made, medium-priced version.

On the whole, it is better to go for a single, good blanket than to use a stack of layers, which rather defeats the object of the convenient, new comforter-style blankets. Extra layers may be needed during cold spells, however. In this case, invest in one or two light under-blankets that fasten at the chest and have their own belly and/or leg straps. Avoid using a roller if you possibly can. If you need to secure the blankets with a roller, make sure it fits well, has no twists, and is always thickly padded at the withers or raised up off the spine completely.

If your horse is unclipped and has room to move in a large stable, he may not need a winter blanket.

Sheets and Blankets

Use a light cotton summer sheet underneath your stable blanket. It is much easier to wash, and the horse will have clean fabric next to his skin.

Obviously, it is just as important that a stable blanket fits as with any other kind of horsewear. Measure your horse as described in the section on outdoor blankets. In addition, assess potential blanket buys for shaping and for general fit, as well as for general durability, warmth, and ease of use in the same way.

Neck Covers

These are available to be used with stable blankets and have their merits for fully clipped horses or others who feel the cold, such as seniors or invalids. Covers have their place but, on the whole, most stabled horses will not gain much from being completely swathed in clothing.

Dual-Purpose Blankets

An innovation in the horse clothing market is blankets suitable for combined indoor and outdoor use. Previously, blankets always needed to be changed for indoors because the old-style, canvas rugs were heavy, wet, cumbersome, and didn't breathe. Modern, breathable fabrics mean it is quite possible for a horse to be comfortable in the same blanket, indoors as well as out.

The danger is in having your horse overheat in the stable, and it may be all too tempting, when pushed for time, not to bother taking the blanket off and shaking it out twice a day. Overall, it may suit you better to have separate blankets for the stable and turnout. This gives you the chance to dry and air each one, rather than having to invest in two expensive "combo" blankets (one plus a spare).

Beating the Stable Blues

Looking at the average stabling situation, it is hard to imagine anything further removed from the life a horse evolved to lead. Before domestication, the horse was a plains-dwelling herbivore, roaming freely over huge areas, searching out and digesting food as he went. He lived within a group of co-dependents, all constantly alert to life-threatening danger. In other words, although a wild horse's day-to-day existence might appear boring to us, to him it is packed full of activity and stimulation. Quite literally, it is a matter of life and death.

Modern materials make stable blankets cozy and comfortable.

Compare this to the enforced idleness and isolation of most stabled horses. A mere few 100 years of domestication have simply not been enough to transform the horse into an animal who enjoys or thrives on solitary confinement with two or three meals a day delivered by bucket.

Instinct vs. Confinement

Contradicting instincts put strain on all stabled horses, both physically and mentally, although being the amenable creatures they are, most horses come to accept and adapt to this life.

However, we should still make every effort to keep stress levels down by reducing the adverse effects of confinement as much as we possibly can, as in the ways described earlier. The fact that any yard will contain a number of horses who seem quite settled in their stables, plus many others showing clear signs of anxiety, shows how tolerance of stress and the coping mechanisms used to deal with it vary enormously from horse to horse.

In a group of humans under pressure, some handle it well, while others go to pieces at the slightest frustration. Which horses cope well with the compromises of stabling? Usually those whose owners have tried to mimic nature as far as possible in their management, and also, most often, those whose lives are full of interest and whose self-confidence and general sense of security is high.

Those who struggle when they are prevented from completely fulfilling their instinctive drives might be the insecure personalities, the sensitive, highly strung types, the animals who have never been properly habituated to confinement as youngsters. It is now believed that horses who suffered a trauma in their early years (such as abrupt weaning) are particularly vulnerable.

Signs of Stress

The way frustration shows itself in horses varies enormously. Signs may be as obvious as the frantic neck-arched air gulping of the wind sucker—one of the many abnormal repetitive behaviors or stereotypes once known (so unfairly) as stable vices. Physical symptoms may be present, which include a failure to thrive, loss of appetite, and susceptibility to colic, allergies, or infections.

But mental stress may also show in more insidious ways, taking the form of depression and a kind of dull resignation or being converted into aggression or riding problems (particularly where excessive confinement is coupled with overfeeding of high-energy concentrated feed).

Even the apparently contented horse may be tolerating an undercurrent of strain he could well do without. Look carefully, and the tell-tale signs will be there, perhaps in a lack of enthusiasm for work, a vulnerability to illness, a slight irritability, or chewed woodwork around the door frame.

Signs of stress vary. The distress of this "wind sucker" is all too evident.

Any one or all of these may be signs of stress:

- physical problems, for example, allergies, digestive upsets, loss of appetite/condition, and stiffness
- depression
- aggression
- abnormal behavior related to eating, for example, chewing wood, scraping teeth on metal, blanket ripping, crib biting, wind sucking, and eating droppings
- abnormal behavior related to movement, for example, weaving and stable walking

When a symptom of stress is obvious enough to be recognizable, the horse is under an unacceptable amount of strain. It is high time to alter stable management to find ways of naturalizing the horse's regime.

Stereotypical Behavior

Stereotypical behaviors are performed by all mammals under stress. It may be the nervous twiddling of a lock of hair, the glassy-eyed pacing of the bear in the zoo, or the mesmerizing head swinging of the horse who weaves. The monotonous repetition of the action begins when the desired action (such as movement in the case of the weaver) cannot be completed, so it is begun again. It then fixes itself into a habit and, by releasing endorphins—the body's natural sedative—into the bloodstream, the action becomes a kind of addictive coping mechanism.

Because such behavior is never seen in free-living horses, boredom was long believed to be the trigger for the stereotypes so commonplace in yards. We now realize that boredom is only part of the equation. Yes, too many stabled horses are, literally, bored out of their minds, but the behavior is now actually known to be a response to sheer frustration.

The stereotyper has a compulsion that his enforced confinement is preventing him from fulfilling. The horse who cannot be free to graze, move, and socialize instead stable walks or weaves; the horse who needs to chew but has no hay left

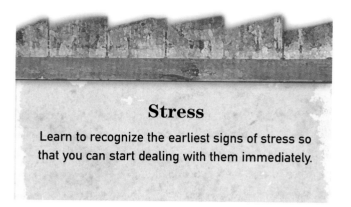

Stress

Learn to recognize the earliest signs of stress so that you can start dealing with them immediately.

instead tucks into whatever's available, even if it's only air, desperate to fill his belly.

Therefore, preventing stereotypical behavior and managing these habits if they have become established is about more than simply amusing the horse. His time in confinement must be filled with activity that is meaningful and satisfying to him. In other words, with activity that mimics natural movement, social contact, and eating.

Another myth to debunk about stereotypes is that these behaviors can be copied. There is no evidence at all to suggest this. However, if a barn full of horses is managed inadequately, it stands to reason that the animals are all under similar levels of stress and will demonstrate it in similar ways. Likewise, a mare that is a stereotyper will become an example to her learning foal and will also have given him genes predisposing him to low stress tolerance like herself.

Stress Reduction

The incredible habit-forming capacity that makes horses so trainable unfortunately works against them when it comes to trying to modify undesirable behavior. Once an abnormal behavioral pattern has become set, it is very hard to alter—even after the stresses that originally caused it are gone. Nevertheless, removing sources of stress can tone down the behavior and, in some cases, even eradicate it; although it may take some time before improvement is seen.

Look at management changes rather than simply resorting to a weaving grille, cribbing strap, or drugs to control stereotypes. Remember that, by this time, the habit itself has become a need. Quick fixes only mask the behavior, denying the horse access to his only means of coping, although a device such as a cribbing strap may play its part in gradually weaning the horse off his behavior when turned out.

As always, prevention is better and easier than cure, and adopting a naturalized management regime will certainly help to prevent undesirable behaviors from ever making an appearance.

Importance of Movement

Wild horses are constantly on the move; steady grazing and walking are punctuated with short bursts of intense activity. A stabled horse needs:

- as much free exercise as possible, preferably loose in the field, but any is better than none
- as large a stable as possible
- plenty of ridden exercise

Social Contact

Wild horses live in a group in which communication is continual. Each individual has responsibilities for herd security and must be constantly alert to danger. A stabled horse needs:

- housing with a stimulating view
- housing that allows for fulfilling social contact and unrestricted communication (for example, touch as well as sight)
- housing that allows a horse to pair-bond with another individual
- time outside the stable, loose with others
- the chance to act as part of a group
- enough personal space not to feel constantly threatened
- plenty of human attention (for example, grooming, massage, etc.)

Break up your horse's routine with periods outside the stable.

Winter Housekeeping

Keep your horse's indoor environment as hygienic as possible by scrubbing barn and stable equipment regularly with disinfectant. The most economical products are made for farms and are available from agricultural merchants. Follow the dilution instructions on the product—usually a ratio of 1:100 or 1:150.

Natural Feeding

Wild horses spend 60 percent of their time eating, taking in a constant trickle of low-grade forage. When a horse is chewing and digesting fiber, he feels happy, settled, and above all, occupied. A stabled horse needs:
• ad-lib forage
• feed he has to work at to get (for example, hay given in a small, mesh net)
• feeding tailored carefully to workload (extreme reliance on concentrated feeds may in itself trigger stereotypical behavior)
• meals given little and often
• feed given from floor level where possible
• feed spread around to mimic natural foraging

Time-Filling Ideas

The measures above will go a long way toward filling the idle hours of the stabled horse. Others include:
• providing some feed in a horseball or a similar device that makes the horse work for each mouthful
• supplying stable "toys," such as giant apples (though I am yet to find a horse that really gets into these)
• some barns keep a radio on to give the horses something to listen to, but choose the channel carefully—remember your horse cannot let himself out to switch it off

Above all, remember such entertainment is the icing on the cake. What your horse wants you to get right are the fundamentals.

There are other more general ways of stress-reduction. These include:
• complementary therapies, such as shiatsu, reiki, Tteam touch, or Bach flower remedies
• feeding calming herbal supplements
• removing major stress factors, such as competitions, until your horse is more settled

Stable Safety

Aside from the issues of stable size discussed earlier, all horse accommodations must be assessed for potential safety hazards.

A horseball will help to keep a horse occupied.

Lighting: Switches should be fitted well beyond a horse's reach, outside the stable, and with a waterproof cover. Light fittings inside must have a protective guard and be well out of reach, either on the ridge of the roof or bulkhead.

Feeding: The fewer fittings in a stable, the less chance of accidents occurring. Removable mangers or feed buckets are safer and easier to keep clean than fixed ones. A permanent manger needs boxing in right to the ground. Avoid positioning mangers and tie rings on an opposite wall, so that a horse must then stand with his rear end to the door.

Hay should be given in a net tied securely at chest height or in a rack so that the horse can eat at a natural head height but not be at risk of catching his face, halter, or a foot. The safest way to feed hay is off the floor, but this is wasteful; a long-and-deep style plastic laundry basket can make a safe but effective compromise.

Watering: Buckets can be fixed using an old tire to avoid using a wall bracket. Check automatic waterers daily to make sure they are not clogged up with feed or bedding.

Protruding Nails, Weak Boards, and Splinters: Check the stable every day. One nail or split plank can cause a very nasty injury. Wood chewers or crib biters will tuck in to all exposed edges, so line these with metal strips (and do something about the boredom and stress at the root of this behavior).

Salt Mineral Holders: These holders are just something else for a horse to catch himself on, particularly when the edges rust and get sharp. Use the kind of lick that has a hole in it and ties to a tie ring.

Windows: All windows must be protected by galvanized grille/mesh.

Doors: Doors should always open outward and be wide and high enough for the horse to pass easily through without frightening himself. Minimum dimensions should be 3 ft 8 in (1.11 m) wide and 7 ft 3 in (2.8 m) high, with the lower door 4 ft 4 in (1.3 m) high. Lower doors require two bolts, one at the top and one at the bottom. A lower bolt prevents equine Houdinis from escaping, but also stops a horse from getting a foot trapped under the door while getting up. This has happened, so use the bottom bolt and make sure doors fit flush with the ground without gaps.

Electrical Supply: Electrical faults cause more yard fires than anything else. Employ only approved contractors and use fittings suitable for exterior use. Position fittings well away from horses and, as much as possible, away from the effects of the weather. Check wiring, cables, and appliances regularly for signs of wear, or damage from mice and rats or other sources. Use a circuit breaker when using any

Horses are all individuals, and some will cope with stabling better than others.

electrical appliance around horses, for example, clippers or a hair dryer. Fit and maintain fire extinguishers in easy-to-reach places and make sure no one ever smokes around the yard.

Tools: Provide a place for mucking out tools away from the horses. Make sure they are always returned there after use, and that they are stacked safely and neatly.

Barn Security

Taking some sensible security measures will not guarantee your barn does not fall victim to thieves, but it will make criminals' lives harder and possibly be enough to put off a break-in attempt. Your local police crime prevention officer will come out and give on-site advice about security measures, many of which will be straightforward and low cost. Safety tips include the following:

- Lock tack, feed, and tool stores (but never stables) with heavy-duty padlocks. Check your insurance policy if tack is kept at the yard; many insurers insist on a certain standard of lock. Then remember to use them. Keep a can of car de-icer handy for iced-up locks.
- Never leave gear lying around. Fix solid iron bars or grilles on windows.
- Deter thieves by publicizing your security measures. For example, post warning notices that horses are freeze-marked, tack is marked, or there is a dog at large.
- Drop into the barn at odd times, rather than always following the same routine.
- Query any strangers hanging around the yard asking for directions, or any out-of-the-ordinary activity nearby. Notify the police and neighborhood watch.
- Keep wheelbarrows and ladders locked away at night. Many a tack thief has helped himself to piles of saddles courtesy of the yard's own fleet of wheelbarrows!

The stable environment should be kept as clean as possible.

- Keep the yard well lit. Movement-sensitive lighting makes life easier for you as well as helping secure your horse, and it is not that expensive to install.
- Permanently mark everything of value to deter theft, and make sure it can find its way back to you if stolen—tack, blankets, tools, and, of course, horses.
- Immobilize and security-mark trailers and other vehicles.
- Large barns in high-risk areas might consider keeping a dog on site or installing security cameras and alarms.

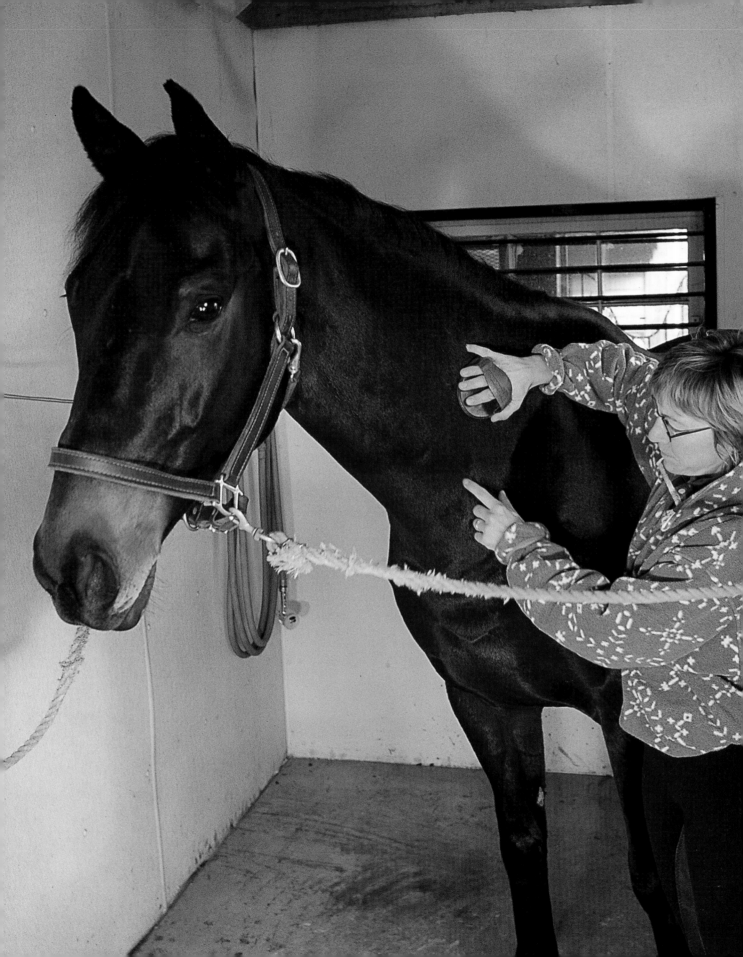

Chapter Twenty-Three

Grooming the Stabled Horse

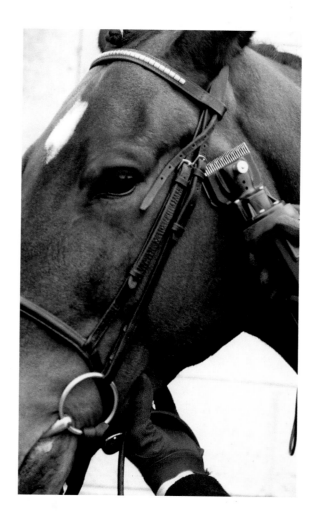

Horses who live part-in, part-out can be given a more thorough grooming than horses who live outside full time in winter. You can go beyond brushing off dry mud with a dandy brush, and you can even use a body brush, as long as the horse is well blanketed. Even so, the skin and coat should still very much maintain themselves with little more than the help of natural exercise and correct feeding.

However, the more time a horse spends stabled, the more significant grooming becomes for his health. Stabling is bad news for skin. Not only is a stabled horse unable to move around to promote circulation, control temperature, and expel waste products via the skin, but he spends his time standing wrapped up in a blanket in an atmosphere full of dust and other pollutants.

Grooming, therefore, takes on a new importance, helping the skin to keep working efficiently as well as contributing to muscle tone and keeping up appearances.

Grooming Guidelines

The less time a horse spends outside his stable, the more grooming he requires. Horses being turned out

Sole Protection

If, for some reason, your horse must be kept in for long periods, use a sole-protecting product to counter the damaging effects of ammonia.

daily need:

- Feet picked out before going out and on coming in.
- Eyes, nose, and dock sponged before going out.
- Quick brush over with a dandy brush if unclipped or a body brush if clipped, when blankets are changed.
- Mane and tail brushed through, if you have time.

Horses mainly stabled need (every day):

- Feet picked out at least twice daily.
- Eyes, nose, and dock sponged at least twice daily.
- Quick body brush over before exercise.
- Thorough body brush after exercise using a curry comb to keep the brush clean. Finish with a wipe-over.
- Mane and tail brushed through.
- Tail bandage can be applied for a few hours only.
- If possible, groom in a sheltered place outside the stable.
- Work from front to back, folding blankets back on a clipped horse so he is never left cold.
- Stabled horses really appreciate freshening-up by sponging the eyes, nose, and dock. Use a different sponge for each area. Fragrance-free baby wipes are a handy, quick alternative.
- Horses' feet weren't designed for standing around in their own dung and urine, so cleaning the feet is all-important. Ammonia from dirty bedding will dissolve the foot/horn wall's natural protective oils, allowing urea to be absorbed and bacteria to get into cracks.

- Pulled tails can be bandaged to smooth the lie of the hair for a few hours only after grooming.
- Don't ignore your horse's "bits" or you could be asking for trouble. Mares need a weekly wipe around the udder, dock, and vulva, applying a little baby oil to help stop the area from drying.

Some geldings seem to get dirtier around the genitals than others, but about once a month give the sheath a thorough cleaning inside and out. It is not as difficult as it seems, especially once your horse is used to it. The easiest way is with a sheath-cleaning gel, baby oil, or petroleum jelly. Put on some rubber gloves, and tactfully but confidently go for it. Leave gel on for a day or two to loosen mucky deposits before sponging the area off with warm soapy water.

Make grooming quality time with your horse. Touch is important to horses, and most love the attention, as long as you are sensitive and tactful (with clipped coats in particular). Don't rush it. Look into massage techniques or methods such as Tteam Touch to make the most of this time spent together.

Fold back the blanket when grooming a clipped horse.

Grooming Routine

A body brush is needed for all-over grooming.

Keep the brush clean by using a curry comb.

A stable rubber can be used for a general wipe-over.

Comb through the mane.

Work through the tail with your hands, loosening tangles and getting rid of straw or shavings.

Clean the eyes with a damp sponge.

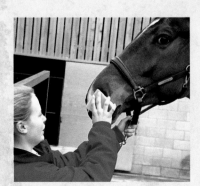

Sponge the nose.

Freshen up the dock.

Pick out the feet.

Chapter Twenty-Four

Time Out

Ever since the early days of domestication, horses have been kept in stables mainly for our own convenience. This is despite the fact that their entire physical and mental makeup is designed for them to survive and thrive roaming free in large social groups. They are most certainly not designed to be confined for long periods in a small, enclosed space.

The problems resulting from this artificial way of life were masked, to a large extent, when most horses spent a large part of their day in hard labor and had to be kept inside to be close at hand and fit enough for work. Today's horses exist in an entirely different world. Although some do still play hard, most live a life of leisure previously unimaginable. Yet, we have continued to see the stable as our horses' principal home.

Fortunately, thinking is starting to change as interest in animal behavior has grown and as the findings of research into equine needs start to filter through to horse owners. Such studies only confirm what common sense could have told us all along. However, many traditionalists have been reluctant to adopt new ideas because it would mean fundamental changes to the way we keep our horses.

Horses made to stand inside a restricted, confined, and dusty "cell" for long periods suffer psychological and physical stress, the degree depending on their individual tolerance threshold. Over a period of time, this leads to health and performance problems that can be extremely difficult and expensive to sort out.

Reducing stress is simple and straightforward. It involves providing a lifestyle for your horse that mimics nature as far as possible, one in which any compromises are made with the horse's interests put first. Most owners would agree this is their aim, but despite good intentions, difficulties crop up when it comes to the practicalities of setting up a more natural regime. For your horse's sake, persevere — most setbacks can be overcome with will and a little lateral thinking.

Turnout: An Essential

Every horse is programmed to think and behave like a horse — and that includes Derby winners, show-jumping champions, Grand Prix dressage horses, and Rolex Kentucky contenders. Each and every one will appreciate, and benefit from, time spent loose outside in the fresh air as nature intended, in the company of his own kind, foraging for his own food, and basically "chilling out."

The only valid reasons for keeping a horse permanently in a stable are to do with health, and these are usually short term, for example, when the veterinarian has advised that a condition is best treated or managed by keeping the horse in.

Arguments against turning out tend to be based on misapprehensions, or else generally have easy, practical ways around them.

My horse is too delicate to stand the weather. There isn't a breed of horse who is *not* physically able to live outdoors 24 hours a day, 12 months of the year, let alone able to spend a few hours a day in it. True, our support will be needed to supplement natural shelter and food where necessary and to replace warmth with blankets where coats have been clipped for thinner-skinned types or more delicate individuals

Daily turnout must be considered essential to proper care.

(such as seniors). But given the opportunity and the tools, every horse is capable of thriving outside; after all, this—and not a stable— is the environment for which he was built.

My horse is too valuable to risk in the field. With care, the chances of injury to a horse at grass can be reduced to a level no higher than those of the knocks risked in a stable. Turned out as part of his daily routine, the horse is unlikely to go crazy as soon as he feels grass beneath his feet. Careful introductions to a group that is settled and free of bullying characters keeps rough play to a minimum. Boots and blankets help to protect against minor injuries.

Indoor living is hardly danger-free itself. Horses

who spend long periods in the bacteria and dust laden surroundings of even the cleanest stable are at far higher risk from a number of health issues than their field-kept companions. These include respiratory disease, musculoskeletal problems, and colic, which can seriously compromise performance. This is not to mention the high incidence of behavioral abnormalities, including so-called "stable vices" seen in horses kept largely or entirely stabled.

My horse needs to focus on his work. Turning out for part, or indeed all, of the day (and night) is far more likely to produce the relaxed animal required for top-level competitive success. If you keep a horse in solitary confinement, in a space in which he can barely turn around, he is far more likely to become anxious or depressed.

Energy and performance ability will not "leach out" if he gets to stretch the stiffness out of his legs for a few hours in the field each day. What may well be noticed, however, is an improvement in willingness and attitude to work, suppleness, and general well-being.

My horse prefers to be inside. The horse who appears to prefer to be inside is far more likely to be either cold, hungry, or being bullied, than he is longing for the four walls of his stable. If owners need convincing of this, they have only to leave their horse's stable doors open one day and see whether he chooses to stay inside or take a walk.

Even given the option of an open-sided shelter, most horses will choose not to use it, preferring the security (from their perspective) of the open air rather than an enclosure.

Genuine issues can arise when introducing horses to a group or within an existing group, but most of these can be tackled successfully.

We need to preserve the grass. Another frequently encountered argument, often from hard-pressed yard owners, is that simply not enough grazing is available or what exists must be preserved or set aside for hay.

In answer to this we do need to question where our priorities lie, and why the horse's right to daily freedom should be made to take a back seat. If sufficient space is not available to allow for all horses to spend time out, then maybe there are too many horses for the available facilities.

Even the most valuable Thoroughbred should be allowed some time out to exercise at liberty in the open air.

The horse who prefers to be inside is probably being bullied in the field.

Creating Freedom

You can maximize available space in a number of ways to provide more freedom for your horse. This might involve both making more and better use of grazing or utilizing yard facilities more effectively so that any time not spent actually out at pasture does not necessarily mean being restricted to a conventional stable.

Making the Most of Limited Grazing

Give thought to how fields that would otherwise be shut off for the winter can be used and managed all year round. Damage limitation might include turning out only a few horses at a time in settled groups, dividing fields into smaller paddocks and using a

rotation system, or improving drainage, particularly around gateways.

Consider fencing off a small area that can be sacrificed and allowed to become poached, then reseeded in the spring. Although the grass will soon disappear, the horses can then be fed extra hay while outside.

Alternative Play Space

Depending on existing buildings and the layout of the yard, numerous options are available for creating alternative leg-stretching space for your horses. Few yards exist that, with a little planning, rearrangement, and creative use of materials, cannot use one or more of the following ideas:

• Remove interior walls to create larger stables or stables in which more than one horse can be kept together (as long as they are friends).

• Indoor and outside arenas can offer a potential turnout space, although it is understandable if your yard proprietor is reluctant to have loose horses rolling and digging up the surface of their expensive investment.

• Utilize a large storage building (or the empty part of the hay barn as the stack gets used up) to allow more than one horse to be kept together in a more open space, either permanently or for part of the day.

• Create a corral-type area where one or more horses can wander about, eating hay out in the fresh air with an open view. Ideally, this should be combined with free access to pasture, but even an enclosed pen is still a vast improvement on full-time stabling. Most yards have various areas, corners, and buildings that can be made into surfaced, at least partially covered, corrals. This allows horses who would otherwise be in their stables to spend a few hours a day out together. Earth floor can be used as it is, or a safe surface created inexpensively by utilizing half-clean or dried-out used bedding. If the layer is thick enough, this will be quite sufficient, but for extra protection over concrete, rubber matting can be used.

Time Out

- If space or layout does not permit you to create a proper corral, then what about creating a more temporary run or "play pen," accessed directly from the horse's stable? As with a larger pen, barriers must be safe and sturdy, but there are various options such as electric fencing, moveable drop-in posts, and slip-rails. Although not real turnout, this arrangement at least offers the stabled horse a chance to make his own choices about being in or out. It is a good way of multiplying the space available by three or four times with very little effort on your part.

An Ideal Arrangement

From everyone's point of view, an ideal arrangement is a large yard opening onto an outside pen which, in turn, accesses pasture. Horses can then be kept in small, amenable groups and are able to choose where they want to be. Meanwhile, owners have the option of closing off access to the field during bad weather or when the horses need to be kept in, knowing they still have plenty of space in the pen and undercover in the yard to move about.

Air Flow

Fitting a chain across the doorway allows the door to be left open on mild days as well as for grooming and other activities. It also creates a greater sense of space and improves air flow.

Considering its benefits and the savings to be made on labor, time, and costs, it's a great pity that the open barn system is not more widely used.

Spatial Awareness

When judging the amount of living space a horse needs, try to look through equine rather than human eyes. As prey animals, horses value their personal space much more highly than we do. Being social animals too, the whole space issue is a complex one.

Isolation is a major cause of stress because any horse on his own cannot help but feel vulnerable. Whether he is in a stable or separated from his companions in the field, few horses choose to be by themselves.

Too close a contact, however, brings its own fears. Depending on individual personality and self-confidence, the personal space most horses like to preserve around them is an oval area of about 33 to 36 ft (10–12 m). With the exception of special friends (horse or human), anyone broaching that invisible boundary without invitation will be

A storage building can be used as a safe exercise area.

219

viewed as a potential security threat and will provoke either avoidance or defensive action.

The first-choice escape option is always flight—moving away from trouble. It follows that a horse can only relax completely when he knows that route is open to him, whether the perceived threat comes from humans or from another horse in the group. Hence, the aggression often seen in overly confined horses forced to be constantly on their guard against violations against their security zone. Confinement too close to other animals can, therefore, be as great a source of stress as separation.

Creating a Happy Herd

Herd living satisfies many of a horse's natural survival needs. Horses also like an easy life and don't go looking for trouble. As long as there is plenty of space and food for all, any group will usually settle down and exist contentedly together—after all, horses want to belong to a group.

In the wild, where herds roam freely, food is everywhere, and affiliations within the group develop naturally over time; cooperation is the name of the game. Maintaining a similarly successful "herd" at home is down to recreating this scenario as far as possible in your field. Just as in the wild, a settled group with sufficient living resources for all will generally get along well, with problems being a rarity.

That is not to say everyone in the herd is equal, whether we're talking mustangs or down at the boarding yard. Keeping things ticking along happily does require some human input and understanding of herd dynamics. Three main principles are involved:

Hierarchy: As in human life, horse society has pushy folks and folks who get pushed, with every shade of character in between. Wild horse groups all feature a leader and hierarchy of underlings ranked by self-confidence and assertiveness (age obviously playing its part in a mixed-age group or in the wild). Once the positions on the ladder are worked out, everyone settles down, secure in that knowledge.

Try to judge living space through your horse's eyes.

When competition for scarce resources (such as food or space) starts, tensions surface. So, it is important not only to reduce any competition, but also to be aware of who is leader and the rankings of individuals in order to avoid stirring up trouble unwittingly.

Friendships: Status is not the only sorting factor at work. A group is also bound by a complicated network of friendships and affiliations, likes and dislikes, as in human society. Some personalities will clash and choose to avoid each other. Others will strike up an affinity, with most horses forming an especially close bond with one other individual whom they will allow to graze very closely or indulge in mutual grooming with. This is known as pair bonding.

Knowing who your horse's friends are (and are not) is crucial to managing a happy herd. Clearly, putting individuals who don't get along into a small field together or in neighboring stables creates

Time Out

unnecessary stress. Likewise, a sense of reassurance and security is provided by keeping good friends together. Creating overdependence does occur, often inadvertently, particularly with less confident individuals. Be aware of this, and take precautions by ensuring that close friends become used to periods of separation.

Introductions: Introductions are important to horses. Many cases of bullying or an inability to settle are due to this crucial meeting-and-greeting phase being rushed or badly handled. Newcomers must be thoroughly sized up by the whole group before being accepted and allowed to find their place within it. Touch, smell, and body language are all vital parts of this assessment, which takes time and inevitably involves some sparring before being settled to everyone's satisfaction.

The process can be smoothed by grazing the newcomer in an adjacent paddock or fenced-off area (see below) at first, then introducing an easy-going, medium-to-high ranking horse to his patch until a

bond has formed before allowing the two access to the main group.

Difficulties that do arise with horses turned out together are often due to either personality clashes or pressure on resources. Admittedly, it is easier when you have control over the whole situation in your own field, but most socialization problems do have a solution. If you keep your horse at a boarding yard, try to discuss options with your yard owner rather than accept a situation that is stressing your horse or putting his safety at risk.

Common Problems
Constant Bickering or Inability to Settle Down

Most groups settle down within a week if given sufficient space and food and the chance to stabilize.

If sufficient food and space is available, a group of horses will coexist happily.

Sometimes a horse will appear isolated from the herd. If your horse is obviously unhappy in the field, look for the underlying reason.

Squabbles that go on longer are usually due to insufficient area per horse (in which case, either provide more room or reduce the group size), too much change, or particularly difficult individuals.

Turning out a different mix of individuals each day, constantly adding new faces or taking away old friends, as happens in many big yards, ignores all the horses' needs for security and stability. It dismisses the length of time required to create this stability, the complexity of equine relationships, and the etiquette of introductions—all so important to horse happiness.

Aggression at Feeding Time

Always create several more feeding stations than there are horses in the field, siting them well apart (remember personal space), and allowing the leader access to food first. This gives lesser-ranked horses a chance to eat their fill in peace. If an individual is still picked on, remove him from the others at mealtimes (see also Bullying).

Handling the Bully

Games can get boisterous, so watch for any serious and prolonged rough behavior, rather than overly enthusiastic play. Out-and-out aggression is unusual and most frequently is the result of the aggressor feeling insecure and defensive rather than dominant. Separate the offender into his own area (electric fencing is useful for this) for as long as it takes him to become completely settled in his new safe haven.

Time Out

This means showing no signs of aggression toward horses approaching on the other side of the fence (which may take a month or more).

Gradually increase the size of his area before moving on to introduce an amenable but confident (medium-ranked) horse to his area for several weeks until these two bond. Then allow them to graze with the rest of the group for short but increasing periods until the bully is fully reintegrated.

The Bullied or Self-Isolating Horse

Horses who get bullied are often those who have never had a proper social education as youngsters—perhaps they were kept by themselves or in a single-age group with others more dominant than themselves. A horse who has not learned the right signals back in adolescence that allowed him to be accepted or to take a place in a group gives off all the vibes of insecurity, making him easy prey for a bully or forcing him to the outskirts of the herd.

The bullied horse needs his own separate safety zone—again, temporary electric fencing is ideal. Graze the highest-ranking available herd member in an adjacent area until the two have become friends (i.e., are happy to graze close together, touch each other, etc.). Then allow both into the same space. When they have fully bonded, reintroduce the pair to the main group, where the confident horse will provide security and protection to the shy one.

Walking the Fence or Standing Alone

If a horse just stands by the gate or walks the fence, think first: Is he cold, is he hungry, or, alternatively, where is his friend? Miserable horses will stand still, hunched up, away from the rest. If you see this, question the horse's behavior, and take action to remedy the cause. Compulsive fence walkers are almost always missing their bosom buddy. Anxieties must be managed by carefully getting the horse used to the idea that separation is no threat.

If a horse has a tendency to bully, he should be separated from the group.

Chapter Twenty-Five

Field Issues

*I*t is a lucky owner whose horse lives in the perfect field, surrounded by pristine plank fencing, grass at its optimum all year round, shady trees, and a purpose-built shelter for protection against wind and weather. Most of us have to compromise, and it is important to remember that, as long as it meets all the essential safety requirements, any kind of turnout is better than none.

Obviously, the more time your horse spends outdoors, and the more he depends on grazing as his principal food source, the closer to the ideal you are, both in terms of environment and pasture quality. Certain features, such as safe fencing, a clean water supply, and some form of shelter, should be considered essentials for all turnout areas, even those only occupied for a few hours a day.

The most unpromising piece of land can be improved with investment of a little time, cash, and some thought put into ongoing management. If you are worried about the way the field at your boarding yard is used or managed, then it's time for a re-think, particularly if your horse lives out all or most of the time.

Horse owners must make the best use of outdoor space that is available.

Fencing and Gates

Field boundaries must be safe, solid, and secure. Horses will lean over to reach a tasty-looking clump of grass. They will stick their head into a gap in the hedge or wire, or get a foot through and pull it out a bit too quickly. When it comes to fencing, imagine an accident that could potentially happen involving a horse and a fence—it will have happened at some point to someone.

Guidelines for Reducing Risk

Safety issues should be monitored and maintained regularly:

- Avoid strands of wire or squared pig/sheep wire if at all possible. The safest fencing for horses is either (or a combination of) well-constructed and maintained wooden or plastic post-and-rail, solid hedging, or purpose-designed horse wire or stud tape.
- If wire must be used, keep it taut.
- Fencing must be high enough to prevent jumping out. The bottom rail or strand should not be so low that a hoof could get trapped between it and the ground.
- Slightly rickety or weak lengths of fence must be backed up by a line of secondary fencing (electric fence is useful for this).

- Lines separating adjacent fields both containing horses must be solid and safe enough to withstand the inevitable bickering over the fence. To keep horses well apart, create an inner fence about 4 ft (1.2 m) away. For temporary separation (e.g., during introductions, sorting out relationship problems, or when restricting grazing), electric fencing is practical, flexible, and cost-effective. Buy a type designed for horses rather than smaller animals, and use at least two strands of wide, high-visibility tape—the top one at around 40 in (1 m) from ground level, the lower at 20 in (50 cm). Check twice daily to be sure that electric fencing is operating properly, and always have a charged battery on standby.
- Check daily for weak spots, protruding nails, breakages, or the thin areas in hedges, which often emerge in the fall. Repair immediately or create an additional barrier if necessary.
- Discourage leaners, bottom rubbers, and other fence wreckers safely by putting up an inner electric-fence boundary to keep them away. Although some people fix a strand of barbed wire

along the top of the fence for this purpose, this rarely deters a determined customer wearing a blanket. Generally, the only result is a shredded blanket.

• Keep gates securely attached and properly fitted so that they are easy to use. When the temperatures are subzero, you are late for work, and your horse is dancing around on the end of his lead rope, you do not want to be struggling with an awkward gate.

• Ditches can fill up and become invisible after heavy snow falls. Horses have been known to get into difficulties in an unseen ditch, so be aware of this danger if your field boundaries include ditches or other potential hazards that might be covered by snow, such as a pond.

Fencing must be high enough to prevent jumping out and should always be kept in good repair. Electric fencing can be used to back up existing, substandard fencing.

Water

Whether it means a self-filling, galvanized trough connected to the main water supply, a hose connected to an old bathtub, or taking buckets to the field, horses at pasture must have a constant supply of fresh water. Ponds or streams are not generally adequate and have too many hazards associated with them; they are best fenced off securely.

Potential autumn/winter watering problems include:

• Troughs clogging up with fallen leaves and other debris. Clear these out regularly and check that the ballcock or filling mechanisms are working.

• Algae can build up even in winter, especially on recycled white bathtubs, so empty and scrub them out every few weeks.

• During severe frosts, water will freeze solid and ice may need breaking thoroughly several times a day, certainly at least twice. Keep a close eye on water levels. In these conditions, horses can easily get dehydrated. Floating a heavy rubber ball in the water can help slow the freezing and create a small space in the ice where water can be reached. Insulate water buckets in field shelters or out in the open by putting them inside an empty plastic feed bag stuffed with straw and tied around the rim. Place the bucket in an old tire.

Shelter

Horses and ponies grow extremely effective insulating winter coats that, together with blankets (if necessary), are perfectly capable of keeping them comfortable in the kind of low temperatures we would find unacceptably cold.

What is more important than trying to overcompensate for the cold is to give protection against

Constant access to a fresh water supply is essential.

nearest roof. So, giving them the chance to stay out, but with some protection, is doing them a real favor.

Field-kept horses will be exposed to weeks and months of the sort of prolonged wind and rain they hate most, so they must be given the opportunity to take respite under more effective weatherproof cover, such as a proper shed-type shelter. That is not to say the horses will always choose to use it, most preferring less "trappy" natural shelter from the elements if it is available.

However, an open-fronted shed does provide somewhere the horse can dry out, stand in more warmth and comfort, and where you can feed hay and provide a dry bed. It will also have the advantage of being able to double-up as stabling if your outdoor horse needs to be brought in for any reason.

wind and wet. If you see horses and ponies huddled up against the rails of a bare, exposed field, desperate for the tiny amount of protection it can afford, you quickly realize the importance of providing shelter.

Free-living feral horses are able to make their own choices about where they graze, and they can seek shelter whenever and wherever they feel need for it, whether that's under a tree or in the lee of a thick hedge or bank. Field-kept horses are totally dependent on what is available within the confines of their field, so effective shelter needs careful thought, particularly for exposed fields with little natural protection.

When assessing a field's suitability, give preference to one offering plenty of its own sheltering opportunities. Where these don't exist, create some; a solid 8 ft (2.4 m) tall windbreak either constructed in an X-shape, or at least positioned to protect against the prevailing wind, is easy to erect and will be much appreciated. Instinct will drive most horses to choose to remain out in the open in weather that would certainly find us rushing for the

When thinking about erecting and using a field shelter, follow these guidelines:

- Site the building carefully, with its back to the prevailing wind. Take into account the field's drainage and ease of access. Avoid overhanging trees or creating a narrow gap between a shelter and fence, which could trap a horse.
- Make sure it is large enough for all the inhabitants of the field to use at the same time without feeling threatened. Entrances must be high and wide.
- If you are building a shelter yourself, make it strong. In addition to the climate, it has to withstand its occupants kicking, rubbing, and leaning against it.
- Angle the roof and use guttering to catch rain runoff. Allow plenty of roof space. Check regularly for dangers, such as protruding nails or broken windows.
- To encourage good use of a shelter, provide a decent supply of hay in there. Horses are programmed to keep chewing throughout most of

Horses will find any natural shelter available. A purpose-built shelter may be needed in a field with an exposed location.

care skills. Without any attention from you (or your yard owner), your horse's pasture will certainly degenerate into little more than a bare exercise area, any grass not only devoid of feed value but also possibly "horse-sick" and actually bad for his health.

The problem with grass is that it is not standard all year round. Spring and early summer grass shoots up like a torpedo and is packed full of water and carbohydrates. Too much grass is more likely to be a problem than too little at these times of the year. But as summer turns to fall, and the fiber content in grass increases, its nutritional value drops. Once the average ambient temperature drops below 42.8°F (6°C), grass simply stops growing altogether. Meanwhile, of course, the horses in the field go on eating at just the same rate.

Failure to manage the excesses and shortages that this changing growth pattern produces is the cause of most pasture management problems for horse owners.

In addition to eating, your horse and his companions also go on walking about, playing, cantering around, and hanging out by the gate during the winter—seemingly in a concerted effort to turn their precious dinner plate into deep mud.

The good news is that a bit of effort put into your pasture will pay dividends in what you and your horse get back from your grass. With planning and the help of a friendly neighborhood farmer or agricultural agent with the right machines for the job, you will find keeping grassland healthy becomes a routine part of your horse-care year. Even boarding-yard clients can improve the pasture their horses graze by optimizing the use of fields.

their day (see Feeding). This will drive them out in appalling weather to continue to graze, rather than standing for hours in a shelter that offers no opportunity to eat.

- Treat a shelter much like a regular stable. Clear droppings out and add fresh bedding several times a week. In the spring, have a good cleanout.
- Check classified ads and farm sales for second-hand shelters.

Pasture Management

Because few of us have access to vast tracts of grazing land, making the most of what you've got is one of the most vital and, unfortunately, neglected of all horse-

General guidelines for managing your pasture are as follows:

- The ideal to aim for is an even pasture of palatable grasses with no weedy areas and no defined lawns (where horses continually graze) and roughs (toilet areas full of rank, sour grasses).
- As a general rule of thumb, if pasture is to form the basis of the diet, allow a minimum of 1.5 acres (0.6 h) for the first horse, and 1 acre (0.4 h) per horse after that. That said, the better looked after the land is, the more horses it can support. Ponies, also, will do well on less grazing than larger animals.
- Depending on the number of horses who have to use it, divide up your grazing into at least two separate areas. Make one in the driest part of the field (to be used in the wettest weather), and the other the wettest part (to be used at drier times).
- Get the optimum from each area by rotating its use if possible:
  - grazing by cattle or sheep (susceptible to different worms to horses, these effectively "vacuum" the pasture, eating weeds and rank grass previously left untouched)
  - harrowing (which aerates the soil, helps gather dead grass, and disperses droppings to dry out)
  - rolling (to iron out any ruts and press healthy roots into the soil)
  - grazing by horses
  - mowing (cutting to maintain the grass at an ideal length of about 3 in [8 cm] and encourage greater density of growth) and, in spring, fertilizing if necessary
  - resting for at least 6 weeks (either with the grass left to grow, or in spring, for hay to be made)
- Control the worm burden by picking up droppings at least twice weekly, cross-grazing with other livestock, harrowing in dry weather, and resting pasture as much as possible. Use an effective deworming program, and deworm all horses before turning out on to clean pasture.
- Have soil and grass analyzed every 2 to 3 years for pH and nutrient levels. This is the only way you will ever know for sure whether any mineral

The area around a gate always gets churned up.

deficiencies are present, and how best to remedy these so that grass growth improves and provides better year-round nutrition for your horse. Analysis is particularly important if you take hay off your own field. The cost is recouped in the long term because you are able to target deficiencies. Your local feed merchant or agricultural extension office will be able to carry out analyses.

- Make drainage a priority, particularly in areas with clay-based soils. Once horses' feet have damaged grass and soil structure, weeds are quick to take over. Keeping a deep, strong root system will help grass withstand damage and wick away moisture.

Field Issues

Soil Testing

Soil testing must be arranged in February to determine whether fertilizer or lime will be needed for the next month. For optimum growth, the pH level should be 6 to 6.5.

Winter Pasture

Pasture management in winter is an exercise in damage-limitation. Prevent or minimize poaching by doing the following:

- Divide the field (see above). Utilize the best-drained part of your land in winter. If necessary, be prepared to write off a section of field to preserve the rest. This allows all horses some daily liberty, and the area can be rolled and reseeded in spring.
- Avoid overstocking. The more space available per horse, the less the ground is going to suffer. In a large yard, smaller groups of horses can be let out in turn for shorter periods.
- Site areas where the horses tend to stand around, such as the gate, trough, shelter, and feeding stations, in the best-drained parts of the field and, if possible, move them regularly.
- Create hard-standing areas at gates, using concrete, stone, or gravel (see below). Even an old rubber-backed carpet laid down before poaching gets too bad can help.
- Avoid riding in the field when it is wet.
- Limit the spread of poached areas by focusing on improving drainage there.

Drainage

Grass cannot grow in cold, wet conditions, and marshy land produces notoriously bad, coarse grazing.

The action required to improve drainage depends on the position and type of soil you are dealing with. There is not much you can do across the whole field, but bear in mind that, to be effective, drainage depends on the water having somewhere to drain to. Simply putting down chalk, gravel, or class I sand onto saturated ground is not enough.

- Make sure all existing drainage routes are clear of vegetation. Organize regular ditch-clearing parties, particularly in the fall.
- In badly affected areas, consider:

Ditches: These should be within your own boundaries, fenced off, and not sited near underground cables or pipes.

Mole-drains: Tiny drains created just beneath the surface by a metal cylinder dragged through the soil by a tractor. Good for clay soil.

Subsoiling: A tractor attachment drives deep blades into the subsoil, breaking up hardened pans of earth that are preventing free drainage.

Soak-Aways: Create a gravel-filled soak-away, covered by a free-draining layer (which will need regularly topping off).

Divide up your grazing so that horses use the best-drained area during the wettest months.

A field where a lot of horses are kept together is bound to suffer.

Drainage work is likely to involve heavy machinery, so tackle it in the spring rather than deep midwinter. Aim to create at least one dry-standing area that the horses can take advantage of if they choose, topped either by concrete or some paving slabs.

Maximizing Grazing Areas

In winter, maximizing grazing areas becomes crucial:

- Pick up droppings at least every 48 hours, so toilet patches where the horses won't eat aren't allowed to spread over most of the field.
- Chain harrow when a bright, dry spell comes along. In milder, moister conditions, avoid harrowing because it only spreads viable worm eggs around, although ultraviolet (UV) sunlight will kill the larvae. Tractors can do a lot of damage to wet fields, however, so wait until March to start your pasture-resuscitation plans in earnest.
- In barns where a large number of horses are housed, think about how groups are segregated to optimize available grazing. For example, even out numbers rather than having a large group of geldings in one field and a couple of mares in another.

Security in the Field

Long, dark winter nights were invented for thieves. Horse-related crimes are increasing at an alarming rate, and not only in areas close to towns and cities. Taking some simple security measures makes sense. Thieves will always go for the easy pickings first, so the harder you make their task, the more likely they are to move on to a softer target and leave your horse and belongings alone.

Simple but effective security measures include:

- Keep fencing in good repair.
- Put padlocks and chains on both ends of the gate, or turn over the top hinge so the gate cannot be lifted straight off.
- Avoid leaving halters on horses.
- Security-mark horses, and put up clear signs

warning this has been done. Microchipping and freeze-branding are the most permanent marking methods, although branding the feet is also effective. For maximum deterrent effect, paint the horse's ID number in large figures/letters on all blankets or use blanket badges supplied by the security-marking companies. Remember to keep freeze marks clipped so they remain visible in a winter coat.

Many a heartless thief has thought nothing of ripping a valuable blanket off a field-kept horse, leaving him shivering. Again, permanently marking your property will lessen its appeal.

Horses at Grass

Keeping a horse or pony in the field for the winter is certainly not as labor intensive as keeping one mainly stabled or on a half-and-half regime. On the other hand, there is more to successful wintering out than throwing a bale of hay over the fence each morning on the way to work.

Routine Tasks

Whatever the weather, visit the field at least morning and evening. If there are no buildings in the field, a small shed or water-tight chest can hold your rubber boots, waterproofs, rubber gloves, and other items.

Each Visit:
- Catch your horse.
- Check your horse over for general well-being, injuries, and signs of illness.
- Pick out feet.
- Remove and replace blankets. Simply adjusting the blanket may do during a strong gale, but you should never leave the same blanket on for days at a time (or longer) without taking it off, shaking it out, and replacing it. Think of your horse's comfort—would you like to wear one set of clothes for 5 months at a time? In prolonged rain, check that wet has not soaked through to the lining; if it has, have a clean, dry blanket on standby.

The field-kept horse can be a vulnerable target for thieves. Catch your horse every time you visit the field and check him over.

- Do a quick once-over of the state of the field, water supply, and fencing.
- Give hay and/or concentrated feed.

Each Weekend:
- Take more time to walk round the field, checking the fencing and picking up any litter that might have blown or been thrown in, and picking up droppings.
- Do any repairs.

Chapter Twenty-Six

Keeping Warm

Nature has equipped your horse to handle the cold. Even fine-bred types have the ability to grow a very respectable winter coat if conditions demand it and they are given the chance. Those with cold-blood ancestry (that is, native and draft types) can produce winter coats that a polar bear would be proud of.

Body Temperature

Maintaining body temperature comes down to two main factors: heat and insulation, just like keeping a house warm. First, the body must create plenty of heat, which it does by utilizing and processing its feed and by constantly moving. It must then minimize heat loss, which depends on insulation provided by layers of fat beneath the skin and the dense, long hairs of the winter coat and a full mane and tail. A thick coat can insulate a horse at temperatures well below freezing— just how effective this is can be seen in the layers of snow found sitting on a hairy pony's back long after a snowfall.

It isn't the cold, but the combination of wind and prolonged rain that saps warmth. Although horses will help themselves as much as possible by turning their backs to the wind and grazing in the more sheltered parts of the field, once a winter coat is wet through, its insulating properties are lost. The body is forced to dig deeper and deeper into its reserves to keep its temperature up.

Nothing makes weight and condition drop off a horse quicker than being cold. And, of course, if we take away his natural insulation by reducing fat layers (either by inadequate feeding or for fitness purposes) and clipping away his coat, then we must provide a replacement in the form of blankets.

What can we do to help boost our horse's natural resistance to cold so that he stays warm in all weathers and can maintain condition?

• Provide a diet high in fiber. Digestion of roughage in the hindgut provides the majority of slow-burning body heat, which is effectively the horse's own "central heating."

A thick coat provides excellent insulation.

• Provide shelter to give him the choice of getting out of the weather and drying off.
• Avoid unnecessary clipping and trimming.
• Put on a carefully selected blanket and/or neck cover.
• Help a cold horse to warm up quickly by gently rubbing his ears with your hands or a dry towel.
• Muscular effort raises the body temperature rapidly and effectively. So, for quick warming, get the horse moving.
• Remove ice completely from troughs and buckets whenever possible. A cold horse doesn't need internal refrigeration from drinking iced water.

To Blanket or Not to Blanket?

Whether or not to blanket a horse who lives out all the time is a point of debate. Owners must weigh up the pros and cons and use their judgment and common sense in deciding what best suits their particular horse's situation.

Advantages

A blanketed horse stays cleaner and is therefore easier to manage if used in regular work. As long as the blanket fits well and is waterproof, it will provide an extra layer that reduces heat loss and keeps condition on by helping the horse retain insulating fat deposits.

Disadvantages

Allowed to grow a full coat and given sufficient food and shelter, most horses and ponies can cope perfectly well without a blanket. A blanket, particularly if it is heavy, flattens air pockets created in a natural coat to keep the horse warm. If the blanket gets wet, it takes far longer to dry than the coat itself, making it more of a hindrance than a help to warmth. No blanket means no rubs or discomfort. There are savings on money and on time spent adjusting/replacing

Keeping Warm

The advantage of blanketing is that mud goes on the blanket rather than on your horse.

one who can really feel the approaching cold.

Checking Warmth

Warmth needs checking at every visit to the field. A very cold horse is easy to spot because he will be hunched up in the best shelter he can find and may possibly even be shivering. This is a miserable horse who must be brought under cover to dry off and given extra protection if bad weather is set to continue. A blanket that is soaked through is doing more harm than good and needs replacing immediately with a dry one.

The best way to tell if a horse is slightly cold is to feel the base of the ears, which should always be warm. The tips are less reliable indicators of body temperature—on a cold or wet day, these extremities are always going to feel damp or chilled.

Blanketed horses can still get cold if their protection is inadequate. Put your hand down inside the shoulder, chest, and flank areas of the blanket. The coat should feel warm and cozy, but not clammy, which would indicate overblanketing for the weather conditions.

Use your common sense about blankets, and be flexible day-to-day. If you decide to wrap up your horse from October onward, be aware that the same blanket does not have to stay on until April—even January or February can have mild days. By putting just as many layers on a horse on a 54°F (12°C) day as on a 28°F (–2°C) day, you are not only making him sweaty and uncomfortable, but you are stopping him from getting the full benefit from the blanket in very cold weather.

Listening to the weather forecast first thing every morning is a good habit to get into if you want to blanket your horse appropriately for the day.

Build up a wardrobe that caters to varying conditions, and change blankets as necessary. On a

blankets each day, and there are also benefits to the health of the skin.

Overprotecting cobby and draft-type horses and ponies can mean they hang on to layers of fat that they would otherwise use up to keep warm, making them vulnerable to obesity when the spring grass comes.

As a general rule, it is probably true to say that most horses and ponies with draft blood can winter out happily without a blanket. Thinner-skinned types, such as those with Thoroughbred or Arab in them, are almost certain to be better off with the added protection of a blanket, as are horses who feel the cold and are less able to deal with it, such as seniors.

If you are unsure, leave your horse unclipped and see how he copes unblanketed. Keep a careful eye on his condition, feed plenty of hay, and provide shelter, and you may be surprised by how well he does. If you are concerned, go for the blanket.

Bear in mind that a horse who is kept in a lot during the late summer and fall, or blanketed early, won't provide himself with as thick a winter coat as

*Check the base of the ears—
they should always be warm.*

*Check under the blanket—the
coat should feel warm to the touch.*

mild day, your horse might be able to go without a blanket, and the fresh air will do his coat good. If you can't face the resulting mud, opt for a lighter weight turnout blanket that day. On colder days, having a supply of underblankets means you can add warmth as required.

Budget for spares too, even if your horse only goes out for short periods, and keep them handy at the barn or in the car. Any turnout blanket can come to grief, although a well-fitting one is less likely to cause trouble. Some horses are notorious escape artists, whereas others think it a huge joke to pull blankets off their field mates. Avoid the situation in which you arrive one freezing, soaking day to find your horse naked and his blanket trampled in the ditch with no spare at hand.

Choosing Blankets

Never before has the owner had so much choice in genuinely horse-friendly gear for his outdoor equine. Most horses would agree that the advances in the

choice and quality of turnout blankets is one of the best things to have happened in the entire history of horse care.

There is no excuse for the once commonplace sight of horses and ponies living, day in day out, in a canvas straitjacket that leaks along the back seam, becomes sodden during the first downpour of fall, drags around their shoulders with every step, and is fastened excruciatingly tightly round their middles with a thin belly surcingle.

Canvas or Synthetic?

Waxed canvas outdoor blankets (known as New Zealand rugs) are still on the market, and those in the medium-to-high price range have now incorporated many design improvements, providing a more streamlined fit and fewer seams to increase weatherproofing. For turnout a few hours during the day, they can be perfectly adequate if comfortable and reproofed yearly. But for permanent wear, canvas cannot compete with the new synthetic turnout blankets. When wet, canvas is extremely heavy and unwieldy to handle and, even with a wool lining, it can never be as warm and insulating as synthetic materials.

Today's turnout blankets are designed and built to be comfortable and provide effective weather protection, so they can potentially be worn 24 hours a day for 6 or more months of the year, taking the worst that the weather and the horse can throw at them.

Selecting Blankets to Buy

Although buying the best you can afford applies to virtually everything to do with horses, it is particularly true with blankets. Turnout blankets must take an incredible amount of punishment. Potentially, a blanket is going to be worn almost permanently for months, being ground into the mud, rubbed up against fences, galloped about in, not to mention being wet much of the time. Through all of this, the blanket must keep your horse warm and dry and not cause him any discomfort.

So there are no bargains to be had in blanket buying. Good blankets are expensive because they incorporate all the advances of modern technology in fabric design, are made to last, and are made to fit. Cheaper ones will have made a degree of compromise on one or more of these areas. When you compare a waterproof riding/walking jacket for human wear with the demands placed on a turnout blanket, and the fabric and work involved in making it, the price of the blanket is a very good value indeed.

An upscale blanket will give you durability and flexibility for your money. Everything, from the fabric to the seams and fittings will be tougher and last longer. The blanket will be designed to fit a horse's shape, but allow freedom to move and graze. Fewer and taped seams mean leaks are eliminated or kept to a minimum. Modern fabrics are lightweight and warm, but also tough, versatile, and very clever.

In addition to being waterproof, most are breathable. They prevent perspiration beneath the blanket by wicking moisture up and through the fabric for it to evaporate into the air without chilling

the horse, while the outer fabric remains waterproof. Thus, the horse can still regulate his own body temperature to a large extent, just as if he was only wearing his own coat. If the weather turns mild, he will not overheat. You can also put a breathable blanket on a horse damp from rain or sweat after exercise, and he won't suffer any ill effects, which is a real time-saver.

Different weights of synthetic turnout blanket can provide different degrees of warmth, so, create a wardrobe based on one or two good blankets adequate for the worst possible conditions, but also include a lighter weight version.

Canvas blankets provide some protection, but they can be cumbersome.

Synthetic blankets are light and breathable.

fingers, and choose those that won't be prone to clogging up with mud. Fastenings range from conventional buckles, metal T's and trigger clips, to various snap-shut versions in metal or plastic. Although metal clips may rust eventually, they generally last longer than plastic ones, which can become brittle and split over time.

Of course, the most expensive blanket in the shop will not be as effective as it could be, or as comfortable, unless you take the time and trouble to make sure it fits your horse. Whatever blanket you buy, it must be shaped to fit a real horse (the cheap ones aren't necessarily!), and it must fit *your* horse. Before buying a blanket, take measurements, and don't be afraid to ask if you can try a blanket on before buying, using a thin summer sheet underneath to keep it clean in case you need to return it. You are making a big investment, so it's worth getting it right.

Blankets are sold in sizes according to length from the point of the chest to the buttock, usually in 3 in (8 cm) increments, but dimensions will also vary between makes and styles in other important areas.

Take your horse's measurements from:
- chest to the furthest point of the buttock
- withers to the dock
- withers to just above the knee
- withers to the front of the chest, across the shoulder

The horse's blanket must be deep enough to keep rain out and drafts away from the vulnerable belly, and it must extend far enough over the tail to protect the dock area. It must lie on the shoulder snugly enough to prevent seepage, but not so tightly as to restrict movement or cause rubbing.

Blanket Rubs

Because the outdoor horse is almost constantly on the move, any friction will soon start to rub off hair and even cause real soreness. Areas most prone to

A huge variety exists in fittings design, including surcingles that cross under the belly, front and back leg straps only, a spider-arrangement of straps, and all combinations in between. A well-shaped and fitted blanket will be self-righting and needs less securing than you may imagine. Straps should be fully and easily adjustable, without bulky buckles that might dig into the horse when he lies down or rolls. Your horse may prefer or dislike certain arrangements—some, for example, are not keen on rear leg straps. The only no-no is any girth-type surcingle, which puts constant pressure on the spine.

With fasteners, go for those that you know will be easy to do up and undo, even with numb, frozen

Choosing and Fitting a Blanket

- Give adequate length for good protection right over the dock. A tail flap helps, particularly for horses permanently outdoors. Too long a blanket will slip, and dangling straps can easily catch a leg.

- Seams should be waterproofed and kept to a minimum. Avoid seams along the back—any leakage here soon wets the whole horse.

- Allow lots of depth to keep the weather out. For wide-barreled horses, ask for extra-deep fitting.

- Surcingles should be broad and easy to adjust. Make sure no twists are present. The correct fit allows a hand to be turned sideways between the strap and the body. Avoid overtightness or fastening too loosely, which risks the horse getting a leg tangled in the strap.

- Tailoring around the quarters keeps out drafts and allows movement.

- The fit at the chest must keep out drafts, but not cut into the base of the neck as the horse grazes. Too loose here, and the blanket will slip back and potentially cause sores. Go for tough, user-friendly fastenings. Well-placed gussets or darts are the key here.

- The fit around the withers must be snug but not tight.

- Shoulders can be a tricky area to fit. The seam should lie flat against the skin to keep wet out, but allow the horse to move freely and not tighten as he lowers his head.

- Look for a design that is shaped along the back.

rubbing are the withers, shoulders, chest, points of the hips, and inside of the thighs (from overtight straps). Friction at the withers can even break the skin, causing a painful sore that is easily infected and may damage nerves.

Thin and sensitive-skinned horses, and those with a certain shoulder conformation, are most vulnerable, but any rubbing should be taken as a sign of a blanket-fit problem that needs urgent action.

Solutions include:
- Change the blanket to one that fits better in the areas being rubbed.
- Opt for designs that are roomier around the shoulders, chest, and/or flanks. Some have an actual gusset here or are elasticized slightly around the neck.
- Styles that extend up the neck slightly take the blanket edge away from the line of the shoulder and the point of the withers, thereby reducing friction.
- Padding or lining the shoulder and wither edge with sheepskin or a satiny fabric can help. This must be kept free of irritating mud.
- Purpose-designed bibs or vests are available to fit beneath the blanket to protect the shoulder/chest area, or the blanket can be lined in these areas with a smooth fabric. However, no lining or vest should be used to make up for an overtight blanket.

Blanket Aversion

Always check fit first if a horse is giving out signals he does not want his blanket on. If the blanket is causing him discomfort, it is not surprising he is objecting to it. Where fit is not at fault, perhaps he is too hot in it. Once this has been checked out, another possibility to consider with a young horse, or one that is new to you, is that he has never been properly introduced to wearing a blanket before. In this case, you will need to go back to basics, gradually getting him used to the feel of having his body covered.

In rare cases, there may be more to a case of blanket aversion. Sensitive-skinned horses can sometimes react to the fabric used in the lining of their blanket. Wool, for example, may become itchy, or synthetic fabrics can create a buildup of static that feels like a never-ending case of pins and needles. You may need to think laterally, but there's always a reason. The ultimate solution is to take off the blanket, and change other aspects of management accordingly.

Covering the Neck

The advent of neck covers has allowed owners who would never previously have considered turning out their horse full-time, or even at all, to do so without fear of him getting cold and plastered in mud. Even a clipped animal can spend most (or all, with adequate shelter) of his time outdoors with the broad, muscular area of the neck kept cozy and clean. To me, a neck cover is well worth the investment.

Detachable Covers

Detachable covers come separately and either fit underneath the blanket, fastening around the chest or front legs, or clip to the blanket itself. The advantage here is that the blanket can be used without the neck cover on milder days.

The type that is open and fastens under the neck is much easier to use than one that has to be pulled on over the horse's head. This is asking for trouble at some point, even if the horse gets used to being in the dark while you struggle on tiptoes to get it over his ears. Avoid zips, which get clogged with mud and, once broken, render the whole thing useless.

Also, check to see if the cover is waterproof, water-resistant only, or neither. Each type is available, so choose the right one or a selection for different conditions. For warmth and water tightness, go for a cover custom designed to fit with your heavy-duty turnout blanket. A light synthetic fabric will be showerproof but give little warmth. The other common type on the market is made of stretch fabric and so clings more closely to the neck. This will resist a light shower and be warm when dry, but will soon be soaked through in a downpour.

Check regularly to ensure the blanket is not rubbing.

Keeping Warm

There is usually a good reason why a horse hates his blanket.

A word of warning about fit: A neck cover should be snug but not tight. It should be attached to the blanket so that it allows movement and neither pulls tight nor slips down onto the ears as the horse grazes. Designs that cover the entire head and even the ears, reaching halfway down the face, are not the great idea they seem at first glance for field use. Additional cover is minimal, yet even if carefully fitted at first, the risk of the cover getting dislodged or creeping up over one (or both) eyes, causing rubbing or outright panic is, to me, not even worth contemplating.

Integral Covers

Blanket manufacturers are now producing a range of designs to suit most budgets that incorporate a partial or full neck cover into the blanket itself. These don't give the flexibility of the detachable cover, but they require less adjusting during visits to the field.

Integral covers tend to be made of lighter fabric than the main part of the blanket, and they can ride back a little when the horse rolls, exposing more neck. Even so, they can add significantly to a blanket's warmth factor—and anything that keeps mud out of even part of the mane is welcome!

Adding Layers

Top-of-the-line modern blankets are very warm. It is generally better to invest in one thick, quality blanket than to put on lots of less effective layers of cheaper ones. Too many layers are awkward to handle, heavy to wear, and prone to slipping.

If you are going to add layers, use thinner blankets or a proper underblanket; plenty of options are available on the market. It's not enough to strap the kids' old comforter underneath.

Some manufacturers have gotten around the versatility issue by providing multilayer designs, which fasten together to provide varying degrees of warmth. They are expensive, but well worth it if you can afford it.

Chapter Twenty-Seven

Grooming the Field-Kept Horse

Field-kept horses get extremely dirty. There's simply no avoiding this fact. The frustration factor is certainly high when you have to remove layers of mud and dreadlocks from a mane before every ride. However, there are ways of cutting down on brushing time. Living out and owning a perfectly tidy and presentable horse need not be incompatible, so extra grooming effort should never be used as an excuse for not turning out your horse. When he buckles his knees to go down on that mud patch the minute you let go of the lead rope, try to take a deep breath and see the sheer satisfaction on his face rather than the hour's brushing that's going down in the dirt!

The good news is that it's not as necessary to groom outdoor horses as it is stabled ones. All-weather equines need every bit of protection they can get. Overly enthusiastic grooming strips the oil from the coat, which does them no favors at all. A healthy horse living outdoors on a balanced diet will have a healthy coat and skin beneath that mud coating and will not need any brushing.

For horses who must be made clean and tidy on a regular basis, the best solution is to keep the mud away with a well-fitting blanket that has an integral or detachable neck cover. Neck covers are one of the best inventions in horse care, saving many minutes of brushing while simultaneously providing additional warmth to a horse with a partly or fully clipped neck. With the neck and body covered, the legs, tail, and head only take a matter of minutes to clean.

Grooming Guidelines

- **Let it dry.** Only brush off dried mud. Attempting to brush the coat when it is wet not only doesn't work, but risks scratching vulnerable wet skin and introducing infection.
- **Minimize body brushing.** Muscled areas of the body are best cleaned using either a stiff dandy brush or rubber curry comb. Keep the body brush for use on the head and for a light flick over the body to finish off.
- **Stubborn mud.** For stubborn lumps of mud, particularly on sensitive areas such as under the belly, get working with your fingers. Stable management lore has it (and quite rightly) that a metal curry comb should never be used on a horse's body. But anyone who has faced the mud monster from Hell knows that there is nothing like a careful, gentle rub with the tips of the metal curry comb to shift huge lumps off the mane or body.
- **Manes and tails.** In the same way, a gentle body brushing is going to have next to no effect on a mane or tail hanging in muddy dreadlocks. Again, your fingers are your best tool, combined with a little judicious help from a curry comb or dandy brush, taking care to break as few hairs as possible.
- **Legs.** It's particularly important not to try to brush wet legs.

Neat and Tidy

In addition to the occasional tail wash, bathing is not advisable for a field-kept horse in winter (or indeed, any horse). Not only will it strip valuable oils from the coat, but the time it takes for the thick winter coat to dry is impractical, even with an insulating blanket to guard against chilling. A combination of keeping the mud at bay, brushing off what is there, and crafty presentation can give you an outdoor horse who will

Winter Issues

- Avoid turning out regularly in brushing boots in muddy conditions. Grit and wet beneath the boots creates perfect conditions for greasy heel. The exceptions are the purpose-designed breathable turnout boots now available.

- Always take gloves off to feel legs and feet. You can't sense any heat through gloves, nor can you feel a small cut or bump.

hold his own against any clipped and stabled companion—all without the need for a bath.

Although the horse's weather protection needs should always be put before glamour, field-kept horses can be tidied up with some trimming and pulling.

Mane and Tail

Manes should not be pulled to within a few inches of the crest, but can be shortened to a tidy and respectable length, especially if a neck cover is worn.

Hair at the dock helps funnel rainwater away and down the tail, so the tails of horses at grass should never be pulled. However, if your horse wears a blanket with a tail flap, you can take away a little of the bushiness here. Alternatively, practice your braiding; a neatly braided tail always looks professional.

Head

Trimming on the head should be confined to under the chin and around the edges of the ears. Long hairs around the eyes must certainly never be touched, and caring owners will leave all whiskers around the muzzle intact for the horse to be able to use them as

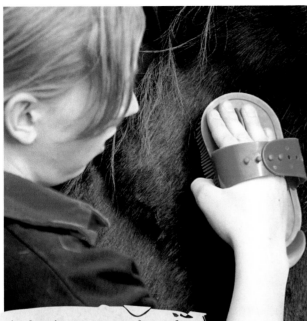

A plastic curry comb works wonders when mud has been allowed to dry.

Your fingers are the best tool for grooming through the tail.

nature intended, as invaluable touch sensors. But it is amazing what a difference trimming the beard off the jaw and taking the fluff off the edges of the ears can make. Never take hair out from inside the ears, which is vital for warmth and for protecting the sensitive inner ear. Gently press the edges together and trim off excess hair.

Legs

Cobby horses can be transformed by trimming off thick feathering on the lower legs. Debate continues about this because the very purpose of this long hair around the fetlocks is to drain water away from the vulnerable heels. However, in the conditions in which cold-blooded horses evolved, horses were free-living animals able to find dry areas in which to stand to allow legs to dry off regularly. Many horses today are kept in conditions in which they have no choice but to stand continuously in the wet. When fields are clay based, great blobs of mud end up hanging from the feathers, thus sealing in the dampness that infection thrives on.

Overall, from cosmetic, practical, and health points of view, trimming back the feathers allows air to circulate around the area and smartens up appearances. Trim carefully with a comb and scissors; clipping down the legs leaves the area too exposed and at risk for greasy heel and chapping if the horse lives outdoors.

Leg and Foot Care

Legs forced to stand about for long periods in wet grass or water-soaked soil are at high risk of skin problems. Once the skin is water-logged, it chaps and cracks easily, which is a perfect opportunity for moisture-loving bacteria to attack.

Make legs a focal point of your care routine, whether your horse is a type prone to greasy heel or not. A balanced diet, with all the correct vitamins and minerals, will help build his general defenses, but the most important preventative measure is to allow legs the chance to dry off as often as possible. For horses who come in at night to a clean, dry bed, this is less of an issue. But for those living out full-time, it means providing a hard standing area both in and outside

247

the field, and regular, thorough leg-drying (this could be a weekend job) to allow you to monitor the situation below the mud layer.

Mud

In dealing with mud, creating a barrier between legs and the wet by applying an oil-based cream (such as petroleum jelly, udder cream, or a zinc and castor oil product) has its advocates. However, it's not simply a case of slapping a handful of it on every morning. The cream must go onto clean, dry legs. Downsides of this tactic are that wet may get trapped next to the skin, and the skin is sealed away for long periods beneath a layer of grease. This soon becomes disgustingly mucky and is difficult to remove except by using cleansing cream.

Other owners religiously hose mud off before and after each ride. This does allow a clear look at what's going on at skin level, but because few people are prepared to spend the time necessary to dry the legs afterwards, the skin never gets the chance it needs to dry. If you do wash legs in winter, do so gently with warm water and dry them thoroughly afterwards using towels or a hairdryer. More practical, on a regular basis, is to let the horse stand in for a while until the mud on the legs dries, then carefully brush and pick it off with your fingers. Remember, never brush wet legs.

Snow

Horses can manage to be perfectly happy out in snow, provided that they have adequate food and shelter. However, deep snow will keep lower legs constantly wet, so be particularly vigilant about skin care during the winter months.

Concave feet aren't the best of designs to cope with snow, which quickly balls up in the sole, making the horse effectively walk on a set of very uncomfortable stilts.

Regular picking out (softening the ice first with warm water) and spreading thick grease into the soles both help to deter ice and snow from building

It is advisable to trim back the feathers on hairy horses.

up in this way, although won't prevent it completely. Again, a hard standing area that can be cleared of snow comes into its own here, giving the horse somewhere dry to stand where snow compacted in the feet will loosen and be knocked out.

Shoeing Options

A better ability to cope with snowy conditions is just one instance where unshod feet have the advantage over shod ones. Feet without shoes—provided that they are given regular attention from a farrier to keep them trimmed and in tip-top condition—will have stronger horn, better grip, and improved anti-concussive ability. Therefore, if your horse does little road work, it is well worth considering taking his shoes off for the winter months (and even all year round). Take care with your barefoot horse when the ground is hard and icy, though.

Grooming the Field-Kept Horse

Discuss different shoeing options for the winter if you plan to continue with a regular exercise program. Consider using:

- Fullered shoes if your horse does not already have these—the ridge gives better grip.
- Anti-slip road nails or studs—permanent studs with hard-wearing borium cores fitted to the branches of the shoe (on both sides, for balance).
- Foot pads for horses regularly working in heavy mud or snow—tough, polyurethane pads widely used in countries where snow is the norm. The ingenious tubular design fits inside a normal shoe. By compressing and expanding with the horse's movement, any buildup of snow or mud is squeezed out of the foot.

Weather conditions affect horses' feet. Excess moisture during long, wet spells can saturate and weaken the horn of the foot/horn wall and sole, making it more flexible and allowing the feet to grow misshapen if left too long between trims. This weakening is responsible for so many lost shoes in the fall and winter because the oozing mud is sucking shoes off.

If your horse comes in at night, he will have a chance to dry off.

Be as conscientious as ever about booking your farrier at least every 6 weeks in winter, even though your horse may be doing less work and his feet appear to grow less quickly than in summer. Worn shoes have poorer grip on slippery roads, and nails lost from shoes are easily buried in the mud ready to puncture a sole. Neglected feet are susceptible to invasion by bacteria through splits or through old and existing nail holes, particularly in the wet.

All outdoor horses need their feet picked out twice daily. It is tempting to skip this job when you are pressed for time, but cleaning the feet gives you a chance to check their condition. You must make sure no cuts or grazes are present on the coronary band, and assess the state of the hoof wall, sole, and frog.

Regular cleaning of the feet also prevents bacteria from infecting the horn. A sharp stone, thorn, or even a nail may have been picked up and pierced the sole; even gravel ground into the sensitive white line can cause no end to problems. Both situations can be easily avoided by daily cleaning out. You should also regularly wash the feet free of mud, which prevents the hoof wall and sole from breathing.

Horses can cope with snowy conditions as long as the snow does not get too deep.

249

Chapter Twenty-Eight

Winter Exercise

When we are knee deep in mud or muck, winter horse owning can feel more like a penance than a pleasure. Struggling with difficult weather and ground conditions and rushing to squeeze exercise into those ever-shrinking daylight hours also takes the edge off the fun of riding during the fall and winter months. But even when it seems as if you spend 10 hours mucking out or brushing off mud for every 1 hour in the saddle, to be out and about on one of those crisp, frosty mornings makes it all worthwhile—that's really living!

Take a Break?

Some owners choose the depths of winter to give their horse his annual vacation, and there is plenty of sense to this. Maybe he is working hard the remainder of the year and deserves well-earned rest and relaxation, both mental and physical. He may be a nervous type who needs frequent breaks from intense training. Or, perhaps it's you who needs the break, especially if you know you simply are not going to have the time to both exercise your horse and do all the necessary care jobs during the winter's shortest days.

In winter, there are times when horse owning can seem more of a penance than a pleasure.

You must ease into this less taxing regime gradually and see that your horse's "chill-out" time does not become his "get-chilled" time. Whatever his management system, he still requires twice-daily attention that includes blanketing and shelter and a maintenance diet that includes plenty of forage.

Shoes can be removed for horses taking a complete break, although your farrier might advise leaving front shoes on for extra support. Just because a horse is on vacation or has no shoes on does not mean feet can be forgotten. Clean feet out daily, trim regularly, and avoid the temptation to let shoes stay on longer, only to become dangerously loose.

Other owners may decide to ease work off a little, but avoid losing too much fitness by reducing ridden exercise but increasing turnout. This suits horses whose temperament suggests they never really relish a total layoff and also suggests conditioning for spring competitions will not take so long.

For other owners, winter is the busiest and best time of year, with a full schedule of indoor events

planned. For these, together with any horses kept mainly stabled, daily exercise is a must, regardless of weather conditions.

In fact, winter riding need not become a chore, whatever the climate throws at you. With some creativity and cooperation, many exercise alternatives are available to choose from without having to dig into your pocket too deeply.

Exercise Your Options

Lucky are the owners whose boarding barn gives them access to a decent, all-weather arena. If that includes you, do beware of restricting your horse's winter world to the walk between his stable and the ring, and the endless chasing of his own tail. Vary his exercise regime as much as possible, planning time schedules to allow for a trail ride or other activity at least once a week.

Winter Exercise

Winter Extras

- If your horse is stuck in the stable due to bad weather conditions, illness, or injury, use the time you would normally spend riding just being with him, grooming, massaging, or leading him out in-hand for some grass. Stretching exercises will help ease stiff limbs and benefit your riding work. Remember to reduce his concentrated feed, replacing it with forage.

- Stop a wet, muddy tail from flapping around and disturbing your horse in competitions by putting it up. Braid the tail, continuing the full length of the dock, and finishing by incorporating the whole length of the remaining tail. Roll up neatly to the end of the dock and stitch firmly. A bandage over the top will keep the tail completely clean, but make sure it's well secured.

- Winter conditions are tough on tack. Look after your saddlery by storing it at home rather than in a damp tack room and by cleaning it regularly and oiling it once a month. If leather tack gets rain-soaked, allow it to dry at room temperature (never in front of a fire or radiator), then use soap and oil to restore its flexibility.

The same goes for those in large yards where facilities include a horse walker. While these machines do admittedly provide a way of getting a horse out of his stable and on the move, any more soul-destroying pastime from the horse's point of view is hard to imagine. You only have to put yourself in his place for more than a few minutes to appreciate that horse walkers are best used as a complement to normal exercise rather than as a staple exercise.

For those without the luxury of an arena, all is not lost. Alternative exercise ideas include the following:

Walkabouts: Make sure all horses have some opportunity to stretch their legs outside the stable every day.

Ring the Changes: Laying soiled bedding in a circle on wet or frosty ground is a traditional way of creating a winter exercise area. Yes, it's hard work to put down and take up, but such rings can be useful, particularly for occasional lungeing. Be imaginative and create a rectangle and figure eight rather than simply a circle, though, or things will soon become dull.

Lungeing and Long Reining: Both activities are useful extras that help increase suppleness as well as having lots of training potential. However, as forms of exercise, they should not be considered as replacements for ridden and more varied work. Keep sessions to no more than half an hour, and make sure you are doing the job properly.

Ride and Lead: This is a handy way of exercising two horses at once and widely used by racing and hunting yards. But in these traffic-laden days, it is best left to experts and those with nerves of steel.

If you are going to ride and lead:
- Use only sensible, well-mannered horses who get on well together.
- If one or both are overfresh, lunge first to take the wind from their sails a little.
- Riders must be secure, calm, and confident riding one-handed.
- Alternate which horse is led and which is ridden to avoid creating one-sidedness.
- Keep the ridden horse on the side closest to the traffic.
- Lead with a lunge cavesson or simple snaffle bridle with the rein passed from the off-side through the near-side bit ring (or single rein with coupling). Avoid using too long a rein.
- Use brushing and knee boots on the led horse.
- Aim to keep the led horse's head level with the ridden horse's shoulder, checking an overly eager

Lungeing is good exercise, but lacks variety for the horse.

horse with intermittent pulls on the rein, or encouraging a lazy one with your voice or a little dig in the ribs with your toe. Set a steady pace that both horses find comfortable, and use voice and hand aids to warn both horses of a change of pace or direction.

• Move an awkward leader along by riding around it a few times.

Joining forces: Find someone at the yard, or someone who keeps their horse nearby, who would like to link up to hire an all-weather or indoor arena in your area. Book an instructor, too, and use the time to help iron out any training problems or prepare for next year's competitions. Many facilities charge by the hour rather than per horse, so as many as six of you can enjoy a good training round on a regular basis at relatively little expense.

Riding on the Roads

Riding on the roads these days is never the safest of activities, but some of us have little option, particularly during the winter months when many off-road paths become too wet to use. Brush up on your road-riding skills well before winter. Check with local horse clubs or societies to see if they offer road safety courses.

Winter presents two additional difficulties for riding on the roads: poor visibility and slippery conditions underfoot.

Poor Visibility

Tightness on exercise time in winter forces many riders out on to the roads in less than ideal light. Most people are aware of the dangers of fading light at dawn or dusk or foggy or misty conditions, but it is also important to be alert to the blinding effects of low sunshine in winter. This can make a rider in the shadows of a hedge all but invisible to a driver as he turns a corner.

It's up to us as responsible riders to make ourselves not merely visible, but impossible to miss whenever we use the roads whatever the conditions

When riding on the road, both rider and horse must be as conspicuous as possible.

but, obviously, especially when visibility is reduced. Many and various ways are available for making yourself and your horse stand out. Easy-to-see, bright riding clothing is fortunately now the fashion and, as potential lifesavers for you and your horse, additional high-visibility gear is reasonably inexpensive.

So no excuses! Your local saddlery shop or mail order suppliers stock a range of easy-to-use high-visibility gear that will include jackets, vests, helmet covers, armbands, gloves, and lights for the rider, and exercise sheets, tail guards, rein sleeves, nosebands, and brushing boots for the horse.

Set Daily Goals

Have a plan and a goal for each day's riding, so that you are not wasting precious minutes deciding what to do or where to go.

General visibility-enhancing guidelines include:

- Be sensible. In darkness, failing light, or when there is any doubt you cannot be seen by motorists at a minimum distance of 100 yards (91.5 m), don't venture out unless you absolutely have to. Find another way of exercising your horse that day.
- Get reflective as well as fluorescent. Fluorescent gear offers high visibility in dull weather, but only purpose-designed reflective material bounces light back from car headlights, making you instantly visible to motorists.
- Research confirms that a motorist's attention is best caught by moving light at low levels, making reflective legwear and exercise sheets two of the most effective items of high-visibility gear.
- Stirrup or boot lights are another effective accessory. These should be secured to the rider's near side if only one is used, showing red to the rear and white to the front.

Go at a steady pace when you are riding on unfamiliar surfaces.

Slippery Conditions

Ice makes riding on the road hazardous for horses, causing obvious problems during prolonged freezes. It also catches unsuspecting riders unaware on early morning rides after a sharp frost. For the few extra minutes it takes, it is well worth the time and effort to fit exercise knee boots in cold weather, as anyone who has ever seen a horse with injuries to his knees from coming down on the road will agree.

Other straightforward precautionary measures include using fullered shoes and/or road or borium studs for improved grip. When ice is widespread and unavoidable, however, it is best to avoid the roads and to find an alternative place to exercise.

When the Going Gets Tough...

Road surfaces have the advantage of being level, but they are also hard, unyielding, and unforgiving on horses' legs and feet. Concussion will not only strain joints, but it will also stress soft tissues such as ligaments and tendons. It will also affect the blood supply, leading to all kinds of problems, from wind puffs to laminitis.

So, go steady on the road for the sake of your horse's limbs and feet, as well as for safety. Stay mainly in walk, saving trot for short, level, or uphill stretches where the horse can stay better balanced and where there is less strain on his tendons and joints.

Hard ground conditions can also be a killer, and are not only a summer problem. Any lengthy spell during which temperatures stay near or below freezing will increase concussion and hammer your horse's feet and legs, both out in the field, and, more intensively, during exercise.

During a freeze, muddy areas will become dangerously rutted. If you feel at risk of twisting an ankle when you walk across the field, then with four legs, additional weight, and carrying a rider, your horse is even more vulnerable. Rutted ground becomes potentially lethal to ride on at any more than a very careful walk and is best avoided completely.

Think carefully about the wisdom of any higher-speed activities, such as hunting or cross-country events if the ground is frosted, because, even if it is level, it will have little give.

The sort of soft, heavy, and wet ground that's part of winter riding for some owners brings its own problems, quite different from those posed by hard going. Constantly wet legs are prone to skin infections. Serious injuries to ligaments and tendons are also more common on soft ground, where there is a greater chance of a mistake making the horse twist or overextend a leg. Boots and bandages may not reduce the risks of tendon strain, but can protect against self-inflicted knocks and cuts like overreaches.

Check limbs carefully after exercise on soft ground because infection can rapidly set into the smallest of cuts, and the heat and swelling of more serious trauma can easily go unnoticed on muddy legs.

Home and Dry

There is no avoiding mud in winter, but it isn't all bad. There is something strangely satisfying, for horse and for rider, about coming home after one of those exhilarating off-road winter rides when you both finish up totally plastered in dirt from head to foot. The only problem is cleaning up afterwards.

As we mentioned when talking about coping with mud earlier, it's not always best to reach straight for the hose to wash off every bit of mud that appears on your horse. However, leaving mud to dry before brushing it off may not be practical after returning from a very muddy ride, when hosing is often a better option. By washing the mud off while it's still wet, you avoid having to use a brush on the legs, although an old wash-up brush does come in handy to help get more stubborn lumps off the hooves. Once the legs are clean, it is easier to clean out feet and check for scratches or other injuries.

A sponge and bucket of warm water (adding a bit of no-rinse shampoo) is the best way to tackle mud on the body. Make sure you don't get carried away and let the wipe-down become a full-scale bath, or you will end up with a very wet, very cold horse. Simply wipe around the eyes and ears, saddle patch, belly, elbows and stifles, and between the hind legs where sweat and mud accumulates but the skin is prone to rubbing. Drying is speeded up by removing excess water from the coat using a sweat scraper and towel.

Make sure your horse is made comfortable after winter exercise.

Winter

Keeping a supply of clean towels handy at the barn is useful for gently drying wet ears and legs. It's particularly important to get the heel area dry; a hairdryer is often the quickest solution (but be careful). A tired horse may appreciate the comfort and support of stable bandages if he is coming in, and this will help to dry the legs quickly.

What you do next depends on the situation, what gear you have, and how wet the horse is. Horses who live out without blankets can simply be turned out—they will move around to keep warm and will soon dry—or else get straight down to roll, thus defeating all your efforts! In cold weather, you can start off the drying process by walking the horse around in-hand for a while. Those horses who are going out, are not too wet, and are the lucky owners of a modern, high-tech, breathable blanket can be dried off as much as possible, then blanketed, and ready to go.

More time must be taken with horses who have older-style blankets without this ability, or if the horse has gotten extremely wet or is now coming into a stable. There was a time when the quickest way to dry off a wet horse took hours and involved stuffing clean straw underneath an inside-out stable blanket and roller. This process was known as thatching, which always appeared extremely itchy as well as near-impossible to achieve. Luckily, today we have such things as cooler sheets, and one of these should be in every horse's wardrobe for winter as well as summer use.

Fasten the cooler securely and comfortably, and put the horse either into a stable or another covered area while he dries off. In very cold temperatures, you can add the stable blanket on top, folding the chest back and securing it under a roller or surcingle to avoid overheating. Once the coat is dry, remove the cooler and replace the stable or turnout blanket as required.

It's very important to keep your horse's heel area dry in cold, wet weather.

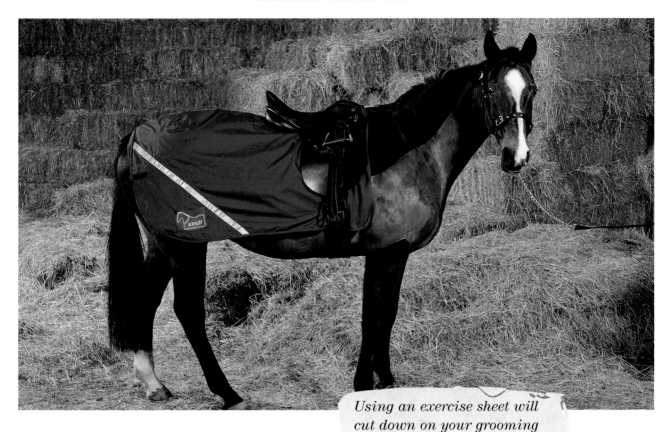

Using an exercise sheet will cut down on your grooming workload.

All this also applies whether the horse is simply wet with sweat or from the rain. It is always best to wipe down a sweaty horse in this way. Dried sweat is uncomfortable for the horse and very difficult to brush off later.

Exercise Sheets

There is a simple, straightforward way to avoid spending too much time on drying off after a rain-soaked ride—use an exercise sheet. No longer the preserve of racehorses on the gallop, exercise sheets are an absolute god-send to the winter rider. They save hours of drying time by providing waterproofing for everyone venturing out in the wet, as well as an extra layer of warmth for fully clipped horses on cold days. So, watch the skies for black clouds and get out the sheet if any look even remotely threatening.

Sheets available on the market vary from warm blanket types to rainproof and fluorescent and/or reflective designs. A fully clipped horse wants

warmth, so he will need a lined sheet, but otherwise you can choose between lined or unlined, showerproof or fully waterproof, high-visibility or not, as your budget and needs allow. Obviously, it pays to go for the most versatile you can afford.

Fit varies with design. Some sheets cover from the shoulders back, sitting underneath the saddle and secured either by integral straps to the girth straps, or by simply folding back the front edges underneath the girth. More recent designs might have a cut-out section where the saddle goes and fasten in front of the pommel, or some fit behind the saddle only, clipping on to the girth straps. These have the advantage of not wrinkling up underneath the saddle, as the older style tends to do. Whichever you have, be sure to use the fillet string to stop the sheet from blowing up, and get a size that gives good cover right to the dock.

Chapter Twenty-Nine

Winter Health Alert

Winter is the time that tests the horse owner to the utmost in knowledge, dedication, awareness, and all-around horsemanship. Hard times ahead are not confined only to horses living out, facing prolonged periods of cold and wet that sap energy and fat reserves. Stabled horses, too, will be coping with the mental and physical stresses that come hand-in-hand with their unnaturally confined lifestyle. Whichever category your horse fits into, he's going to need all the help and support you can give him through the tough months ahead and the inevitable stresses on his health and well-being that they will bring.

Skin Conditions

A horse's skin and coat is his first and most important line of defense against winter conditions, whether that be the cold and wet or spending long periods standing in inactivity, blanketed up in a stuffy, possibly less than clean stable. A number of skin conditions can affect horses during the winter months, all of which should be easily avoided through thoughtful management.

Rainrot

This is a superficial skin infection caused by the bacteria *Dermatophilus congolensis* (the same organism is often implicated in mud fever/scratches). Hair loss, oozy scabs, and crusting are seen over the body and neck, where the coat has repeatedly been moistened by rain or by sweating under blankets. Most frequently, the condition is seen in horses left unblanketed outdoors and exposed to heavy, persistent rain.

Wash the affected areas thoroughly in chlorhexidine or povidone iodine solution, and dry the coat carefully. Make sure the horse is kept dry and out of the rain. Severe cases will even appear dull and lethargic, lose weight, and need treatment with antibiotics.

In large yards, it may be necessary to consider isolating affected horses and disinfecting tack and grooming equipment.

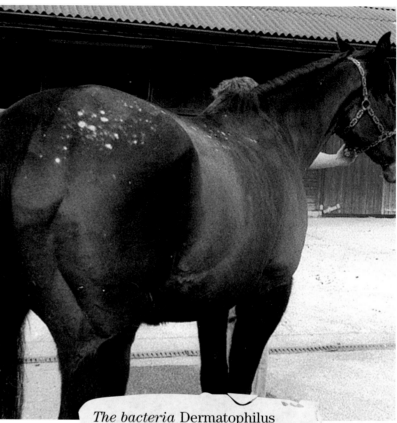

The bacteria Dermatophilus congolensis *is responsible for the skin infection rainrot.*

Pastern Dermatitis (Scratches)

Affecting the heels and pastern area, this is perhaps the most common of equine skin problems. It occurs more frequently during the winter months, when the feet and legs are constantly being exposed to wet, muddy conditions. Superficial bacterial infection by *Dermatophilus* is often complicated by the bacteria *Staphylococcus*, which causes a very painful, inflammatory, and purulent skin infection.

All over the lower legs, but especially around the heels, pasterns, and fetlocks, localized areas of matted, tufty hair can be seen, with thick, heavy scabs that ooze pus and serum. Not surprisingly, the whole area is sensitive, painful, and often swollen and, in severe cases, there can be secondary lameness.

Treatment must begin with bringing the horse into dry conditions. To have a chance of successful healing, he must stay in the dry, away from mud, wet grass, and bedding until all signs have cleared and his skin has had a chance to make a full recovery. This means that alternative arrangements will have to be made for horses who normally live outside so that they can be stabled until completely better.

The bacteria involved thrive in moist conditions, but are vulnerable to exposure to dry air; therefore, the first step is to clip the affected area as much as possible, using sedation if necessary. Scabs and crusts can be picked off gently with the fingers, but take care because this help is not always appreciated by your horse. With more stubbornly crusted areas, applying a warm poultice for 24 hours can help soften the crusts enough for easier removal.

Once air can reach the pink, healthy skin underneath, wash the area with an antibacterial solution and dry it thoroughly, patting it with clean towels or using a hairdryer. The area then must be kept meticulously clean and dry.

Antibiotics and anti-inflammatory drugs may be needed to give that bit of extra help to heal the infection, and even then cases can take weeks to resolve. Remember that crusts and scabs should be disposed of carefully to prevent reinfection or the spread of infection to healthy animals.

Chorioptic Mange

Heavily feathered breeds with a generous dose of draft breeding are most commonly affected by chorioptic mange, usually when stabled during the winter months. Intense itching caused by mites will make the horse not only restless, stamping his foot frequently in irritation, but even driving him to chew, rub, and bite his legs, leading to hair loss, scabbing, and matting in the affected area of the leg, and a general moth-eaten appearance. Sometimes the abdomen and groin are affected.

The condition is usually controlled by clipping away the long hair and washing with insecticidal shampoo. The mite infestation can be reduced by dosing orally with an ivermectin-based dewormer. Where an infested horse is present, it is always worth treating all the residents because some animals act as carriers without showing symptoms themselves, thereby acting as a reservoir for reinfestation.

Lice

Horses can be affected by two types of lice (biting and sucking), which can be seen on the neck, tail, body, and sometimes on the limbs of infested animals, causing irritation that leads to patchy hair loss, sores, anemia, and loss of condition.

The most effective way to tackle an infestation is with insecticidal washes, powders, sprays, or pour-on preparations. Again, it makes sense to treat all horses in contact with this individual at the same time, because infestation can be spread easily by blankets and grooming equipment, as well as by direct

Pastern dermatitis, also known as scratches, affects the lower leg.

contact. Because the louse can survive in the environment for several weeks, repeat the treatment every 10 days.

Problems with lice are more likely to be seen during the winter months, when horses are kept inside, close together, and in relatively warm conditions. Horses who are stressed, very young or elderly, or in poor physical shape are more likely to develop a heavy infestation.

Ringworm

Ringworm can appear at any time of the year, but because this fungus relishes moist conditions, it is particularly prevalent over winter, when many animals with stressed or rundown immune systems have lowered resistance to the disease.

Lower resistance to disease can make a horse vulnerable to ringworm.

What Is Ringworm?

Ringworm has no connection with parasitic worms. It is a fungal infection that can affect horses of all types and ages, although the young and debilitated tend to be affected most severely. Infections often start in areas that get sweaty and rubbed by tack, such as the girth and saddle. Initially, the horse is simply itchy and irritable, showing some patches of hair standing up on end. These areas soon progress to the classic "ring-like" ringworm lesions or areas of hair loss and crusting.

Action

Call the veterinarian if you suspect ringworm because he will need to take hair samples to confirm the diagnosis. Although this may take several days, treatment often starts immediately using topical, prescribed washes and shampoos (commonly enilconazole or miconazole), sometimes with the addition of griseofulvin powder in the feed. It is crucial to thoroughly disinfect the horse's environment to tackle this most highly contagious of diseases effectively. The fungal spores are most infectious in wet, humid conditions and can survive for years, spreading directly from horse to horse, horse to human, and indirectly via clothes, tack, blankets, grooming equipment, bedding, soil, fencing, and the like. The whole environment and all equipment must all be decontaminated as thoroughly as possible by exposure to ultraviolet light (bright sunlight will do) and scrubbing with antifungal solutions. While treatment is going on, make sure affected horses are properly isolated and their equipment kept separate from other horses.

Chronic Obstructive Pulmonary Disease

Visit any barn in the winter months and, before long, you'll hear coughing. Although owners worry, understandably, about the possibility of bacterial or viral infections of which coughs are a symptom (such as equine influenza), the fact remains that 99 percent of all coughs are a symptom of chronic obstructive pulmonary disease (COPD).

Why Do Horses Cough?

COPD, or heaves, is entirely a manmade condition in that it results entirely from our bringing horses in from their natural, fresh-air environment into the relative stuffiness of stables, where their air supply is contaminated by dust and spores from hay and bedding that irritate the lining of the lungs.

COPD is the most common of all respiratory disorders. It is most often seen in the older horse, whose sensitivity has built up over years of being stabled, and in the winter, when more horses tend to be housed. Typically, horses are over the age of 4 when they first show signs of the disease, which involves a hypersensitive reaction to inhaled particles, stored hay and straw being the most usual sources.

Mildly affected horses may only show a reduction in performance or tolerance of exercise and may not cough or have any nasal discharge. Most horses with COPD, however, do have a definite cough, which is worse at the start of exercise, together with a watery nasal discharge, which frequently worsens as exercise continues.

A severely affected horse will cough even when resting. He will often show a characteristically abnormal breathing pattern, making a double effort to exhale (abdominal lift) as he struggles to force air out of the narrowed, inflamed airways of the lungs. The extra effort this forced expiration requires means that, over the years, muscles in the abdomen develop abnormally, resulting in the tell-tale heave lines that mark the sides and flank areas of the "broken winded" horse.

Over time, the tissues of the lungs may become permanently damaged from constant overinflation. Excess fluid is produced, which can be detected in the lungs as a crackling sound when breathing is listened to with a stethoscope. Another symptom is a resting breathing rate that is slightly elevated, at around 20 breaths per minute (bpm) compared to the normal of around 16 bpm. The inflamed airways also produce a thick nasal discharge, although this is not always seen because some horses manage to swallow secretions.

The vet will make a diagnosis based on the horse's history and a thorough examination, possibly using a breathing bag held around the muzzle. This forces the horse to take deeper breaths, emphasizing abnormal respiratory sounds, such as wheezes and crackles. An endoscope may be used to take a closer look at the upper airways. Samples of fluid from further down the respiratory tract can be taken using tracheal or bronchial washes, and these can be used to analyze what cells are present in the airways. This will indicate whether the problem is inflammatory or due to an infection.

Clearing the Air

In the short term, horses with severe signs of COPD can be given anti-inflammatory medication, bronchodilators, and mucolytics to give some relief. However, the only effective long-term answer is to remove from the horse's environment all the

allergens that are triggering the reaction in his airways—that is, all dust and spores. Dust-free feed (for example, hay soaked in clean water for 30 minutes before draining and feeding, haylage, dust-extracted chaff or chopped hay, hay pellets, or complete cubes) and bedding (shavings paper or rubber matting) will help, but it must be stressed that any stable will be stuffy and dusty to a degree. Without a doubt, turnout for as much of the time as possible, with the necessary blankets for warmth, is the best environment for the horse with COPD. If horses must be kept stabled, the ventilation must be excellent.

Care also must be taken that a horse with a meticulously planned, dust-free environment is not housed next door and sharing air space with one

Respiratory ailments like COPD are a direct consequence of stabling horses for prolonged periods.

bedded on straw and fed dry hay. Sometimes, airways can be sensitized by viral or bacterial infection and then go on to develop COPD.

Some horses respond very well to drugs delivered directly to the respiratory system via a nebulizer, mask, and pump, which can help to prevent episodes of COPD.

Never ignore a cough or runny nose hoping it will go away like a human cold. Always act on the signs of COPD by looking at how your horse is managed and how you can make changes to improve the quality of the air he breathes. Left untreated or poorly managed, COPD will get worse and can become extremely debilitating.

Winter Foot Problems
Thrush

Because thrush tends to be found in horses forced to stand in unhygienic, damp, dirty bedding, it is more likely to be seen during the winter when horses spend long periods stabled. The poorly ventilated clefts of the frog become infected and deepened, the culprit generally being the *Fusobacterium necrophorum* bacterium, which produces a black, foul-smelling discharge.

A horse with the first stages of thrush does not usually become lame right away, but starts becoming unlevel as the infection progresses into the deeper, more sensitive soft tissues of the foot. If it reaches extensively into the area beneath the horny sole (underruns of the sole), the infection can cause the sole to actually separate from the rest of the foot.

Treatment for thrush involves scraping away any dead or separated tissue and applying antibacterial solution to the affected areas daily after cleaning the foot thoroughly. This must be continued until the infection is under control; the horse must be kept on very clean, dry bedding. Regular foot trimming and steady exercise will help to promote and maintain a healthy frog. Most importantly, the horse should never have to stand on a dirty, wet bed.

Abscesses

Infections within the foot are among the most common causes of lameness and can happen whatever the weather or season. However, persistent wetness softens and weakens the protective horn of the hoof wall and sole, often giving bacteria the opportunity to enter the vulnerable, sensitive structures inside. In addition, damp, dirty conditions underfoot will contain more bacteria and increase the risk of a foot abscess during the winter, when more horses are stabled or standing in muddy paddocks.

Most infections enter the foot along the white line, the junction between the horn of the hoof wall and the sole. The white line is normally only 1/8 inch (2–3 mm) wide, but it is considerably wider in horses with chronic laminitis, especially in the toe region,

Regular foot trimming and steady exercise will help to promote the growth of a healthy frog.

The time you spend caring for your horse will make all the difference when spring comes around again.

due to rotation of the pedal bone. The crumbly, flaky horn in this toe area is more prone to infection, known when it occurs here as seedy toe.

Any object that penetrates the sole (e.g., a nail, thorn, or sharp stone) can introduce the bacteria that will cause an abscess to form. Most serious are penetrations of the middle third of the frog because these can puncture important structures of the foot. Prompt veterinary attention is needed here. Hoof wall cracks and incorrect nail hold placement when shoeing can also introduce infection into the foot. Corns and bruises may also become infected and develop into an abscess.

In the early stages, an abscess may produce only a slight, barely detectable lameness. But, in the same way that an infection building up under one of our own fingernails can suddenly become unbearably sensitive, so a foot abscess develops until it causes extreme pain, with the horse unwilling to put any weight on that hoof. The horse might sweat, have a

high pulse rate and, in the worst cases, even show signs of suffering a bout of colic.

To detect the location of the abscess, the vet or farrier will need to remove the shoe and use hoof testers to pinpoint the site. A hoof knife is then used to pare away the sole and/or hoof wall in that area until pus can be released and a channel created to encourage ongoing drainage. Poulticing over the next couple of days should ensure that all the pus is drawn out. Thankfully, the horse is usually much more comfortable on the release of the worst of the pressure.

Very deep abscesses can be difficult or impossible to reach by paring and may travel up the white line to break out at the coronary band. These are trickier to drain successfully and complete recovery may take longer.

Index

Index

271

Index

Acknowledgments

Special thanks to Fiona Poole BVSc, MRCVS and Lesley Ward for expert help with factual content.

Photo Credits